Feminist Approaches to
Interreligious Dialogue

Perspectivas feministas acerca del diálogo interreligioso

Feministische Zugänge zum interreligiösen Dialog

*Journal of the European Society of Women
in Theological Research*

*Anuario de la sociedad Europea de mujeres en la
investigación teológica*

*Jahrbuch der Europäischen Gesellschaft für
theologische Forschung von Frauen*

Volume 17

**Bibliographical information and books for review
in the Journal should be sent to:**
Dr. Ursula Rapp, Kirchweg 12
A - 6800 Feldkirch, Austria

**Articles for consideration for the Journal
should be sent to:**
Christine Gasser, Kaschlgasse 6/17
A - 1200 Wien, Austria

Feminist Approaches to Interreligious Dialogue

Perspectivas feministas acerca del diálogo interreligioso

Feministische Zugänge zum interreligiösen Dialog

Editors:
Annette Esser, Katharina von Kellenbach,
Annette Mehlhorn, Sabine Bieberstein,
Christine Gasser, Ursula Rapp

PEETERS - LEUVEN - WALPOLE, MA

A CIP record for this book is available from the Library of Congress.

Journal of the European Society of Women
in Theological Research, 17

© 2009, Peeters Publishers, Leuven / Belgium
ISBN 978-90-429-2290-7
ISSN 1783-2454
eISSN 1783-2446
D/2009/0602/125
Cover design by Margret Omlin-Küchler

All rights reserved. No part to this publication may be reproduced, stored in a retrieval system, or transmitted, in any form of by any means, electronic, mechanical, photocopying, recording or otherwise, without the prior permission of the publisher.

CONTENTS – INHALT – ÍNDICE

Introduction
Annette Esser, Katharina von Kellenbach and Annette Mehlhorn   5

Thema – Theme – Tema
Helene Egnell
The Messiness of Actual Existence: Feminist Contributions to Theology of Religions 13

Annette Mehlhorn
Gleich und doch verschieden – getrennt verschieden oder gemeinsam? *Intra*religiöse Debatten und *inter*religiöser Dialog im Wechselverhältnis zwischen Religion, Politik und Gender . 29

Manuela Kalsky and Katharina von Kellenbach
Interreligious Dialogue and the Development of a Transreligious Identity: A Correspondence 41

Christa Anbeek
The Beauty of Ten Thousand Blooming Flowers: Towards a Feminist Approach to Buddhist-Christian Dialogue 59

Annette Esser
Salir en busca de espiritualidad feminista en el diálogo interreligioso 69

Forum – Fórum
Nadja Furlan
Women in Interreligious Dialogue: Transformation of Negative Gender and Religious Stereotypes 89

Humera Khan
Exploring Women's Rights in Islam through Interfaith Dialogue   99

Alice Schumann
Experiences of Inter-religious Dialogue as a German Hindu Woman   105

Uta Blohm
Women Ministers and Rabbis in London: Intra- and Inter-Faith Relations 123

Rachel Herweg, Gisela Matthiae und Rabeya Müller
Erfahrungsbericht aus dem Ersten Interreligiösen Feministischen Lehr- und Lernhaus 135

Helene Egnell and Annette Esser
European Projects and Initiatives for Women's Interreligious Dialogue 145

Women's traditions – Frauentraditionen – Tradiciones de mujeres
Larissza Hrotkó
Ungarische Frauen im Aufbruch zwischen Religion(en) und Politik. Ein Überblick über die Entwicklung der ungarischen Frauenbewegung 153

Nuriye Duran Özsoy
Die Frauenbewegung in der Türkei 165

Naime Çakir
Muslimische Frauen in Deutschland: zwischen Viktimisierung, Kriminalisierung, Rechtfertigung und Selbstbehauptung . . . 183

From the Countries – Aus den Ländern – Desde los distinios Países
Pilar de Miguel, Lucía Ramon Carbonell, Rosa Cursach Salas
Logros y retos de la teología feminista en España 195

Book market – Büchermarkt – Feria de Libros
I. **European Electronic Journal for Feminist Exegesis: Lectio difficilior celebrates its 10th anniversary** 209
Ulrike Sals
Reading the Difficult Way – for Ten Years 209

II. Selected Bibliography: Feminist Approaches to Interreligious Dialogue 215
III. Bibliographie – Bibliography – Bibliografía 219
IV. Book Reviews – Rezensionen – Recensiones 229

Introduction

A majority of attendees at the ESWTR-Conference in Budapest (2005) voted to make interreligious dialogue of women the topic of a forthcoming volume of the Society's Journal, adding that the notion "feminist" should be included in the title. Subsequently, during the Society's meeting in Naples in 2007, a call went out soliciting members who would be interested in collaborating in this joint venture. This core group of authors/editors met twice in the fall of 2008 to assemble the articles for this volume and to solicit additional authors to increase our religious and national diversity. We were committed to examine feminist interreligious dialogues from different theoretical angles, various religious backgrounds, as well as different European national perspectives. The contributors speak from the Jewish, Christian, Muslim, Hindu and Buddhist perspectives and reflect German, British, Dutch, Spanish, Slovene, Hungarian, Turkish and US American cultural contexts. As befits the topic, the editors remained acutely aware of the Society's predominantly Christian character and ongoing struggle to achieve equity and just representation among its European national contingents. At the same time we recognized, that we ourselves, like the ESWTR in general, are mostly Christian and primarily of Northern European (especially German) extraction.

During its twenty-five year old history the ESWTR struggled with its identity as a Christian theological organization and the meaning of its (expanding) European boundaries. Founded by Christian scholars engaged in European ecumenical contexts, especially within the Ecumenical Council of Churches (ECC), the ESWTR was challenged early on by Jewish women. Already during the eighties (Helvoirt, NL 1985; Arnoldshain, DE 1989), the desire to include Jewish women's voices led to the curious decision to include "Israel" into the European fold and to make Israel a member-country in the statutes of the ESWTR. During the nineties (Hofgeismar, DE 1999), Muslim women were encouraged to join the Society as members and invited to serve on the Board as well. Nevertheless, neither Jewish nor Muslim scholars have joined the Society in any measurable numbers. To date, the name, structure and programming of the ESWTR affords Jewish and Muslim participants little more than token status. As far as we know, no Buddhist or Hindu women have asked to join the Society.

The ESWTR gathering in Budapest (2005) proposed the topic of "feminist interreligious dialogue" apart from the question of membership and the religiously homogenous makeup of the Society. The topic suggested itself because many recognized the relevance and urgency of this theme for any kind of theology, including feminist theology today. Interreligious or intercultural dialogue has moved from the sidelines of religious studies to the centre of theological reflexion. Nevertheless, dialogue has remained promoted and dominated by male religious leaders and scholars. While some of them have integrated feminist theological thoughts during the past years, and although questions of gender are broadly recognized as important subjects in thinking about diversity, there is little sustained feminist focus. With the present volume we want to start to fill this gap.

All of the contributors to this volume refer to a cultural context dramatically changed by the globalization of the economy and massive population migrations. Where one might have supposed interreligious dialogue to be a conversation between strangers living in different countries on faraway continents, such interreligious dialogue now occurs among neighbours, co-workers and family members. Although Europe never existed as an exclusively Christian culture, this nostalgic ideal is relinquished only very slowly. Europe has long struggled with the presence of religious minorities in its midst, but we now confront the "religious other" in a global context and as societies committed to democratic ideals of human rights and respect for religious self determination. At the same time, equal representation and basic human rights remain an unfulfilled promise for many women in the world. Interreligious dialogue envisions and practices a new approach to religious differences based on equality and human rights. Where in the past, religious disputes were solved by torture, forced conversion, expulsion, *auto da fes,* and crusades, contemporary practices of interreligious dialogue envision tolerance, empathy and an embrace of difference. Nevertheless, despite such political commitments to religious tolerance and equal human rights, several of the non-Christian contributors in this journal report their fear of violence and experiences with discrimination that have shaped their lives as members of minority religions in Europe. Western Christian feminists struggle with appropriate responses to religious differences that involve traditions that perpetuate the discrimination and second class status of women in the religious sphere. Pulled between acceptance of religious differences and rejection of central patriarchal tenets within those religions, feminists struggle to find solidarity in the midst of diversity, discrimination and conflict. Non-Christian women in Europe face multiple levels of discrimination and negotiate competing loyalties as members of minority religions or immigrant communities who confront external stereotypes as well as internal role-expectations. As feminist theology enters into interreligious dialogue, the empowerment of women, respect for and curiosity about women's experiences, and commitment to women's liberation can serve as guiding principles.

This volume of the Journal is committed to giving voice to the growing religious diversity in Europe and to nudge the ESWTR towards greater openness and inclusion of non-Christian religious scholars. Several of our contributors are not theologians but Hindu and Muslim scholars who are trained in academic disciplines other than theology or religious studies (anthropology, political science, history). They may not pursue academic careers because of the politics and institutional structures of European university systems. Should the ESWTR commit itself to increasing religious diversity, we may need to consider the further expansion of European boundaries (by including Turkey, e.g.) along with disciplinary and methodological expansions. As long as the name and programming of the ESWTR is centred on (Christian) theology, we remain unattractive to non-Christian women as a professional organization. Interfaith dialogue strives for common ground between religions even as it acknowledges profound differences. "Theology" may not be the most appropriate access point for dialogue since it remains a predominant Christian approach to religion. This may even be true for a pluralistic "theology of religion" that understands itself as a common platform for all religions. Nevertheless, specific points of view – including Christian theological thinking – will also in future be important for an enriching and differentiated dialogue that confronts the necessity to respect diversity and at the same time searches for a common global ethics and responsibility.

In our attempt to respond to this challenge, we looked for a reflection of the plurality of religious and cultural traditions, perspectives, contexts and approaches that characterize the actual European situation. On our way we had to recognize that such pluralism requires openness and flexibility in handling the diversity of languages, working-styles, expectations, and modes of presentations. We tried to fit this diversity into our concept without forcing or equalizing the contributions. In the end, we are glad to have found a way to present a mosaic which represents the plurality without leaving the readers completely lost – at least this is our hope.

Based on her dissertation research on Christian feminist approaches to religious plurality, Swedish theologian *Helene Egnell* opens the **Theme** section with a plea for greater dialogue between feminist theologians and those engaged in dialogue – often men. She maintains that key insights and concepts of feminist theology, especially women's experiences of marginality and insistence on the "messiness of actual existence" are critically relevant for the emerging theory of a "theology of religions." Interfaith dialogue that starts with thick descriptions of the religious life will prove more promising than approaches rooted in doctrine and systematic theories.

For German Protestant practitioner of interreligious dialogue *Annette Mehlhorn* this "messiness of actual experiences" means that individuals who engage in dialogue negotiate not only disagreements with representatives of the "other religion" but also internal divisions among co-religionists. *Interreligious* dialogue necessitates simultaneous *intrareligious* dialogue. No "religion" is ever homogenous. Each religious community is made up of individual religious subjects who navigate internal conflicts along with external relations with "others."

Manuela Kalsky and *Katharina von Kellenbach,* however, challenge the very existence of "insider" and "outsider" in contemporary Western European societies. Their letter exchange questions the notion of "interreligious dialogue" from the perspective of migrants who cross national and religious borders. A rising number of people are unaffiliated with any particular religious community and claim the freedom to "pick and choose" marriage partners, countries, religious traditions and observances as they fit into their lives. New religious identities are being forged in the maelstrom of globalization. The realities of multicultural societies and of religious pluralism are fast overtaking the timid steps undertaken in official interreligious dialogue settings.

Christa Anbeek, a Buddhist feminist scholar from the Netherlands, retraces interreligious dialogue by way of her own journey and proposes several "travel guides" that emerged from her own adventures across the Buddhist and Christian borderlines. Starting with the philosophical-theological travel guide that exposed her to the comparative academic study of Buddhism and Christianity, she branched out into Zen meditation using a "practical-spiritual travel guide." As a pastoral care provider in a psychiatric institution, she applied an "interhuman travel guide" meeting each human being at the level of their spiritual needs and finally, she suggests an "ecosophical travel guide" to frame the "multireligious adventure" of human togetherness and dependence on the resources of planet earth.

German theologian *Annette Esser*, finally, addresses the role of spirituality in interfaith dialogue and asks whether the search for feminist spirituality serves to draw women into dialogue or whether it is a particularly divisive topic among dialogue activists. She notes that while on the one hand, individuals who are interested in spirituality seem to be especially attracted to spiritual practices in other religious traditions, on the other hand the prospect of celebrating together across religious traditions or of creating religious rituals together is often accompanied by great tension and awkwardness. "Spirituality" and religious celebration are both a place of great attraction as well as of profound division among women engaged in feminist interreligious dialogue.

The second section of the *Forum* contextualizes a variety of experiences in feminist interreligious dialogue in different religious and national settings. *Nadja Furlan,* a Slovenian feminist theologian, argues that women's interfaith dialogue takes on special political urgency "to heal the war wounds" in the aftermath of the Balkan wars. She is especially concerned with the persistence of negative stereotypes and prejudices that always threaten to legitimate further violence and calls on women to come together in order to create trusting relationships across the divisions.

Raised in the secular pluralist atmosphere of the UK, *Humera Khan* credits interreligious dialogue meetings in Bendorf, Germany with her development as a Muslim and a feminist. These Jewish-Christian-Muslim encounters forced her to weather internal conflicts within the small number of Muslim representatives hailing from different contexts but also to develop a coherent position on the topic of "women in Islam" in dialogue with Jewish and Christian feminists. As a child of immigrants in the UK, her religious journey is fundamentally dialogically, forged in the interstices of various Muslim constituencies, European secular culture, as well as feminist political, Jewish and Christian discourses.

For *Alice Schumann*, a German convert to Hinduism and devotee of Krishna Bahkti-Yoga, the religious path proved to be equally fundamentally dialogical. The granddaughter of a Lutheran missionary and daughter of a Roman Catholic father begins her narrative with reflections on the "internal dialogue" that propelled her towards Indian philosophy and meditative practice. Her "intrareligious" battles involved the subordination of women that eventually led her to open a missionary temple in East Germany where she encountered racist hostility and xenophobia. As resident expert on Hinduism she was often invited to interreligious dialogues with church representatives who remain intent on framing Hindu communities in Germany as dangerous cults and sects. In her conclusion, Schumann reiterates that each level of dialogue is indispensable for overcoming ignorance and prejudice.

The third essay looks at the extent of interfaith practice among Christian ministers and rabbis in London. For her dissertation Protestant theologian *Uta Blohm* conducted in-depth interviews with female rabbis, priests and ministers and found high levels of interfaith collaboration at the local level irrespective

Introduction

of theological or political outlook. Nevertheless for some, sharing liberal political values trumps denominational and religious allegiances. Hence, politics – and current divisions between liberals and conservatives within religions – prove to be in greater need for sustained efforts at dialogue than interfaith dialogue.

The last essay in this section reports on the first, feminist, interreligious "teaching and learning institute" (*Lern- und Lehrhaus*) in Germany. Led by a Jewish, Muslim and Christian feminist religious scholar, this course involved seven modules and exposed participants to the basic teachings of each of the Abrahamic religions as well as of feminist efforts at reforming these teachings. *Rachel Herweg, Gisela Matthiae* and *Rabeya Müller* present an overview of this course and draw preliminary lessons at to its successes.

In conclusion, *Annette Esser* and *Helene Egnell* have collected a list of the most important and best-known projects involved in feminist interreligious dialogue in Europe at the current time.

The third section is dedicated to the presentation of **Women's Traditions**. *Larissza Hrotkó* provides short historical portraits of prominent Jewish and Christian women who became leading figures in the women's movement/s in Hungary, especially in Budapest. She shows that the Hungarian feminist movement, for better or worse, had deep roots in the religious communities as they transformed women's charitable organizations into political forums for the improvement of women's political situation.

For all its obvious cultural and religious differences, the history of the Hungarian women's movement is remarkably parallel to the history of the (Ottoman) and later Turkish women's movement. *Nuriye Duran Özsoy* points out that women's political activism preceded the establishment of the secular state by decades and that women in the Ottoman Empire fought valiantly for political rights. The history of the establishment of the secularist state is important to understand current political battles among secular and religious feminists in Turkey and the heated debates over women's headdress in the public sphere. *Nuriye Duran Özsoy* argues persuasively that contemporary women who don Islamic head-cover are far from passive victims but choose to forge a modern path for religious women in an urban context.

Naime Çakir points to a similar development, looking at the situation of Muslim immigrant women in Germany. Confronting several layers of discrimination they develop diverse strategies to overcome these difficulties. A reflected religious practice, often supported by academic studies of religious traditions gives them a new and emancipated view on their religious and cultural roots.

Introduction

The last essay hails from Spain under the heading ***From the Countries*** and traces the exciting development of Spanish feminist theology against the historical backdrop of the patriarchal institution of the Roman Catholic Church in that country.

While certainly not exhaustive, the editors have compiled a short ***Bibliography*** of relevant titles in the area of feminist interfaith dialogue. These entries contain our personal favourites and should be accepted with that limitation, as they reveal a predominantly Christian bias. We would ask that readers recognize the need for further study and growing awareness that in the future feminist discourse on religions must include more non-Christian perspectives.

Finally, we would like to thank all those who translated and proofread the various articles and abstracts into different languages: Gisela Boehm (Heidelberg, Germany), Jenny Daggers (Liverpool, UK), Teresa Forcades i Vila (Sant Benet de Montserrat, Catalonia / Spain, and Berlin, Germany), Mary Phil Korsak (Linkebeek, Belgium), Charlotte Methuen (Oxford, UK, and Hanau, Germany), Margaret A. Pater (Greifswald, Germany), Susan Roll (Ottawa, Canada) and Aysun Yasar-Cebeci (Bamberg, Germany). We cannot implement our vision of dialogue across religious borders without the expertise of those guides who can navigate the linguistic barriers. We are deeply indebted to their reliable, speedy and able work.

Annette Esser, Katharina von Kellenbach and Annette Mehlhorn
Bad Kreuznach, Maryland and Rüsselsheim, May 2009

Helene Egnell

The Messiness of Actual Existence
Feminist Contributions to Theology of Religions

What does feminist theology have to do with interfaith dialogue and theology of religions? So far, feminist theology has not to a great extent dealt with the issues of theology of religion, that is, how to view other religious traditions from the point of view of one's own tradition. How do we understand other religious traditions: as heresies, as competitors, as other sources from which we can learn something about the Divine? How can we learn to live in harmony with adherents of other faiths? How can the followers of different religious traditions work together for a better world? These, in short, are the questions with which theology of religions deals.

It is true that feminist theology from the outset was interreligious in its character; Jewish and Christian feminists as well as those who seek the Goddess were among the pioneers, and there has been reflection and dialogue on interfaith issues. However, on the whole, this has not been an area of concern for most feminist theologians.

I would argue that it is necessary for feminist theologians to take part in the increasingly important field of theology of religions, and that these two fields can mutually enrich each other. Key questions to be considered include: what could a feminist theology of religions look like? How could it show the way forward for the reflection of religious plurality and the praxis of interfaith dialogue? What elements of feminist theory might prove useful in the theology of religions? What new issues and concerns can feminist theology bring to interfaith discourse? And conversely, how can theology of religions enrich and challenge feminist theology?

In this essay I will offer some tentative answers to these questions. As this is virtually uncharted territory, I hope that there will be many further explorations in this field. It will be especially important that such explorations are done from the vantage point of other religious communities, since my perspective is Christian.

Thema
Theme
Tema

Lack of connection between theology and practice

In my doctoral thesis, *Other Voices: A Study of Christian Feminist Approaches to Religious Plurality East and West*,[1] I found that although more work has been done in this area than is generally realised, there still is not a lot, especially in the area of systematic reflection on religious plurality from a feminist perspective. Moreover, I found that there was very little connection between feminist dialogue praxis and feminist reflection upon religious plurality.

Women have met for dialogue according to the fundamental feminist rationale that women have been absent from interfaith dialogue, and that their involvement would bring up new issues having to do with women's subordination in religious communities and in society, as well as new ways of doing dialogue. However, there has not been much effort to bring feminist theory to bear on the structure of the conferences, or the discussions. On the other hand, feminist reflection in the area of theology of religions has seldom drawn on the experiences of women in interfaith dialogue, or offered a theoretical analysis of the learnings from them. This lack of connection between dialogue praxis and theology of religions is a serious flaw, not least because feminist theology has always emphasised the need to be praxis oriented, to take its starting point in experience, and to contribute to the liberation of women.

A number of themes that appear in the conferences and projects I study in my thesis,[2] are treated in depth in feminist theology. Supported by the experiences in my material, these could be developed further into a feminist theology of religions.

The first and primary theme that echoes in the reports of women's interreligious conferences is that close relations were built and cherished, and that a "common we" very soon was established, which was felt to be stronger than the divisions caused by different religious belonging. This did not mean that all was harmony. On the contrary conflicts abounded, showing real differences in opinion, often connected to geographical and social location. However, these conflicts were handled constructively and not seen as a threat to the relationships that had been built. It was rather the opposite: the establishment of good

---

[1] Helene Egnell, *Other Voices. A Study of Christian Feminist Approaches to Religious Plurality East and West* (Studia Missionalia Svecana 100: Uppsala 2006).

[2] The main ones being Women, Religion and Social Change at Harvard University in 1983, the WCC consultation Women in Interfaith Dialogue in Toronto in 1988, and The Women's Interfaith Journey carried out by the Henry Martyn Institute 1998-2003.

relationships prompted the participants to take each other seriously, neither glossing over nor building walls.

The role of conflict
It is quite often asserted that women avoid conflict, because they are anxious to preserve harmonious relations. However, the role played by conflict in all these projects was striking, as was the common explanation that conflicts were possible and could be handled precisely because the participants had built up relationships and cared about each other. The fact that conflicts arose, however, seemed to be attributable to the fact that some of the women, often those from a non-western and/or non-white context, insisted upon making differences visible, pointing out that their perspectives and aims were different from those of white, western women. That is to say, although a "common we" was established, it was not a homogenous entity. Difference and similarity were held together.

The "common we" was created through methodologies developed by the women's movement: sharing life stories in small groups, starting in the realm of concrete experiences rather than with abstract problems or dogmatic statements, paying careful attention to seating arrangements and to the planning of introductory sessions and rituals in order to create a "safe space".

However, the shaping of the "common we" did not simply result from methodologies geared towards relation-building. There were indeed commonalities to be found between the women. Although this is a contested concept, I have chosen to summarise them under the label "women's experiences". As long as the concept is used in the plural, in order to allow a wide spectrum within it, I think it is useful to talk of women's experiences both in the sense of "women's traditional experiences" and of "women's feminist experiences".

With "women's traditional experiences" we mean those connected to women's biological functions and the social roles assigned to them, while "feminist experiences" are those connected with the oppression of women, giving rise to anger and the urge to struggle for change. Both these kinds of experience played a part in the building of the "common we", but the "feminist experience" appears to have been the more decisive. There were examples in parts of my material, which lay outside the scope of my main interest,[3]

---

[3] One such example can be found in Annette Wilke, "Interreligiöses Verstehen. Rahmenbedingungen für einen gelingenden christlich-muslimischen Dialog", in: Doris Strahm / Manuela Kalsky (eds), *Damit es anders wird zwischen uns. Interreligiöser Dialog aus der Sicht von Frauen* (Matthias Grünewald: Ostfildern 2006), 14-26.

Thema
Theme
Tema

that suggest that "traditional experience" alone would not have allowed for the acknowledgement of differences, which made conflict possible to handle.

Critique of institutional religion
What distinguished these dialogues from malestream[4] interfaith dialogue, was the feminist critique of religion. All participants came with the experience of belonging to a religious tradition which had denied women access to the writing and interpretation of sacred texts, the performing of sacred rites etc, and many had struggled to achieve the right to do so. There was also a shared conviction that religious traditions are not static, but constantly changing, and that change is desirable.

Another way to express this is the notion of marginality. The women experienced themselves as being on the margins of their religious traditions, and this was seen as an asset: they did not have as many "vested interests" as those holding centrist positions.

At the same time, they had experienced faith as comfort and inspiration in their personal lives as well as in their struggle for justice and peace. The stress on lived faith rather than doctrine was another distinguishing mark of women's interfaith projects. One reason for this is that these were not theological conferences in a strict sense. Some participants were theologians, but many were social workers or educators, and all were, in one way or another, activists. Consequently, what is known as "the dialogue of life" played a more important role in these projects than in malestream dialogue. It also appears that "the little tradition" or "religion as practised" – that is, religion as understood and practised in everyday life, as distinct from "the great tradition" or "religion as prescribed" – was more prominent.

Another concept, which has to do with this connection to lived faith, is messiness – "the messiness of actual existence". The women taking part in dialogue questioned the very concept of interfaith dialogue as implying that religious traditions were clearly defined entities, "boxes" from which the dialogue participants negotiated well-defined standpoints. Their own experience was that it was not so easy to find a "representative" who fitted into the box of a certain tradition. Their spirituality was inspired by many traditions, and

---

[4] I have borrowed the term "malestream" from Elisabeth Schüssler Fiorenza. It exposes the fact that in a male-dominated society, what is considered mainstream is male dominated, and that what is considered universal is in reality particular.

they were well aware that insofar as they identified with a tradition, they could only represent part of that tradition.

The themes I have identified above are all fundamental themes in feminist theology: the critique against institutionalized religion, relationality, difference, the role of experience, marginality, messiness, the theology of lived faith. But in the reflections upon, and the analysis of, these projects, these themes have seldom been developed in a dialogue with current feminist theology. I will now try to chart the intersection between feminist theology and theology of religions at these points.

The hermeneutics of suspicion

The most obvious contribution of feminism to the theology of religions is the "hermeneutics of suspicion", the critique of institutional religion. Theology of religions needs to learn from feminist theology how to criticise religious traditions, while at the same time holding on to their liberating and life-enhancing potential, and work for change within them. For too long interfaith dialogue and theology of religions has suffered from mutual and one-sided apologetics, in which the courage to face the adverse sides of religious traditions has been absent.

It is understandable that the first stages of interfaith dialogue must focus on presenting and discovering the positive traits in each others' traditions. Mutual understanding must begin with mutual appreciation of what is good and beautiful in the other's way of expressing our faith – what Krister Stendahl has called "holy envy". However, if interfaith dialogue is to be able to contribute to world peace – as Hans Küng put it "no world peace without peace between the religions" – it is not enough to go on explaining that Christianity is not about crusades, and Islam not about jihad interpreted as holy war; nor is it enough to highlight the parts of our scriptures that talk of peace. We must have the courage to scrutinize our scriptures and theologies to understand why they are in fact such eminent tools for inspiring hatred and violence, why indeed crusades and jihad in the sense of holy war against infidels are part of Christianity and Islam in history as well as in our world today.

Feminist theology has not only developed the tools for scrutinizing the negative sides of religion, but also has some experience of doing this interreligiously. There is still a long way to go, but Jewish-Christian dialogue between feminists has grappled with the Christian habit of contrasting the "patriarchal God of the Old Testament" with "Jesus the feminist". The similarities and connections between misogyny and anti-Judaism have shed light on both phenomena.[5] While respecting that the two traditions have different interpretations of common texts and concepts, Jewish and Christian feminists have been able to carry out fruitful joint critique of such texts and concepts, and suggest new interpretations and new images.

An important task for feminist theologians is to analyze and criticize how women function as cultural and national markers, and thus as symbols in conflicts in society. Whether a woman covers herself or appears naked, her body is the field where political and economic conflicts are played. How we dress (up) as women – with hijab or mini-skirt – can be interpreted as being simultaneously a sign of, and a resistance against, the significance attributed to women's bodies. This is a question that especially Muslim and Christian women must tackle together, so as to avoid being the symbol that the "clash of civilizations" is focused upon.

Christology

Much of the Christian feminist critique has concerned christology. Rosemary Radford Ruether's question "can a male savior save women?" has not yet received a definite answer. However, it is not only that the maleness of Jesus has been a problem for feminist theologians – other ingredients of traditional Christology have been questioned as well, including imperialistic or exclusive claims for Jesus as the only saviour.

"Saving Jesus from those who are right" is a contribution to the rethinking of christology from Carter Heyward, which can show the way for theology of religions as well.[6] In the Preface, she explicitly addresses her book to adherents of other faiths.[7] She cautions against a Christology that "too often obscures the Christic – redemptive – meanings of the Jesus story" and claims that "it is hard for us not to get stuck in the faulty assumption that Jesus was, and is, *the* Christ in a unique and singular way that applies to him alone; to imagine that he – not anyone else with, before, or after him – was and is *The* Savior, who saves only those Christians who hold this "right" view of him."[8] Heyward

---

[5] The standard work in this area is Katharina von Kellenbach, *Anti-Judaism in Feminist Religious Writings* (Scholars Press: Atlanta 1994).
[6] Carter Heyward, *Saving Jesus From Those Who Are Right. Rethinking what it means to be Christian* (Augsburg Fortress Press: Minneapolis 1999).
[7] Heyward, *Saving Jesus*, xvi-xvii.
[8] Ibid., 32.

goes on to confess: "With you, I see that neither you nor I, nor any person or culture, nor any tribe or religion or species, nor past, present or future holds the keys to heaven, and that only together can we save this earth and liberate one another from those who are right – thank you Jesus, sweet sister."[9]

The critique of the notion of Jesus as the only saviour also comes from Asian feminist theologians, who choose to bypass the christological developments of the early councils, and construct a christology in dialogue between the biblical stories and soteriological motifs found in their native religious traditions. Kwok Pui-lan claims that Jesus' question, "Who do you say that I am?" must be answered anew in every new context, and that there can be many answers to that question. With the help of post-colonial theories, she proposes Jesus/Christ as a hybrid concept as a viable christology. Jesus/Christ has always been a hybridized concept, as it has travelled between the human and the divine, between the Jewish and Hellenistic world, and through the quests for the "historical Jesus", always set firmly in their own historical context. Today hybrid images of Christ are consciously produced in new contexts, like the Black Christ of the Afro-American community, the Shakti of Asian feminists or Jewish theologian Susannah Heschels's notion of Jesus as a "theological transvestite".[10]

Wisdom christologies are another option for feminist theology as well as for theology of religions. Hochma of the Hebrew Scriptures provides us with a female metaphor for God, which, though not unambiguous, is closely connected to creation and to a holistic concept of knowledge. Understanding Jesus as "Sophia's prophet"[11] or as Wisdom incarnate offers a less triumphalist image than traditional christologies. As there are female personifications of wisdom in other religious traditions, including Hinduism and Buddhism, a quest for wisdom in a feminist key opens a new road for the theology of religions.[12]

Salvation

Closely related to the issue of christology in the Christian tradition is that of salvation. Feminist theologies have criticised traditional soteriologies for being

---

[9] Ibid., 33.
[10] Kwok Pui-lan, *Postcolonial Imagination & Feminist Theology* (Westminster John Knox Press: Louisville 2005), 168-185
[11] Elisabeth Schüssler Fiorenza, *Jesus: Miriam's Child, Sophia's Prophet. Critical Issues in Feminist Christology* (Continuum: New York 1994).
[12] I have developed this idea in an unpublished M. Phil thesis at the Irish School of Ecumenics, *Sophia in Interfaith Dialogue* 1997.

too focused on transcendent, after-life, end-of-time salvation. In its place, they have advocated an imminent concept of salvation, concerned with well-being here and now, a "now and then" instead of "once-and-for-all", a process rather than a product.

Christians have, says Carter Heyward, "had great difficulty living as participants in an unfinished, imperfect creation," and "the church has tried to complete the redemption story by suggesting that, in Jesus' death, God's desire for right relation with creation was finally completed or 'satisfied'."[13] Instead of being the completion of God's saving work, Heyward understands the uniqueness of Jesus as "a window into the ongoing processes of a creation that is unfinished, and as a partner in the saving work of healing and liberation."[14]

The theme of salvation as a process in which humans participate, easily lends itself to a pluralist understanding. Jeannine Hill Fletcher develops this idea in *Monopoly on Salvation*: "through active attention to solidarity and liberative relations to others, humans are agents in co-creating salvation. In the Christian story, none other than Jesus of Nazareth provides the pattern for salvation in solidarity and wholeness".[15] However, as the Jesus story is told and interpreted in today's multireligious context, salvation understood as restoring the world to wholeness must be "'worked out' in solidarity with the religiously other."[16]

Difference

Feminist theology has criticised the way in which gender has been constructed through the categories of hierarchy and difference. There are parallels in the way religion has been constructed, where in triumphalist versions of Christian theology other religions have been constructed as not only different, but inferior. Therefore, theology of religions could learn from the way feminists have grappled with central concepts like "difference", "relation" and "the other".

In its infancy, feminist theology had strong universalising tendencies, which were challenged by womanists and feminists from the Third World. Since then, an affirmation of diversity, and reflections on how to live with differences

---

[13] Heyward, *Saving Jesus*, 25.
[14] Ibid., 24.
[15] Jeannine Hill Fletcher, *Monopoly on Salvation? A Feminist Approach to Religious Pluralism* (Continuum: New York 2005), 122.
[16] Ibid., 126.

without glossing over tensions due to power relations, has been part of feminist discourse. Only through acknowledging difference can relations be built, argues Audre Lorde: "it is not those differences between us that separate us. It is rather our refusal to recognize those differences, and to examine the distortions which result from our misnaming them and their effects upon human behaviour and expectation."[17] Additionally, the idea of multiple, hyphenated or hybrid identities has arisen from women's experiences of never being completely at home in any context, for example as a feminist in the church, or as a Christian in the women's movement, and their need to negotiate these situations of inclusion and exclusion, of identification and "othering".

Feminist theologians like Maura O'Neill and Jeannine Hill Fletcher have criticised theologies of religion for their universalising tendencies and failure to affirm diversity. Current theologies of religion stand in an impasse of sameness and difference, says Jeannine Hill Fletcher,[18] because they view difference as a problem to be overcome, not as a theological resource. Either differences between religious traditions are collapsed into an essential sameness, or the differences are seen as so essential as to preclude dialogue. The solution would be to cease viewing religious traditions as bounded wholes, and instead see them as diverse and fluid. The feminist experience of, and reflexion upon, hybrid identities, and of not being able to identify with a religious tradition in its totality, but always being "the other" can show a way out of the impasse.[19]

Kwok Pui-lan offers the term "theology of religious difference" instead of "theology of religions" as a means of moving beyond the pluralist paradigm and bringing postcolonial as well as feminist insights into the discourse. Like Hill Fletcher, she wants to move away from the idea of "religions" as bounded wholes, stressing that "religion" is a Christian theological category, which has been constructed within a colonial framework. She calls on theologians to make use of religious studies and cultural studies, to study how religious difference has been constructed, and "[i]n the age of globalisation, how religion intersects with gender, race and transnationalism."[20] In such a study, the reality of hybridized religious identities must also be taken into account. The feminist contribution to a theology of religious difference would be to analyse

---

[17] Audre Lorde, *Sister Outsider* (Crossing Press: Trumansburg, N.Y. 1984), 115.
[18] Fletcher, *Monopoly,* 62-81.
[19] Ibid., 82-101.
[20] Kwok, *Postcolonial Imagination*, 207.

how gender has played into the construction of Christian identity and religious difference.[21]

Relation

Relationality is a key concept in feminist theology, and here too feminist theologies of relation have much to offer the discourse on interfaith relations. A relational ontology, according to which we understand God in relational terms and see human existence as being-in-relation, has consequences for how we perceive the religious "other". The philosophy of Levinas exerts a certain influence on theologies of religion today. For Levinas, the foundation for ethical behaviour is the radical demand of "the face of the other". However, the problem for Levinas is how to enter into relation with the other without either dominating or being crushed by it. The feminist critique would point out that for Levinas' male enlightenment subject, constituted by separation, to enter into relation to the other is a threatening project. By contrast, in a relational ontology, the self is constituted by its relations.

Additionally, feminist experience of being "the other" and reflections on the construction of woman as "other" ("the second sex") can help deconstructing the "religious other", and make mutual relation possible. Carter Heyward in her theology of mutual relation identifies "self-absorption", to be turned in toward oneself, as a detrimental consequence of western individualism. Redemption from this self-absorption comes through God understood as "power in relation".[22] Heyward understands reality as radically relational, interconnected in such a way that "all parts of the whole are mutually interactive". "Mutual" is understood metaphysically as well as ethically: everything is interconnected, but we must also struggle against self-absorption to notice and make this mutuality the basis for our existence and acting in the world. God, then, is to be found in this mutual relation: "God *is* the movement that connects us all".[23] This sacred power of mutual relation can be understood through the Buddhist concept of "dependent co-arising", as well as through the image of the Trinity: "A Trinitarian faith [...] would never require that people be Christian in order to be saved."[24]

---

[21] Ibid.
[22] Heyward, *Saving Jesus*, 5.
[23] Ibid., 61.
[24] Ibid., 73.

Carter Heyward understands self-absorption as not only concerning the individual him/herself, but also one's family, property, race, class, gender and religion. By extension then, we can understand Christianity as a self-absorbed religion, as long as it does not understand itself in relation to other religious traditions. Only by realising our interconnectedness with people of other faiths can we develop mutual relations, which will bring us closer to the mystery of God as "power in relation".

Marginality

In the women's interfaith events I studied for my dissertation, marginality was a significant feature which was often commented upon. The women operated from the supposition that women are marginal in religious traditions; the very impetus for the events was a reaction to the fact that women are marginalised in interfaith dialogue so that they have not had much impact on malestream interfaith dialogue. At the same time, marginality was turned into an asset. "The margins is a good place for dialogue" said Diana Eck, commenting upon the WCC women's interfaith consultation in 1988, "the reach is not so far, the investment in centrist positions is not so great".[25]

Standpoint epistemology has been a contested issue in feminist theory. It has been questioned whether the marginalised perspective is a truer, or better perspective, why should a marginalised perspective be privileged? I would, however, like to exclude the question of standpoint epistemology from my reflections on marginality. For me, Diana Eck's words "the reach is not so far", conflate the image of the margin with that of the border or boundary. If we consider what happens at borders of cultures, this opens up exciting perspectives which can also be applied to religions..

Contemporary cultural theory increasingly puts a focus on what happens at the boundaries of culture, arguing that this is where culture is shaped and renewed through interaction with surrounding cultures. Cultures are not seen as sharply bounded, self-contained units, but as fluid and constantly changing. In this process of change, a culture is held together, not by sharp boundaries or consensus, but by a common focus of engagement, in the struggle over the meaning and place of cultural elements. In this understanding, cultural elements can cross boundaries without jeopardizing the distinctiveness of a culture. Cultural identity is then constituted by the way these elements are to be

---

[25] Diana Eck, "Moderator's Report", in: *Current Dialogue* 16 (1989), 20.

appropriated or resisted within the culture. This is an interrelational, hybrid understanding of cultural identity.

Kathryn Tanner has applied this to Christian identity, as it is shaped by its interaction with the surrounding culture. Christian identity is not constituted by sharp borders, as proponents of neoliberal theology claim. Instead, argues Tanner, the boundary is "one of use that allows Christian identity to be essentially impure and mixed, the identity of a hybrid that always shares cultural forms with its wider host culture and other religions (notably Judaism). [...] Christianity is a hybrid through and through; nothing need be exempted out of fear that the distinctiveness of Christianity must otherwise be lost. Moreover – and most significantly – [...] the distinctiveness of a Christian way of life is not so much formed *by* the boundary as *at* it; Christian distinctiveness is something that emerges in the very processes occurring at the boundary, processes that construct a distinctive identity for Christian social practices through the distinctive use of cultural material shared with others".[26]

Tanner's argument is that Christian tradition is not fixed, but can and must change as the surrounding culture changes. Christian practices change, but are held together by "the common reference to the God to whom they all hope effectively to witness"[27] and new practices can not only be found within the tradition, but also from outside it. Such borrowed elements should not, argues Tanner, "always be subordinated to Christian claims; they should be permitted, instead, to shake them up where necessary."[28]

Tanner's use of cultural theory could also be applied to how Christian theology is developed in the interaction with other religious traditions. If the word "border" is allowed to retain something of its geographical meaning, then religious traditions might be understood as countries, with capitals in the middle – which is the place of established theology, authorized scriptures and liturgies, guarded by the religious dignitaries – and a borderland, where people, as often happens in a borderland, have more in common with those living on the other side of the border than with those in the capital, where languages merge and all kinds of more or less legal transactions take place. The capital could equal what in religious studies is called "the great tradition", or "religion as

---

[26] Kathryn Tanner, *Theories of Culture. A New agenda for Theology* (Augsburg Fortress Press: Minneapolis 1997), 114-115.
[27] Ibid., 136.
[28] Ibid., 150.

prescribed", and the borderland as "the little tradition", or "religion as practised". Alternatively, the capital might equal orthodoxy and the borders new, still marginal(ized) developments in theology, such as feminist theology, creation theology or queer theology. Then the margins become a creative space, the place where religious change takes place, where religious identity is shaped, and the dialogue that goes on there would point the way forward, whereas in the capitals it would just reify old patterns.

"Religion as practised" and the messiness of actual existence

Finally, feminist theology should take more account of "religion as practised", and work in an interdisciplinary way with anthropology and religious studies. From the beginning, "women's experiences" and "theology of lived life" have been the starting points of feminist theology. However, with the increasing suspicion against the notion of women's experience, it has withdrawn to theoretical discussions, at least in the West. Necessary as this development has been, maybe it is time to return to the experiential method, but in a new way. Besides working from personal experience, we could draw on the work of feminist anthropologists, who have studied how women live their faith in everyday life. Susan Sered's work on Jewish women as "ritual experts" and religions dominated by women are examples of such sources of knowledge.[29]

Feminist theologians in the Third world have concerned themselves more with ordinary women's religious practices. The Korean interest in shamanism is a case in point. There is sometimes a tendency to romanticise "people's religion", but with the insights of anthropology and religious studies, the destructive sides of religion as practised can be criticised, just as are those of institutional religion, while the life-giving practices can be a source of inspiration. The point, however, is not so much to pass judgements as to create a theology of religion that takes account of the religion that real people actually practice, in all its messiness.

"Messiness" is another concept that appears in feminist theology, not least in its reflection on religious diversity. In Asia, says Chung Hyun Kyung, "there is a messy and fluid process of cross-permeation among the different religions."[30] In the same vein, Marjorie Suchocki warns that we should not seek

---

[29] Susan Starr Sered, *Women as Ritual Experts: The Lives of Elderly Jewish Women in Jerusalem* (Oxford University Press: New York 1992); *Priestess, Mother, Sacred Sister: Religions Dominated by Women* (Oxford University Press: New York 1994).

[30] Chung Hyun Kyung: "The Wisdom of Mothers Knows No Boundaries", in: *Women's perspectives* (WCC Gospel and Culture Series: Geneva 1996), 31.

Thema
Theme
Tema

to control life through too clear definitions: "They are useful abstractions from the messiness of lived experience that leave the fullness of that experience behind. [...] Seeing the world through concepts, we become blind to whatever does not fit into our conceptual scheme."[31] The implications for a theology of religions then, is that if God is not to be found in conceptual systems, "but in the messiness of evolutionary life, the expressions of this God, and the ultimacy thus represented, will necessarily be pluralistic."[32]

A feminist theology of religions should then not only concern itself with "religion as prescribed", but with "religion as practised", lived faith. It should make use of the insights of feminist theology concerning the hermeneutics of suspicion, relationality, and difference, as well as feminist reflection upon Christology, soteriology and other areas of "classical" dogmatics – and above all, it should dare to dwell on the margins, in the borderland where everything is in flux, and in a creative state of becoming. In this way, it can challenge malestream theology of religions as well as lingering exclusivist and supremacist tendencies within feminist theology.

Feministische Theologie hat bislang keinen großen Einfluß auf die Theologie der Religionen ausgeübt. Sie hat auch kaum auf die Fragen der Theologie der Religionen reagiert. Außerdem besteht kaum ein ernst zu nehmender Austausch zwischen feministischen Praktikerinnen im interreligiösen Dialog und feministischen Theologinnen. Dieser Beitrag legt dar, dass Einsichten der feministischen Theologie, insbesondere die Hermeneutik des Verdachts sowie die Diskurse über Relationalität und Differenz, notwendige Beiträge zur Theologie der Religionen liefern können. Konkret kann feministische Theologie die Theologie der Religionen herausfordern, sich an die Ränder der religiösen Traditionen zu begeben, wo sich Traditionen im kreativen Grenzbereich verändern und das „Chaos realer Existenz"greifbar wird.

Hasta ahora, la teología feminista no ha tenido gran influencia en la teología de las religiones. Y tampoco ha respondido a las cuestiones de la teología de las religiones. Además, hay una grave falta de comunicación entre las practicantes del diálogo interreligioso y las teólogas feministas. En este artículo se sostiene que la teología feminista puede ofrecer una importante contribución a la teología de las religiones a través de cómo percibe la hermenéutica de la sospecha, el discurso de relacionalidad y diferencia. En especial, la teología feminista puede desafiar a la teología

---

[31] Marjorie Suchocki, *Divinity and Diversity. A Christian Affirmation of Religious Pluralism* (Abingdon Press: Nashville 2003), 41.
[32] Ibid., 51.

de las religiones para que se sitúe en los márgenes de las tradiciones religiosas, en una zona fronteriza creativa en la que cambian las tradiciones y se admite el "caos de la existencia real".

Helene Egnell (*1957) is a Bishop's Adviser at the Centre for Inter Faith Dialogue in the Diocese of Stockholm, within the Church of Sweden. She was ordained as a minister in the Church of Sweden in 1988, and has served as a parish minister for many years. She studied at the Irish School of Ecumenics in Dublin 1994-1995, and wrote her M. Phil dissertation on *Sophia in Interfaith Dialogue*. She earned her doctorate at Uppsala University in 2006 with the dissertation *Other Voices: A Study of Christian Feminist Approaches to other Faiths*. She is chair of IKETH, Interreligiöse Konferenz Europäischer Theologinnen.

Annette Mehlhorn

Gleich und doch verschieden – getrennt verschieden oder gemeinsam?
*Intra*religiöse Debatten und *inter*religiöser Dialog im Wechselverhältnis zwischen Religion, Politik und Gender

Eine der Organisationen in Deutschland, die auf eine besonders lange Geschichte (über 40 Jahre) im interreligiösen Dialog aufbauen kann, ist das Bendorfer Forum für ökumenische Begegnung und interreligiösen Dialog e.V.[1] Hier habe ich gelernt, wie wichtig es ist, bei *inter*religiösen Begegnungen Räume für den *intra*religiösen Dialog zu öffnen. In den Bendorfer Begegnungen gehört die Versammlung in intrareligiösen Gruppen zum grundlegenden Prinzip des Dialoges.[2] In den folgenden Ausführungen möchte ich der Frage nachgehen, in welcher Wechselwirkung inter- und intrareligiöser Dialog stehen und welchen Erkenntnisgewinn ein bewusster Umgang mit dieser Wechselwirkung verspricht. Es wird deutlich werden, dass die Genderthematik dabei einen Dreh- und Angelpunkt darstellt, an dem sich entscheidet, inwiefern Konflikte ergebnisoffen ausgehandelt werden können.

Zwischen Zugehörigkeit und Abgrenzung
Die Erfahrung zeigt: Wenn interreligiöse Begegnungen von einem Geist der Wahrhaftigkeit getragen werden, brechen durch die Begegnung mit den „anderen" scheinbare Selbstverständlichkeiten bezüglich des „Eigenen" auf. Oft wird dadurch das „Eigene" sehr viel mehr zur Diskussion gestellt, als das „Andere", dem man eine gewisse exotische Fremdheit durchaus zubilligt. Zugleich können völlig neue interreligiöse Allianzen entstehen, wenn zentrale ethisch-moralische Fragen, Themen der Lebensform oder der persönlichen Orientierung ins Gespräch kommen. Gräben in Debatten führen oft nicht an den Grenzen zwischen Religionen entlang, sondern gehen mitten durch sie hindurch. Wie mit solchen Widersprüchen umgegangen wird, ob sie tabuisiert,

---
[1] www.bendorferforum.de
[2] Vgl. auch den Beitrag von Humera Khan in diesem Band.

Thema
Theme
Tema

auf Sündenböcke projiziert oder als Konfliktfelder offen ausgehandelt werden, ist ein entscheidender Indikator für einen „erwachsenen" Umgang mit Interessens- und Orientierungskonflikten.

Zwei Beispiele:
1. Die interreligiöse Frauengruppe „Sarah und Hagar – Religion, Politik, Gender" traf sich seit 2001, um Impulse für die Sozialpolitik in den Themenfeldern Arbeit, Familie und Bildung zu erarbeiten.[3] Qualifizierte Beraterinnen unterstützen die Gruppe bei ihrem Meinungsbildungsprozess. Die Debatten waren zum Teil hitzig, aber sie führten die Gruppe Schritt für Schritt dem Ziel eines gemeinsam verantworteten Impulspapieres entgegen. Als es im Herbst/Winter 2003/2004 in Hessen zu politischen Debatten um das Kopftuch kam, entstand in einer Sitzung die Idee, als interreligiöse Frauengruppe eine gemeinsame Erklärung in Solidarität mit den Kopftuch tragenden Frauen zu veröffentlichen. Diese Erklärung wurde von einigen Frauen erarbeitet und beim nächsten Treffen eingebracht. Dabei stellte sich heraus, dass drei Frauen, die beim vorangehenden Treffen gefehlt hatten, sich nicht vorstellen konnten, eine solche Erklärung mit zu tragen. Bei diesen drei Frauen handelte es sich um eine Jüdin, eine Christin und eine Muslimin. Ein politischer Graben war aufgerissen, der sich durch die Religionsgemeinschaften zog. Es wurde offensichtlich, dass keine der Frauen für sich in Anspruch nehmen konnte, „die" Positionen ihrer Religionsgemeinschaft zu vertreten. Da in der diskutierten Frage kein Konsens zu erreichen war, das Vorgehen der Gruppe aber ansonsten nach dem Konsensprinzip geregelt wurde, war klar, dass es keine gemeinsame Erklärung zur Kopftuchfrage geben würde. An der heftigen Debatte, die folgte, wäre die Gruppe fast zerbrochen. Einzelne Frauen verabschiedeten sich. Diejenigen, die blieben, entdeckten eine neue Freiheit und Verantwortlichkeit für die gemeinsame Zielsetzung. Es gelang, wesentliche Aspekte der Interessen Kopftuch tragender Frauen in das Impulspapier einzuschreiben, ohne in der grundsätzlichen Frage eindeutig Position zu beziehen. In diesem Konflikt machte die Gruppe wichtige Schritte zum „Erwachsen-Sein".[4]

---

[3] Vgl. das Ergebnis dieses Arbeitsprozesses, die „Impulse für eine geschlechtergerechte Sozialpolitik auf der Basis jüdischer, christlicher und muslimischer Traditionen", in: *epd-Dokumentation* 6 (2006), 10-18.
[4] Das bestätigt auch die Einschätzung der hinzugezogenen Konfliktmoderatorin, die während des Konfliktes im persönlichen Gespräch äußerte, die Gruppe befände sich noch immer in

2. In Rüsselsheim gibt es einen „Arbeitskreis Interkulturelles Friedensgebet" in dem neben mir und einer katholischen Gemeindereferentin ca. 20 Männer aus katholischen, evangelischen, freikirchlichen, orthodoxen und verschieden ausgerichteten muslimischen Gemeinden mitwirken. Zu Beginn meiner Tätigkeit als Pfarrerin der Stadtkirchengemeinde Rüsselsheim wurde ich gebeten, bei einem der jährlich stattfindenden interreligiösen Gesprächsabende als evangelische Referentin aufzutreten. Das Thema des Abends „Was ist uns heilig?" hatte sich aus dem Karikaturenstreit entwickelt. Die Moderation hatte der katholische Vorsitzende des Arbeitskreises inne. Außer mir saßen ein Alevit und ein Sunnit auf dem Podium. Mein Beitrag zielte darauf ab, dass das gleiche Recht aller Menschen auf Würde und persönliche Entfaltung für mich zum unhinterfragbar „Heiligen" gehört. Diesem Recht für Menschen unterschiedlicher Religionen und Weltanschauungen, unterschiedlicher Kulturen, unterschiedlichen Geschlechts und unterschiedlicher sexueller Orientierung zur Geltung zu verhelfen sei ein wesentliches Ziel meines Engagements als evangelische Pfarrerin. Ein muslimischer Mann im Publikum stellte daraufhin die Frage, ob diese Haltung im Blick auf Homosexuelle in meiner Religionsgemeinschaft geteilt wird. Ich verwies auf eine synodale Entscheidung meiner Landeskirche zur Segnung von Homosexuellen. Sofort meldeten sich zwei evangelikal orientierte Männer im Publikum zu Wort, um klarzustellen, dass diese Entscheidung nicht von allen evangelischen Menschen gebilligt würde. Von diesem Moment an fand das Gespräch im Saal ausschließlich unter Männern statt, ohne dass ich weiter zu Wort gekommen wäre. Auch der Moderator wirkte dem nicht entgegen. Im Anschluss an die Diskussion bemerkte der sunnitische Podiumsteilnehmer mir gegenüber im Vier-Augen-Gespräch, selbstverständlich müsse man über die Frage der Gleichberechtigung von Frauen und Homosexuellen ins Gespräch kommen. Es hatte hier also entlang einer gemeinsamen Einstellung zur Homosexualität eine vorübergehende Interessensgemeinschaft zwischen Männern unterschiedlicher religiöser Orientierung gegeben. Dabei waren – ausschließlich in der christlichen Gruppe – intrareligiöse Differenzen sichtbar geworden. Diese waren durch normative Dominierung unter den Teppich gekehrt worden. Der für Gleichberechtigung von Frauen und Homosexuellen begrenzt offene muslimische Podiumsteilnehmer hatte nicht gewagt, der

---

einem unreifen Zustand der Abhängigkeit von der Gruppenleitung. In der Tat war ich als Leiterin und Initiatorin der Gruppe bis dahin von den anderen Frauen oft als die „Gruppenmama" betitelt worden – eine solche Rollenzuschreibung wäre inzwischen nicht mehr vorstellbar.

Thema
Theme
Tema

normativen Dominanz in der Öffentlichkeit etwas entgegenzustellen. Zum „Erwachsenwerden" im intra- und interreligiösen Dialog würde gehören, dass der Dissens benannt wird und die ihm zugrunde liegenden unterschiedlichen Interessen offen diskutiert werden.

„Wir" und „Ihr" auf wechselnden Seiten
Es ist wichtig, sich zu vergegenwärtigen, „dass im Dialog nicht ‚die Religionen' miteinander reden, sondern Menschen, die ihnen angehören. (…) Interreligiöser Dialog stellt demzufolge nicht einfach eine Beziehung zwischen zwei (gemeinschaftlichen) Religionen her, sondern bereits im einfachsten Fall eines Dialogs zwischen zwei Personen unterschiedlicher Religionszugehörigkeit entstehen Beziehungen zwischen vier verschiedenen Größen…".[5] Diese lassen sich modellhaft grammatikalisch in den ersten beiden Personen Singular und Plural abbilden.

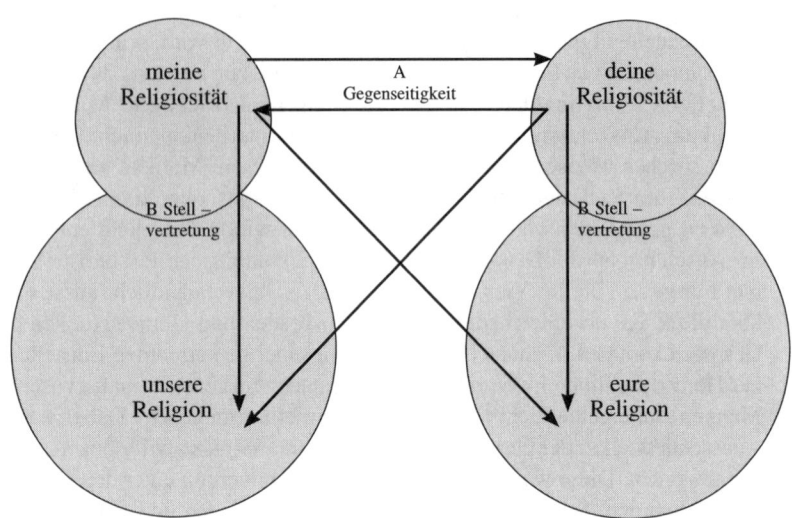

Interreligiöser Dialog nach Andreas Feldkeller

---

[5] Andreas Feldkeller, „Interreligiöser Dialog und Pluralistische Religionstheologie – ein Traumpaar?", in: *Ökumenische Rundschau* 49 (2000), 273-285.

Das Modell[6] verdeutlicht mehrere Ebenen der inter- und intrareligiösen Verständigung, die sich folgendermaßen zusammenfassen lassen: obwohl jede einzelne im interreligiösen Dialog stellvertretend für das Ganze der Religion steht, „ist das, was auf dem Spiel steht, fast ausschließlich ‚meine Religiosität'". Dialogbereitschaft heißt, das Risiko einzugehen, sich auf die andere Seite einzulassen, zuzuhören, sich in der eigenen Religiosität als einer in letzter Konsequenz persönlichen und individuellen Haltung befragen zu lassen. Auf diesem Weg werden wir auf die Grundlagen unseres Weltverstehens verwiesen. Da wir diese im Feld „Religion" mit anderen teilen und dieser Gemeinschaftsfaktor auch zur Religiosität grundlegend dazugehört, suchen wir nach Vergewisserung: Gibt es „unsere Religion"? Wie sieht sie aus?

Bei allen Religionsgemeinschaften handelt es sich um höchst komplexe Gebilde mit einer großen Variationsbereite an innerer Differenz und Pluralität, an Widersprüchen und Kontroversen zwischen den verschiedenen Traditionen, die zu der jeweiligen Religion gehören und zu ihren jeweiligen individuellen Vertretern/Vertreterinnen. Im Grunde gibt es innerhalb einer Religion so viele Glaubenswege wie es Menschen gibt, die für diese Religion eintreten.

Wenn ein „Ich" mit dem Anspruch auftreten kann, für das Ganze eines „Wir" zu sprechen, handelt es sich in der Regel um ein Gespräch auf institutioneller Ebene. In solchen Fällen werden zu gewichtigen Anteilen gruppenbezogene Macht- und Interessenskonflikte verhandelt. Die Suche nach einem ergebnisoffenen und damit persönlich risikoreichen Dialog spielt demgegenüber eine geringere Rolle. Hier geht es um Einfluss und Deutungshoheit und um die Verteilung von Privilegien, z.B. im Blick auf das Recht auf und die Aufsicht über den Religionsunterricht an öffentlichen Schulen, die Repräsentanz im öffentlich-rechtlichen Rundfunk, die Anerkennung als offizieller politischer Gesprächspartner. Vor allem dort, wo in Institutionen Hierarchien noch nicht klar sortiert sind – wie z.B. in und zwischen den muslimischen Verbänden in Deutschland – haben solche institutionellen Dialoge aber ebenfalls Rückwirkungen auf den intrareligiösen Dialog innerhalb der Gruppierungen und ihren Institutionen.

Auch jenseits institutioneller Beauftragungen, dogmatischer Festlegungen oder offizieller Religionsgespräche gibt es im Dialog eine „Wir"-Ebene. Auf sie beziehen sich die Angehörigen verschiedener Religionsgemeinschaften im

---

[6] Feldkeller, *Interreligiöser Dialog*, 275.

interreligiösen Dialog. Doch zugleich gibt es diese „Wir"-Ebene möglicherweise in mehreren Zusammenhängen, die nicht in jedem Fall *religiöse* Unterschiede markieren. Im oben geschilderten Konflikt der Sarah-Hagar-Gruppe gab es in einem bestimmten Augenblick ein gemeinsames „Wir" der Kopftuchgegnerinnen, das aus einzelnen Frauen aller drei Religionen gebildet wurde. Ähnlich schlossen sich die Gegner der Gleichberechtigung im zweiten Beispiel zu einem religionsübergreifenden „Wir" zusammen.

Die genannten Beispiele zeigen, dass „Wirs" oft weniger entlang von Glaubenslinien entstehen als aufgrund von Macht- und Interessenskonstellationen. Um diese zu benennen und zu diskutieren, helfen intrareligiöse Debatten im interreligiösen Dialog. Von dort ausgehend lassen sich diese natürlich – wie ebenfalls an den beiden Beispielen ersichtlich – auch in interreligiösen Debatten benennen und diagnostizieren.

Differenz und Gleichheit

Es braucht *intra*religiöse Debatten, um in *inter*religiösen Fragen voranzukommen. In einer sich pluralisierenden und differenzierenden Welt gilt zugleich: Es braucht *inter*religiöse Debatten, um sich *intra*religiös auszudifferenzieren und zu entwickeln. Unterschiedliche Zugehörigkeiten (unterschiedliche „Wirs") kommen auf diese Weise in den Blick und können als Teil einer gemeinsamen Realität angenommen werden. Auf diese Weise unterstützt der Dialog die Entwicklung eines emanzipierten Selbst- und Menschenbildes, in dem das individuelle Recht zur Entfaltung – also die volle Akzeptanz aller Aspekte der Menschenrechte – an erster Stelle steht. All das ist Voraussetzung für das Gelingen eines Pluralisierungsprozesses, wie er in der „Charta der Grundrechte der Europäischen Union"[7] auf vorbildliche Weise angelegt ist.

Hinter dem Antidiskriminierungsparagraphen der *Charta* steht ein zukunftsweisendes Verständnis von „Diversity" (Vielfalt/Verschiedenheit). Es sucht nach einer Balance zwischen Unterschiedenheit und Zugehörigkeit. Antidiskriminierungsrichtlinien und die praktisch-politische Maßnahme des Gender Mainstreaming haben die konsequente Verwirklichung der Menschenrechte in

---

[7] „Charta der Grundrechte der Europäischen Union", in: *Amtsblatt der Europäischen Union C 303/1* (2007) Art. 21 Abs.1: „Diskriminierungen insbesondere wegen des Geschlechts, der Rasse, der Hautfarbe, der ethnischen oder sozialen Herkunft, der genetischen Merkmale, der Sprache, der Religion oder der Weltanschauung, der politischen oder sonstigen Anschauung, der Zugehörigkeit zu einer nationalen Minderheit, des Vermögens, der Geburt, einer Behinderung, des Alters oder der sexuellen Ausrichtung sind verboten."

Europa zum Ziel. Diese ist, so das Postulat, das hinter den Richtlinien steht, nur möglich, wenn Menschen in ihrer Verschiedenheit gleichberechtigt sein können. Es geht also um vollen Respekt gegenüber jeder Form von kultureller, weltanschaulicher oder biologischer Besonderheit im Unterschied zu einem wie auch immer für „normal" gehaltenen Grundverständnis vom Menschsein.

> „Die neuen Regeln richten sich gegen die seit Jahrhunderten tradierten geistigen und sozialen Orientierungen: Das Eigene und das Fremde, das Gesunde und das Kranke, das Rechtgläubige und das Heidnische, das gottgefällige, der Fortpflanzung der Menschheit dienende Eheleben und die als Perversion geächtete sexuelle Ausschweifung (…) Das Ziel (…) ist nicht die Schaffung einer Gesellschaft der Gleichen, sondern einer Gesellschaft, die in Anerkennung der Verschiedenartigkeit der Menschen jedem ein Leben in Würde sichert."[8]

Die Antidiskriminierungsrichtlinien sollen real oder potentiell Diskriminierten das Handwerkszeug an die Hand geben, dieses Ziel zu verfolgen. Sie gehen davon aus, dass die Entwicklung und Durchsetzung gemeinsamer Interessen und der Verfolgung gemeinsamer Ziele im demokratischen Zusammenspiel voraus setzt, dass Interessen voneinander unterschieden und gebündelt werden können. Gegenseitige Anerkennung von Verschiedenheit braucht die Orientierung an der notwendigen Komplementarität von Gleichheit und Differenz. Es geht darum, „heterogenen Lebensweisen *gleiches Recht* (zuzusprechen). Gleichheit ist also (…) *Bedingung der Möglichkeit von Differenz.* (…) Differenz ohne Gleichheit bedeutet gesellschaftliche Hierarchie, kulturelle Entwertung, ökonomische Ausbeutung. Gleichheit ohne Differenz bedeutet Assimilation, Anpassung, Gleichschaltung, Ausgrenzung des ‚Anderen'".[9]

Der intrareligiöse Dialog unterstützt im interreligiösen/interkulturellen Dialog einen bewussten und gleichberechtigten Umgang mit dem Wechselspiel

---

[8] Eberhard Eichenhofer, „Diskriminierungen der Rasse, ethnischen Herkunft, des Alters und der Behinderung. Vieldeutigkeiten und Operationalisierungsprobleme aus gemeinschaftsrechtlicher Sicht", in: Ursula Rust / Wolfgang Däubler / Josef Falke / Joachim Lange / Konstanze Plett / Kirsten Scheiwe / Klaus Sieveking (Hg.), *Die Gleichbehandlungsrichtlinien der EU und ihre Umsetzung in Deutschland* (Loccumer Protokolle 40; Evangelische Akademie Loccum: Rehburg-Loccum 2003), 73-90, hier 86f.

[9] Annedore Prengel, „Gleichheit versus Differenz – eine falsche Alternative im feministischen Diskurs", in: Ute Gerhard / Mechtild Jansen / Andrea Maihofer / Pia Schmid / Irmgard Schulz (Hg.), *Differenz und Gleichheit. Menschenrechte haben (k)ein Geschlecht* (Ulrike Helmer: Königstein 1997; Erstaufl. 1990), 120-127, hier 124.

Thema
Theme
Tema

zwischen Religion(en), Politik (Macht, Interesse) und Gender. Der Gender-Faktor stellt in jedem religiösen und kulturellen Milieu einen internen Differenz-Faktor dar, der hilft, das Diversity-Thema mehrschichtig zu erörtern. Im Dreieck Religion-Politik-Gender kann die Differenz-und-Gleichheitsthematik in ihren existenziell grundlegenden und sozial bestimmenden Aspekten diskutiert werden.

Dass diese Chance auch auf Europäischer Ebene weiterhin ergriffen und entwickelt werden muss, zeigt der fortgesetzte Diskussionsprozess um ein demokratisches Management kultureller Vielfalt, wie er z.B. im „White Paper on Intercultural Dialogue" vom Mai 2008 sichtbar wird.[10] In dieses Papier wird Gleichberechtigung der Geschlechter als „nicht verhandelbare Voraussetzung" eingeschrieben (1.3.) und als für alle Religionen und Kulturen noch einzulösendes Desiderat herausgestellt (3.4.3). Dennoch wird das Thema Diversity in allen übrigen Passagen primär als Thema ethnischer, kultureller und religiöser Prägung verhandelt. Der Faktor sexuelle Identität scheint demgegenüber kein relevantes Differenzierungskriterium darzustellen. Das legt die Vermutung nahe, dass in diesem Papier noch immer eine heterosexuelle Einheitsnorm für das Verständnis der Geschlechter und die Unterordnung geschlechtlicher Gleichberechtigung unter andere Gleichberechtigungsforderungen prägend bleibt.

Wer Diversity ernst nimmt, muss auch die Differenz innerhalb von ethnischen, kulturellen oder religiösen Gruppen thematisieren. Dazu eignet sich in besonderer Weise der Genderfaktor. Ich werde abschließend der Frage nachgehen, warum gerade in diesem Faktor dem Pluralisierungsprozess am meisten Widerstand entgegengesetzt wird.

Gender-Differenz als intrareligiöses Differenzierungskriterium
Es ist kein Zufall, dass in den oben genannten Beispielen intrareligiöser Diskussionen jeweils die Infragestellung einer patriarchalen Einheitsnorm und die Anerkennung der vorhandenen Differenzen zur Verschiebung der Trennlinien zwischen den Religionen und zum Aufbrechen intrareligiöser Unterschiede geführt hat: An der Infragestellung eines patriarchalen Menschenbildes setzt die Frage nach Deutungshoheit und Überlegenheitsanspruch des vermeintlich „Normalen" als erstes an.

Martin Riesebrodt zeigt, dass fast alle „Spielarten des Fundamentalismus, ob charismatisch oder legalistisch-literalistisch, ob christlich oder muslimisch

---

[10] www.coe.int/dialogue

(sich) darüber einig zu sein (scheinen), dass die ideale Sozialordnung auf patriarchalischer Grundlage zu ruhen habe, dass die patriarchalische Familie und nicht das Individuum die soziale Einheit darstelle, auf der Gesellschaft aufbaut und dass die Geschlechterrollen von ‚Gott' oder von ‚Natur' aus unterschiedlich, aber aufeinander bezogen konzipiert seien."[11]

Dabei spielen Frauen oft eine hervorragende Rolle als Agitatorinnen / Missionarinnen dieses Gesellschaftsideals. In begrenztem Umfang werden also gerade Frauen in öffentlichen Funktionen eingesetzt, um das patriarchale Sozialmodell fundamentalistischer Gruppierungen nach außen zu vertreten:

„Die aktive, öffentliche Teilnahme von Frauen in fundamentalistischen Bewegungen stellt (...) ein besonders interessantes Phänomen dar, weil sich darin ein zweifaches Paradox auszudrücken scheint, ein normatives und ein strukturelles. Das normative Paradox besteht darin, dass sich Frauen für etwas engagieren, was gemäß westlichen Emanzipationsvorstellungen ihre eigene Unterdrückung beinhaltet. Das strukturelle Paradox liegt darin, dass der Fundamentalismus die Frauen auf die häusliche Sphäre beschränken will, sie aber gleichzeitig zu diesem Ziel politisiert und massenhaft in die Öffentlichkeit bringt."[12]

Betrachtet man das Phänomen fundamentalistischer Bewegungen und Tendenzen mit Martin Riesbrodt als „Vergemeinschaftungen in einem Kulturkonflikt", die auf wachsendes Unbehagen in der Moderne und die Unübersichtlichkeit pluralistischer Gesellschaften zurückgehen, so wird an den oben genannten Beispielen deutlich, dass sich im interreligiösen Dialog auch fundamentalistische Haltungen innerhalb kultureller Vielfalt positionieren und nach neuen „Wirs" suchen. Zur Rettung einer fundamentalistischen Einheitsnorm werden dann sogar religions- und kulturübergreifende Koalitionen möglich.[13] Die Chance liegt darin, solche interessensgebundenen Haltungen offenzulegen und zur Debatte zu stellen. Das gelingt letztlich nur, wenn sie auch innerhalb der religiösen Gruppierungen ausgetragen werden können. Dass dies nicht nur innerhalb einiger muslimischer oder evangelikaler Gruppierungen und Verbände schwierig ist, sondern ebenfalls die größte institutionalisierte

---

[11] Martin Riesebrodt, *Die Rückkehr der Religionen. Fundamentalismus und der „Kampf der Kulturen"* (Beck: München 2000), 117.

[12] Riesebrodt, *Die Rückkehr der Religionen*, 119f.

[13] Vgl. die Ausführungen von Uta Blohm in diesem Band, in denen ebenfalls deutlich wird, wie am Gender-Faktor die Grenze zwischen politischen Positionierungen sichtbar wird und dabei die Grenze zwischen den Religionen oft an Bedeutung verliert.

Thema
Theme
Tema

christliche Gemeinschaft in Europa betrifft, zeigt das fortgesetzt am Rande dieser Gemeinschaft stattfindende Ringen katholischer Frauen um das Priesteramt und der dort weiter unter dem Mantel der Doppelmoral verborgene Umgang mit sexueller Abweichung von der Einheitsnorm.

All solche Versuche der Dominierung von Abweichungen durch eine nach außen postulierte „Normalität" können Entwicklungen nicht aufhalten, deren erreichten Aggregatzustand Peter L. Berger den „Zwang zur Häresie"[14] nennt, die Notwendigkeit eigener Wahl und Freiheit. Denn selbst in eher traditionell und kollektivistisch orientierten Kulturen wird durch Informations- und Kommunikationsmedien das ganze globale Angebot an Orientierungsmöglichkeiten verbreitet. Damit stehen Alternativen zur jeweils konkret vorgegebenen Norm zur Wahl.[15]

Globales Zusammenwachsen und weltweite Migrationsbewegungen haben dazu geführt, dass ethische Vereinbarungen, in deren Rahmen die Beziehung von Recht und Pflicht im sozialen und politischen Kontext bestimmt wird, neu sortiert und aufgebaut werden müssen. Religiöse Traditionen *können* hierfür geeignete Reflexionskontexte bieten, die durchaus miteinander kompatibel sind. Bereitschaft zum kritischen Diskurs und Dialog mit anderen – auch innerhalb der eigenen Gruppe – ist die Vorraussetzung dafür. Sie braucht Eigenverantwortung und Mut zur Entscheidung.[16] Die oben aufgeführten Beispiele zeigen die Schwierigkeiten, Positionen zwischen Zugehörigkeit und Abgrenzung auszuloten. Es bedarf dazu persönlicher Verantwortungsübernahme, der Bereitschaft, in Fragen der Orientierung und Weltgestaltung „auf eigenen Beinen" zu stehen und zugleich Verbindlichkeiten im Blick auf soziale Prozesse einzugehen. Die Entwicklung und fortgesetzte Diskussion von gemeinsamen Werten und Grundlagen ethischer Ziele und Maßstäbe für die Gestaltung des Zusammenlebens in einer globalisierten Welt ist ohne eine solche Bereitschaft zur Verantwortungsübernahme nicht vorstellbar. Das individuelle und soziale Handwerkszeug dafür muss vielerorts noch entwickelt

---

[14] Peter L. Berger, *Der Zwang zur Häresie. Religion in der pluralistischen Gesellschaft* (Herder: Freiburg i. Br. 1992), sowie ders., *Sehnsucht nach Sinn. Glauben in einer Zeit der Leichtgläubigkeit* (Gütersloher Verlagshaus: Gütersloh 1999)

[15] Das gilt, wie am Beispiel China deutlich wird, selbst dort, wo rigide totalitaristische Regimes versuchen, den Zugriff auf Information und Kommunikation zu behalten.

[16] Nicht zufällig findet der größte Teil interreligiöser Begegnungen bisher vorwiegend auf Grassrootebene statt. Dass darüber aber Wichtiges erreicht werden kann, zeigt sowohl das Parliament of the World's Religions, das im Juli 2004 zum vierten Mal in Barcelona tagte (www.cpwr.org), als auch die Aktivitäten der „United Religions Initiative" (www.uri.org).

und aufgebaut werden. Interreligiöse und gendersensible Bildungsprozesse sind dafür besonders geeignet.

Fazit
Pluralisierung und Individualisierung der Lebenswelten im globalisierten Kontext stellen ebenso hohe Anforderungen an das individuelle Orientierungsvermögen wie an soziale Prozesse und die sie organisierenden Institutionen. „Religion" bzw. „Glauben" (das „was uns unbedingt angeht") stellen einen Ernstfall existenzieller Selbstvergewisserung in einem Gemeinschaftszusammenhang dar. Darum ermöglicht der *inter*religiöse Dialog die Entwicklung von Fähigkeiten der Unterscheidung im Blick auf persönliche Präferenzen, Interessensklärungen und Solidarzusammenhänge. Der *intra*religiöse Dialog unterstützt dabei die weitere Ausdifferenzierung dieser Klärungsprozesse. Zugehörigkeit und Abgrenzung können in der Komplementarität des inter- und intrareligiösen Dialoges justiert werden. Die Genderfrage spielt dabei eine Schlüsselrolle, weil sie einen intrareligiösen Differenzierungsfaktor darstellt, der zugleich interreligiöse Gemeinsamkeiten sichtbar macht.

The pluralisation and individualisation of life in the globalised context make equally high demands on the individual's ability to find orientation and on social processes and the institutions which organise them. "Religion" or "faith" (that which is our "ultimate concern") constitute a test case for existential self-assurance in a community context. Hence, inter-religious dialogue facilitates the development of the capacity to decide in reference to personal preferences, clarification of interests and links of solidarity. Intra-religious dialogue also supports further differenciation in this process of clarification. Membership and delimitation can be adjusted in the complementarity between inter- and intra-religious dialogue. In this, the gender issue plays a key part because it constitutes an intra-religious factor for differentiation which simultaneously brings common inter-religious characteristics to light.

La pluralización y la individualización de nuestras vidas en el mundo globalizado exigen mucho tanto de nuestra capacidad de orientarnos como de los procesos sociales y de las instituciones que organizan dichos procesos. La "religión" o la "fe" (lo que nos "concierne absolutamente") son un caso de urgencia del autoaseguramiento existencial en una comunidad. Es por ello que el diálogo interreligioso hace posible aprender a discernir preferencias personales de intereses y de contextos solidarios, sirviendo aquí el diálogo intrarreligioso para seguir adelante con este proceso de clarificación. La complementariedad del diálogo interreligioso e intrarreligioso ayuda a encontrar un ajuste entre formar parte de algo o demarcarse. La cuestión del género juega aquí un papel decisivo, debido a que es un factor de diferenciación intrarreligioso, que pone de manifiesto a la vez lo que se tiene en común a nivel interreligioso.

Annette Mehlhorn (*1958), Studium der Theologie und Theaterpädagogik in Jerusalem, Frankfurt, Heidelberg und Berlin, schauspielerische Tätigkeiten in Berlin, Rom und quer durch Europa. Promotion mit einer religionswissenschaftlichen Arbeit über Verbindungen zwischen Theater und Religion. Pfarrerin und Studienleiterin in Frankfurt, Arnoldshain und Rüsselsheim, Vorsitzende des Bendorfer Forums für ökumenische Begegnung und Interreligiösen Dialog e.v., Mitbegründerin der Initiative „Sarah und Hagar. Religion-Politik-Gender". Jüngste Publikation gemeinsam mit Gisela Matthiae, Renate Jost, Claudia Janssen und Antje Röckemann (Hg.), *Feministische Theologie. Initiativen, Kirchen, Universitäten – eine Erfolgsgeschichte* (Gütersloher Verlagshaus: Gütersloh 2008).

Manuela Kalsky and Katharina von Kellenbach

Interreligious Dialogue and the Development of a Transreligious Identity
A Correspondence[*]

Dear Manuela,
When I entered interreligious dialogue as a student of Protestant theology, the theoretical framework and theological expectations were clear: the solidly trained and identified Christian would reach out, engage in conversation and learn about the different practices, traditions and beliefs of the religious other – in my case those "others" were Jews. Missionary efforts were declared anathema, nobody was to be converted and those on each side were supposed to maintain their religious distinctiveness as Jews and Christians. True, the Christian engaged in such dialogue in anticipation of having her Christian anti-Judaism challenged. She was prepared to amend her anti-Jewish biblical hermeneutics, to suffer the loss of theological heroes and teachers over their anti-Semitic attitudes, and to struggle with Christology and the trinity. But dialogue was supposed to deepen one's original religious identification. It was neither supposed to lead to conversion nor to syncretism and *mishmash,* as the anglicised Yiddish would put it.

But a dream, early in my career in interreligious dialogue during the mid-eighties, alerted me to the fact that my interreligious practice was beginning to affect deeper and unconscious levels. It was a dream that made no sense in Christian symbolic and ritual language and could only be interpreted within a Jewish framework. I had been invited to my first Orthodox Jewish Passover in Allentown, PA. I was nervous and dreamt during the preceding night that I arrived at the door of my friend with a large suitcase. She became suspicious and told me that she had just cleaned her house of all *hametz* (no yeast may remain in the house, and all bread, noodles, flour, etc has to be removed) and that she wanted to make sure that I had nothing in my suitcase that would

---

[*] The letters were written between spring and late fall 2008.

Thema
Theme
Tema

break the laws of Passover. When I opened the suitcase, it contained cakes and loaves of bread. The crumbs were falling all over the threshold of her house. This dream not only expressed my fears of breaking Passover laws, but more significantly, it re-enacted a ritual of *Rosh HaShana*. During the Jewish New Year, observant Jews put breadcrumbs in their pockets and walk to a moving stream. There the breadcrumbs symbolizing one's sins and trespasses are thrown into the water in preparation for *Yom Kippur*, the Day of Atonement. I had participated in such a Rosh HaShana observance the fall before and had been moved by this ritual of cleansing and renewal. The dream fused these two rituals and I realized for the first time that I would have to pursue my family's history during National Socialism if I wanted to enter the houses of my Jewish dialogue partners without guilty baggage. My dream of being forced to open a suitcase full of breadcrumbs on the threshold of a house prepared for Passover proved to be prophetic of my later research in German family history during National Socialism.[1] But I am telling this story to show how deeply Jewish ritual symbolism had ingrained itself into my unconscious. This dream was the beginning of a slow border crossing between the Jewish and Christian religious traditions.

My story is not exceptional. A good number in my cohort of Protestant theologians who started on the path of Jewish-Christian dialogue have since converted to Judaism – an option that I have contemplated occasionally and rejected (so far).[2] Instead a third way suggested itself between the either/or of conversion: the go-between, *Grenzgänger*, the smuggler who makes a living on the border and maintains homes in two places.[3] Smugglers move goods

---

[1] Katharina von Kellenbach, "Vanishing Acts: Perpetrators in Postwar Germany", in: *Journal of Holocaust and Genocide Studies* 17 (2/2003), 305-329; Ead., "Vergangenheitsbewältigung: Familienlegenden und Archivforschung", in: Brigitta Huhnke / Björn Krondorfer (eds), *Das Vermächtnis annehmen: Kulturelle und Biographische Zugänge an den Holocaust. Beiträge aus den USA und Deutschland* (Psychosozial Verlag: Hamburg 2002), 275-299.

[2] Walter Homolka (ed.), *Nicht durch Geburt allein: Übertritt zum Judentum* (Knesebeck: München 1995); Leo Trepp / Gunda Wöbken, *Denn dein Gott ist mein Gott: Wege zum Judentum und zur jüdischen Gemeinschaft* (Kohlhammer: Stuttgart 2005); Pnina Nave Levinson, *Aus freier Entscheidung: Wege zum Judentum* (Hentrich & Hentrich: Teetz 2002). Several personal narratives presented in these anthologies document extensive Christian theological training and exposure to Jewish-Christian dialogue that prepared the path towards conversion to Judaism.

[3] Katharina von Kellenbach / Susanne Scholz (eds), *Zwischen-Räume: Deutsche Feministische Theologinnen im Ausland* (LIT Verlag: Münster 2000).

across borders and are considered criminals in the eyes of those charged with protecting the integrity of the community. Because they subvert religious (national) boundaries they pose a threat to interreligious dialogue.

What may interreligious dialogue mean in a secular world where the boundaries between religious communities have become porous and fluid as a matter of course? For many, religious identity and communal identification have become matters of choice and conflict. We experience loyalty and spiritual connection not only with our religious families of origin but also with new friends in the global marketplace of religious and philosophical traditions, as well as social and political movements. Jews celebrate Christmas and Christians celebrate Passover, communities are led by Jewish-Christian pastors and Christian-Jewish rabbis, Jews practice Buddhism and Christians identify as Wiccans. The women's movement has become a spiritual home for many of us, and these ties prove often stronger than the bonds with our respective faith communities. The keepers of orthodox doctrine and catholic consistency have sometimes more in common with each other than with their respective wayward flocks. Can the smuggler legitimately represent the community in dialogue?

* * *

Dear Katharina,
My first interreligious encounter also took place in the context of Christian-Jewish dialogue. During my theological studies I made the move from Marburg to Amsterdam, where subjects were taught at the university that did not yet exist in the early 1980s in Germany: women's studies and liberation theology. I had also heard that there was a rabbi in Hilversum at the Folkertsma Foundation called Yehuda Aschkenasy, who was a survivor of the Shoah and offered seminars on Judaism for German students. I did not yet know that these seminars would influence my theological approach to such an extent. They were confrontational, existential encounters and instructive moments in which I was more or less forced to engage with my identity as a German. No escape was possible: I was living in a country that had been invaded by Nazi-Germany and tangled up in a war, and before me stood a rabbi who had survived Auschwitz and made it his aim in life to work with young Germans so that it would never happen again.

In the Netherlands I was confronted with the prevailing anti-German mood: my car with its German license plates repeatedly received mysterious dents; my neighbour, who had fought in the Princess Irene Brigade against the "Moffen" (a disparaging Dutch term for Germans), regularly showed me the weapons collection that he preserved in his apartment two floors down. He would draw a knife from its sheath and would only reinsert it when he had made a small cut in his arm and it was sticky with blood. I avoided inviting my parents to visit as I was afraid of what might happen should my neighbour speak to my father, who was about the same age, if they happened to meet on the stairs.

These experiences and encounters caused me to feel increasingly personally involved and conscious of responsibility to help remove anti-Judaism from Christian theology. Converting to Judaism, as you had considered doing yourself, was not something I thought of, however. The challenge in engaging with Judaism lay for me more on intellectual and theological level and this was reflected in my dissertation on the re-vision of Christology from a feminist theological perspective.[4]

Christian identity

The analysis of anti-Judaism in Christian theology brought me to the realization that Christian identity had to emerge in relation to and no longer in contrast to the 'other'. The longer I engaged with Christology, the clearer it became that it was not enough to interpret Jesus within the context of Judaism in order to escape anti-Judaism in Christian theology. I owe a lot to the feminist theological work of Rosemary Radford Ruether. She set me on the track of understanding that Christian anti-Judaism had something to do with the search for Christian identity.[5] In order to be authentically Christian, one's own yearnings for salvation must be found in Jesus. And so it happened that in the 20th century Jesus of Nazareth became the Arian, the Communist, the feminist, the black liberator, etc. In the stories of Jesus, people were not looking for *inspiration* for a contemporary Christian identity – they wanted to seek and find *legitimization* for their hopes for salvation in the modern age. After all, these values could only be claimed as Christian values if Jesus embodied them too. This process of defining Christian identity occurs then – and now – at the expense of Judaism and other religions that are unwilling to accept the uniqueness and novelty of God's revelation in Jesus as the redeemer of the whole of mankind.

---

[4] Manuela Kalsky, *Christaphanien. Die Re-Vision der Christologie aus der Sicht von Frauen in unterschiedlichen Kulturen* (Gütersloher Verlagshaus: Gütersloh 2000).

[5] Rosemary Radford Ruether, *Faith and Fratricide. The Theological Roots of Anti-Semitism* (Seabury Press: New York 1974).

Christianity's claim to superiority and this hierarchical and dualistic notion of Christian identity was and still is the object of my critique. Instead of such a closed concept of identity, I am looking for a relational identity that is fundamentally open to the wisdom of other religions and wants to learn from them without anxiously setting itself apart from "the others."

Community and individual
You have chosen for yourself the position of smuggler, the one who slips through the holes in the barbed wire of religious traditions and thus fosters the "exchange of religious goods and values". The smuggler undermines the separation between religious traditions and gradually loosens the barriers between religious communities that become porous and fluid. And finally, you ask the question whether only the guardians of orthodoxy and unity have the right to speak on behalf of the community or whether those who, as smugglers, mix up the different religions into a *mishmash* also have this right.

I would like to ask a question, which arises from your query into who has the right to speak as representative of a certain community. Do you think that in the future we will be able to assume the existence of religious *communities* at all, in a culture that has become so individualistic? Do you consider participation in a community a precondition for the practice of a religion or can one be a Christian or a Jew without being an active member of a religious community? The situation in the Netherlands seems to be moving in this direction.

Although religiosity is a 'booming business' in the Netherlands, the number of church members is constantly declining. People are turning their backs on the church as an institution. Incidentally, this also applies to political parties, associations, trade unions etc. Many young people have no idea what Christianity is actually all about. While 60 percent of Dutch people still claim to be faithful, according to surveys, only 4 out of 10 mean a traditional faith. The rest fall into the category of "unbound spirituality". They are far from being smugglers who secretly draw on two traditions. For some time now they have been quite openly patching together their own religion from the wisdom sayings of differing traditions. 75 percent of the Dutch people are convinced that this is the way forward for religion in the future.[6] To be honest, I think that when smugglers speak they no longer do so in the name

---

[6] Ton Bernts / Gerard Dekker / Joep de Hart, *God in Nederland*: 1996-2006 (Ten Have: Kampen 2007).

Thema
Theme
Tema

of a whole gang of smugglers but as individuals who have picked out wisdom sayings from the religious traditions of Judaism, Christianity, Islam, Hinduism, Buddhism or Voodoo religion that suit their lives. They do not represent a group but only themselves, or perhaps two or three others that belong, though no longer as part of a religious community in the classical sense. How does this development fit with your question as to whether the smuggler can legitimately represent the whole community? I look forward to your reply.

* * *

Dear Manuela,
You are correct to point out that the metaphor of the smuggler depends upon the continued existence of borders and a sense of communal identity. And you are also right to note that membership in religious communities is waning in Europe where citizens experience themselves primarily as individuals without strong commitments to or sense of obligation towards particular religious communities. In secular societies, where individuals feel empowered to pick and choose religious wisdom from different traditions, the keepers of orthodox boundaries lose authority and smugglers become obsolete. But I am not convinced that we (already) live in such an open and borderless world in which individuals may think, pray and move freely. I want to provide two examples why I think that the subversive border crossing of smugglers will remain a relevant metaphor.

On the one hand, our borders have shifted from religious institutions to the secular realm of nation states. The image of the smuggler hails not accidentally from the world of nation states which has absorbed the desire for community and (almost) replaced religious markers of identity. This is especially true for Europe. The United States is different because religious communities continue to flourish despite (and because of) the individualism of the modern capitalist economy. But in both the European and American settings, religion has been relegated to the private sphere of personal sentiments. The public political realm of communal affairs is shaped primarily by secular, national, liberal and rational discourses. This arrangement is currently being tested by the political awakening of evangelical Christianity under George W. Bush and Republican candidate for Vice President Sarah Palin. The Republican ticket of 2008 strikes fear in the hearts of many liberals committed to religious freedom and interreligious exploration because evangelical Christians act as a unified force, and hence politically, in order to challenge the political and legal foundations of the state. They refuse to accept the marginalization of religion to the private, individual realm and reclaim public, political relevance. Political Islam poses a similar threat to the established border between "state and church", the secular world of politics and the private world of individual spirituality.

My sense is that your description of personal interreligious exploration depends upon the safety of borders that are currently threatened by Evangelical Christianity in the US and political Islam in Europe. The Dutch may pick and choose nuggets of religious wisdom from various religious traditions. But they also feel threatened by Muslim representatives who demand political representation and social equality. European Islam is perceived as a threat to the secular political foundations of Europe. The current wave of Islamophobia sweeping Europe is a testament to the frantic search to secure the borders of communal identity. Suddenly the Christian roots of Europe have become relevant in public political discourse. I am less convinced than you that we are on the verge of dispensing with boundaries of communal identity. While I share your vision of a world of free religious agents, I am weary of the threats to individual spiritual exploration. In the meantime, it seems to me, we will continue to need smugglers who subvert borders in order to move people, goods, ideas and practices across the frontiers that divide us.

I have one "gang" of subversive interreligious smugglers in mind. Feminist theologians and activists are often maligned as outsiders and carriers of external notions, suspected of smuggling foreign ideas into a pure and pristine patriarchal tradition. Christian feminists were considered handmaidens of secular enlightenment and revolutionary philosophies. Jewish feminists were accused of assimilating into mainstream culture and Muslim feminists are considered carriers of Western colonialist ideologies. The patriarchal keepers of orthodoxy perceive the radical vision of women's religious agency and human subjectivity as an external threat to tradition and community cohesion. And they are right to fear global feminist networks that support women across religious differences. There is an intrinsic interreligious component to the world wide sweep of feminism: despite local differences, women face similar issues in each religious patriarchal tradition: rights of access to religious education, to leadership roles and positions of authority; hermeneutics and the reinterpretation of sacred texts, marital law and sexual ethics, etc. Feminists cross religious borders routinely, both individually and in the name of a "smuggler's gang", if you will.

* * *

Thema
Theme
Tema

Dear Katharina,

It is probable that Europe is far less secular than was long thought. The present revival of religion comes as a real shock to many European "enlightenment fundamentalists". Above all, because it makes it clear that the reigning theory of secularization according to which the greater a country's affluence, the less the citizens feel the need for religion, is a myth. This theory has never quite applied to the United States – as you have already indicated: "America is rich *and* religious." In Europe, however, this prediction was widely believed to be true, and the consistent decline in church membership seemed to confirm it. Now, though, sociological studies show that there is a religious upswing to be noted worldwide, and even Europe does not represent merely a little secular island in a huge religious ocean but is experiencing its own religious revival. In the Netherlands, one of the most secular countries in Europe, a sense of helplessness can be observed, arising in a desperate quest for an identity of their own.

With trepidation one observes Muslim solidarity and sense of "we", feared because of September 11, 2001 and subsequent terrorist attacks by Islamic extremists, and one realizes that one has no comparable sense of common identity to counter it. What do we actually believe in, and are we actually still proud of our own country and our own culture? In the demarcation from others – above all from Islam – there has been a recurrence of national feeling, a desire for a well-defined identity and pride in the achievements of Dutch history, which are then immediately laid down in a cultural canon that children are to learn at school. National consciousness is "in". But this often disregards the fact that many Dutch people's histories originated elsewhere. They have their roots in Turkey, Greece, China, North and South America, Asia, Africa etc. and their cultural and religious legacy will help to determine the future of the Netherlands. There are Asian, African and oriental-looking young women and men who, when they open their mouth, have an unmistakable local Amsterdam accent, as though their ancestors had never lived anywhere else than in the "Jordaan" district, the heart of Amsterdam. They are migrant children who have grown up bi-culturally and are now in the second or third generation, bearers of a hybrid identity who, if they mix with a lover from another culture, are the hope of a cosmopolitan and cosmoreligious future.

This is no longer strictly a matter of interreligious dialogue, in which representatives of the different religions exchange commonalities and differences in their understanding of Buddha, Krishna, Mohammed and Jesus. Here, differing cultures and religions flow together in one and the same person. This is not a matter of an inter-subjective dialogue, but of inner-subjective loyalties towards several cultures and religious traditions, which are directly linked in the person's self, their parents, siblings or life partners. Such people embody multiple religious and cultural identities.

I have referred to this because I recently came across a book with interviews, entitled *Let's make love – 27 impossible love relationships*.[7] It contains reports by bicultural and bireligious couples about the problems and opportunities of multicultural and multireligious relationships. The story of Susan und Yahya stayed with me for a long time. She is a Danish Jew and he is a Muslim from Morocco. They met at a pantomime training course in Amsterdam. Like many other couples who experience what looks like an "impossible love", Susan and Yahya experienced hostilities from the community – their relatives, friends and acquaintances – that made things hard for them. They not only have to deal with personal differences but are forced to take on the burden of the entire political situation in the Middle East. They are not willing to give up their love because of the Israeli-Palestinian conflict, however, and with the help of their pantomimes, which they perform with and for children, they strive to eliminate stereotypes that typecast the enemy. They have given their own daughter a Yiddish-Arab name: Blume/Yamina. They consider her a sign of hope in the midst of a hopeless war and intend to raise their child biculturally and bireligiously in order to give her the best of both traditions. A contribution to peace between the peoples, under the slogan: the *Juslims* are coming!

While this initiative is primarily an individual action, it is highly political. To be honest, I have always held out greater hopes to small personal encounters than to big, top-level interreligious conferences. As you notice, I am less negative about "individualization" in Europe than you are. I get the impression from your letter that you regard the development that many Europeans nowadays determine the measure and origin of their religious connection themselves as a kind of religious "fast food", a superficial consumerism of religious values, which you reject. I am less critical of this trend, or at least more ambivalent about it, as it seems to me to be a logical consequence of our late-modern European society. People are now forced to make their own choices, not only in the sphere of economics but also in other areas, since concepts of

---

[7] Annet de Groot / Frénk van der Linden (eds), *Let's make love – 27 onmogelijke liefdes* (Uitgeverij Contact: Antwerpen / Amsterdam 2008).

life previously held as matter of course are now gone and life has become very flexible, with all the advantages and disadvantages that this entails.

Under the impact of secularization, but above all of individualization, Europe has undergone a transformation of religious identity, and the consequences are now particularly visible thanks to globalization and its accompanying migration. Not only are the churches as institutions under pressure, but also political parties, trade unions and other associations are losing members. Europeans have become vocal citizens and will no longer be told what, or how, they are to believe. Feminism has made a crucial contribution to this dissolution of dogmatic truths. This also applies to the individualization that has made it possible for women to withdraw from the group pressure of a patriarchally structured society and religion, and to decide for themselves how they want to live and what they want to believe. The personal is political – women's experience has become the hermeneutic key to a new theology of women's liberation. Certainly the consistent implementation of these demands of the (religious) women's movement of the 1960s helped lead many women to turn their backs on institutionalized religion.

Europe today faces the challenge of an incisive paradigm shift, from a mindset of unity to a mindset of diversity. If the citizens of Europe are not ready to offer a home to the people of other cultures and religions who come to Europe as migrants, there is a danger that Europe will be torn apart in the tussle for cultural and religious differences. The nostalgic attempts to recreate a long-gone European culture of nation states, based on unity of language, territory and religion, must therefore be replaced with a culture made up of multiple identities in all areas of life.[8]

I completely agree with you: we need to intensify relations with one another, forge links where we still fearfully avoid one another. Our latest research project at the Dominican Study Centre for Theology and Society is a multimedia, interreligious website, intended to promote religious flexibility: www.reliflex.nl.[9] Before I tell you about the website though, I would like to

---

[8] See Manuela Kalsky, "Wahrheit in Begegnung. Die Transformation christlicher Identität angesichts kultureller und religiöser Pluralität", in: *Christian Identity / Christliche Identität I* (Forum Mission, Jahrbuch Band 2/2006; Brunner Verlag: Luzern 2006), 29-52.

[9] Manuela Kalsky, "Religiöse Flexibilität. Eine Antwort auf kulturelle und religiöse Vielfalt", in: Reinhold Bernhardt / Perry Schmidt-Leukel (eds), *Multiple religiöse Identität. Aus verschiedenen religiösen Traditionen schöpfen* (Theologischer Verlag Zürich: Zürich 2008), 219-242.

hear whether you agree that we should give more attention to the bireligious experiences of the second generation of migrants, and less to the theoretical interfaith dialogue between representatives of different religious schools of thought? I have the impression that the concept of "interreligious dialogue" is no longer suited to expressing what we need in the 21st century and what I have tried to express in the concept of a paradigm shift, from a mindset of unity to a mindset of diversity.

* * *

Dear Manuela,
I agree completely with you that the definition of interreligious dialogue ought to begin with those who struggle to create a home between idealized notions of national, religious and cultural unity. Maybe it would be helpful to spell out our scepticism of interreligious dialogue and clarify our misgivings. The following description may be an unfair exaggeration but it exemplifies what I see as the limitations of traditional conceptions of interreligious dialogue. Typically, interreligious dialogue involves representatives of religious institutions (churches, synagogues, mosques, temples) who initiate and facilitate meetings in which the respective theological traditions are explained in formal settings, such as dialogue groups or conferences. The invited experts are authorized to speak on behalf of their communities and present the dogmatic "high-tradition" of their faiths. Topics revolve around central dogmatic tenets such as theology, authority and interpretation of scripture, prayer and festivals, or religious law and ethics. Those who attend such panels, conferences, or local dialogue groups receive basic knowledge and learn to respect the authenticity and distinct nature of another religious tradition. Dialogue often relies on religious dignitaries who are predominantly male and such dialogues invariably reproduce patriarchal conventions. The theory of dialogue believes that increased knowledge of the other creates greater tolerance and appreciation of religious difference.

Such theories of dialogue fail to capture the much more chaotic conversations among the ordinary multitudes, especially migrants who do not belong to the educated elite and are not among sanctioned religious dignitaries. Their encounters demand an expanded, religiously pluralistic theory because they involve different agents, settings and contents. "Who" the experts are, "how" religious difference will be negotiated and "what" constitutes the primary items on the agenda will differ substantially. In a second step, we must ask whether such interreligious practices can still be called dialogue or should be given a different name altogether.

Thema
Theme
Tema

The "Who" – Subjects of Dialogue

Global migrants must cultivate some level of inter-cultural and interreligious competency and flexibility. They are engaged in dialogue on an existential level and their identity is transformed by their intimate negotiations of interreligious conflicts. They interact daily and form deep and lasting relationships in the context of love or work across cultural and religious differences. Such hybrid, interreligious existence is deeply challenging. But their presence in the midst of majority cultures also compels changes among their "hosts" as they develop strategies to adjust, co-exist and accept neighbours, lovers and co-workers. Are such interreligious survival strategies developed by women and other ordinary folk included in our definitions of interreligious dialogue? In what ways do such "dialogues" differ from those among religious functionaries?

The "How" – The Settings of Dialogue

Dialogue guidelines call for clear boundaries and warn against two main dangers: first, no missionary attempts and efforts to convert the partner by "proving" the superior truth of one particular religious path. The principles of dialogue repudiate evangelism and condemn the history of "disputations" that intended to force the "other" to concede defeat and to embrace the truth of Christianity. Second, dialogue warns against the dangers of "syncretism" and any "illegitimate mingling of different religious elements."[10] Such "mixing" of faiths is perceived as a dilution and reaching for the lowest common denominator. Syncretism, so the argument, compromises the authenticity of religious traditions and fails to do justice to either party. By definition, dialogue partners agree to respect the integrity of each religious system and commit to forgo missionary ambitions and syncretism.[11]

But the interreligious reality of migrants includes conversion and syncretism. People fall in love and convert in order to marry – or they maintain the religious commitments of their families of origin and negotiate competing religious festival calendars and the religious education of their children.[12] By definition they fall outside the boundaries of dialogue, because they have

---

[10] http://www.ciid.ca/Articles/Baker_1.pdf (June 24, 2008).
[11] http://www.wcc-coe.org/wcc/what/interreligious/77glines-e.html (June 24, 2008).
[12] Cf. the autobiography of Lauren Winner, who first converted to Orthodox Judaism, following the upbringing in her Jewish father's tradition, and subsequently to evangelical Anglican Christianity in the tradition of her mother's Southern family. Along the way, she developed a strong

converted and/or mixed and matched religious obligations to rival communities – and yet they, more than anyone else, mediate conflicting religious truth claims and moral systems. How must the definition of dialogue change in order to support and critically accompany the syncretistic and religiously mobile in times of economic globalization?

The "What" – Content of Dialogue

The intermarried Jewish-Muslim couple you mentioned is forced to negotiate competing loyalties and suspicions of their families and communities. As a couple, they are also required to make daily decisions about food (luckily, *halal* meat is considered *kosher*), sex (menstrual taboos and Ramadan restrictions, etc), which particular festivals to observe during the liturgical year and the basic education of their daughter. A committed interreligious relationship requires extraordinary religious knowledge. Most religious institutions condemn interreligious relationships. They demand conversion and threaten excommunication for those who fail to submit to one religious regiment. The intermarried tend to be abandoned by their respective religious communities and often drop out of religion altogether.

Sometimes new communities emerge. For instance, a group of intermarried Jewish-Christian families has regularly observed the Passover Seder at my house for years. None of the intermarried couples felt competent and knowledgeable enough to host a Passover Seder. As resident religious expert, my home seemed the perfect neutral space for this celebration despite my Christian pedigree. To my children, Passover has become an expected and integral part of their liturgical year, although they are baptized and confirmed Lutherans. Such syncretism is anathema to purists of interreligious dialogue. Yet, the interreligious reality of love and work prepared the way for this community. Dialogue nurtures its spiritual life as this intermarried band of smugglers prepares the house, distributes cooking tasks, reads the Seder and observes the laws of remembrance of Israel's Exodus from Egypt.

For religious hybrids "dialogue" should provide a reflective space where interreligious relationships and practices can be critically examined. Such dialogue moves beyond respect for distinct and authentic religious traditions and provides critical tools for people engaged in processes of integration and acculturation. Individuals assimilate, mix and match, or switch primary religious

---

attachment to both religions and negotiated disappointments and hostilities from both communities. Lauren F. Winner, *Girl Meets God* (Algonquin Book: Chapel Hill 2002).

allegiances. Syncretism and religious mobility are not the enemy. Oppression, injustice and fanaticism are. As economic and political globalization proceeds, ever greater numbers of people will move, acculturate and experiment with religious paths into which they were not born.

And there will be backlash! Individual mobility and mass migration (e.g. the Turkish Muslim minority in Germany or the Arab Muslim community in France) break up traditional institutions and undermine established communities. Such mobility creates instability and insecurity. While some welcome and benefit from the introduction of diversity and flexibility, others retrench and long for clear boundaries and structures. We witness similar phenomena in the renewal of nationalist secularism among indigenous European (post-)Christians and the rise of religious-ethnic fundamentalism among European Muslims.

Better education helps during unsteady times of transition. Basic instruction about the history and beliefs of Islam, Christianity, Judaism, Buddhism and Hinduism belongs in every school and university curriculum (it is currently in neither!). But the communication of knowledge is not to be the primary task of dialogue. Its principal task consists of the establishment of trusting relationships that serve to negotiate conflicts peacefully. The conflicts we are currently witnessing in Europe revolve not around issues of theology, scripture or religious observance, but rather around sex and gender, dress and religious architecture, social justice and violence, education and immigrant welfare. These are not coincidentally the primary conflicts that every intermarried couple has to solve. Such decisions about "right practice" (orthopraxis) are the daily bread of migrants who negotiate different sets of cultural expectations and religious loyalties. You correctly referred to them not as "inter-subjective" but "inner-subjective" dialogues. Interreligious dialogue should create the space to examine and reflect on the daily negotiations of interreligious life.

* * *

Dear Katharina,

Your thoughts about the Who, What and How sum things up again: interreligious dialogue has entered a new phase and it is time to check on the shelf-life of the concept and related content and ask: where do we go from here?[13]

---

[13] On the development of interreligious dialogue see: Reinhold Bernhardt, *Ende des Dialogs? Die Begegnung der Religionen und ihre theologische Reflexion* (Theologischer Verlag Zürich: Zürich 2005).

Interreligious

Can we really still speak of "interreligious" dialogue? Religious identities are becoming hybrid or they already are, and that does not apply only to migrants. The established citizens of Europe are developing multiple religious identities in everyday life through their encounters with people of other religions and through the information flow in the "worldwide web". These identities no longer conform to the law of purity and unity. Boundaries are blurring and identities are becoming fluid. The insight of post-colonial thinkers that there is always "an other" in "the other" has made clear that the dualist separation between rulers and ruled, colonizers and colonized, is an oversimplified analysis of the real power relations. The role we play in life is far from clear.[14] This observation of multilayering also applies in the religious sphere. Religions too are not clearly defined entities, to be tidily sorted into clearly defined categories. All religious traditions are products of intercultural and interreligious processes, according to Michael von Brück, a scholar of religious studies, and I agree with him. As soon as there are alternatives to the cultural rules and to basic values of a society, new identities are constructed.[15] The purity of a truth or doctrine of faith yields to the mixing of different religious truths, which are generally rejected as syncretism in official theological and ecclesiastical quarters.[16] However, when a normative tradition is no longer the rule, but rather a religious *bricolage* constructed out of the elements of different religious traditions, then the concept of interreligious dialogue is no longer apt.

Dialogue

Is dialogue still the right expression for what should happen in the encounter of people with differing religious and cultural backgrounds? I would like to maintain that the relation between people of different religious and non-religious views of life should be one of dialogical understanding. Dialogue is not to be

---

[14] Manuela Kalsky, "Embracing Diversity", in: *Studies in Interreligious Dialogue* 17 (2/2007), 221-231, here 224-226.

[15] Michael von Brück, "Identität und Widerspruch. Bemerkungen zu einer Theologie multipler religiöser Identität", in: Bernhardt / Schmidt-Leukel (eds), *Multiple religiöse Identität*, 291-328, here 313.

[16] On the concept of syncretism see: Reinhold Bernhardt, "Synkretismus als Deutungskategorie multireligiöser Identitätsbildung", in: Bernhardt / Schmidt-Leukel (eds), *Multiple religiöse Identität*, 267-290.

equated with discussion, though the term strongly suggests a verbal relationship with others. Yet the encounter should not primarily be about discussion of one's own religious convictions and the central truths of a certain normative tradition, but rather about the establishment of mutual trust and understanding. In my view, the term points too strongly to the cognitive aspect of encounter and too little to common action, the realization of small, specific projects together. How do we create a common "we" in our immediate environment? A "we" that does not immediately produce a "they" by excluding others; a new "we" that makes cultural and religious differences fruitful and enables a more holistic view of what "the good life for all" means; a "we" in which we learn to see with the eyes of the others and are thus in a position to expand our own limited view with the other's perspective in personal relationships.

In other words: fruitful intercultural and interreligious interaction begins not with one's own – in our case – Christian-dogmatic beliefs, but with everyday life and the ethical action grounded therein. This attitude is, incidentally, also quite possible at meetings of official representatives of respective religions, as I have shown with the example of Rita Gross and Paul Knitter in my article "Embracing Diversity".[17] Knowledge of the different religions and cooperation on projects give rise to friendships, which are important pillars of interreligious encounter and nourish theological reflection. First comes practical encounter and confidence-building and then theoretical theological reflection. This methodological path that was paved in the 1970s by liberation theologians who put practice before theory, appears to be the right one, i.e. setting small goals and expressing them in terms of the participants' everyday life – though this is not an argument for navel-gazing. The same rule applies for transreligious encounter: Act locally, think globally.

The good life for all
Theoretically we agree: the hermeneutical and epistemological place for what is important in interreligious dialogue lies in the life and faith experiences of people who live and survive in the daily life of a multicultural and multireligious society. But who are they, in fact? Migrants and their hosts, you will say, and, in principle, I agree with you. But being a migrant is not the same as

---

[17] Manuela Kalsky, "Embracing Diversity", 226-228. Also on this topic see: Helene Egnell, *Other Voices. A Study of Christian Feminist Approaches to Religious Plurality East and West* (Studia Missionalia Svecana: Uppsala 2006).

being poor and oppressed, just as being a host is not the same as being affluent and privileged. People can no longer be easily divided into groups with a clear indication of their aspirations and their standard of living. The dividing line between people often runs not between the different religions or between atheists, agnostics and religious people, but between people who are willing to work for the "the good life for all", including their own, and people who exclusively focus on their own well-being. This means that everyone who lives in a particular suburb or village, rich and poor, male and female, Hindu and Muslim, hetero and homo will be invited to a communal meal. Without establishing a bond between all the people living there it will not prove possible for the less powerful in the land to flourish. Here too I think that we must transform the paradigm shift from an "either-or" to a "both-and" approach. Spiritual poverty can kill just as material poverty does. Both must be combated. And that is why Sophia – the personification of divine wisdom in the Hebrew Bible – invites everyone to the table:

"Come, eat the bread I give you, drink the wine I have mixed! Leave your foolish ways, and live. Walk in the way of understanding." (Proverbs 9:1-6).

* * *

Dieser Briefwechsel nimmt die interreligiöse Realität vieler in Europa lebender Menschen zum Ausgangspunkt und befragt gängige Theorien und Praktiken des interreligösen Dialogs. Die herkömmliche Definition des interreligiösen Dialogs verlangt die Existenz stabiler religionsgemeinschaftlicher Identitäten. Dies ist aber in der mulitkulturellen, individualistisch geprägten und säkularen Gesellschaft Europas nicht mehr gegeben. Stattdessen bahnen sich interreligiöse Paare, Nachbarn, Kollegen, Gemeinschaften neue Lebenswege und Identitäten, die multireligiös, synkretistisch und grenzüberschreitend sind. Damit forden sie die klassischen Grenzen des Dialogs heraus. Die Autorinnen meinen, dass diese Entwicklung zukunftsweisend ist und von Dialogpraktikern und –theoretikern ernst genommen werden muss.

El punto de partida de este intercambio de cartas es la realidad interreligiosa de muchas personas que viven en Europa. En él se analizan teorías y prácticas comunes del diálogo interreligioso. La definición tradicional del diálogo interreligioso requiere que existan comunidades religiosas estables. Sin embargo, ello ya no es natural en la sociedad europea multicultural, individualista y secular. Al contrario, las nuevas parejas, vecinos, comunidades y compañeros de trabajo interreligiosos van buscando nuevos caminos e identidades, que son multirreligiosos, sincretistas y pasan de un lado a otro de las fronteras, con lo que son un desafío para los límites clásicos del diálogo. Las autoras son de opinión que este desarrollo va a ser decisivo en el futuro y que tiene que ser tomado en serio por los prácticos y teóricos del diálogo.

Manuela Kalsky (*1961) is director of the Dominican Study Centre for Theology and Society in Nijmegen, the Netherlands, and chief editor of the multimedia websites www.reliflex.nl and www.nieuwwij.nl. For more information, see also: www.manuelakalsky.nl.

Katharina von Kellenbach (*1960) is Professor of Religious Studies at St. Mary's College of Maryland, USA. For more information, see http://faculty.smcm.edu/kvonkellenbach.

Christa Anbeek

The Beauty of Ten Thousand Blooming Flowers
Towards a Feminist Approach to Buddhist-Christian Dialogue

For twenty years or more I have been involved in interreligious dialogue and multi-religiousness. In this essay I would like to report on how the journey has been up until now with the aid of the travel guides that I have been using. The first travel guide is philosophical-theological in essence. I shall explain how such a guide works and what its perspectives and blind spots are.

My second travel guide deals with the practical-spiritual areas that are inherent in every religious tradition. Peaks and abysses which are explored with great effort and sometimes joy form the starting point for this guide. Suggestions are made about ways to move from one religious tradition to areas of another one.

The third travel guide is not initially directed at inter-religiousness at all, but rather deals with ordinary contact between human beings and poses questions such as "Who are you? What have you experienced? Which were the peak experiences in your life, and what were the bad ones? How have you dealt with them? What was it that supported you and what carried you through?" To my astonishment this guide revealed a new layer of interreligious exchange and multi-religiousness, showing that amidst great differences there is also immense solidarity. The uniqueness and glow of each separate believer or non-believer contribute to the radiance of the whole, which is not only a collection of individuals but also a wonderful network of connections.

Whilst working with this guide, I recently became aware of another increasingly popular travel guide for the interreligious and multi-religious adventure. This has as starting point the whole of living nature and the care and responsibility that we share together. Although I have not used this guide to a large extent, I would like to portray its possibilities.

Finally, I would like to explore the growing feminist perspectives in the travel guides that I have been using.

Thema
Theme
Tema

Experience with the philosophical-theological travel guide

The philosophical-theological travel guide for interreligious dialogue is directed at important insights and dogmas from religious traditions and tries to compare them with each other. The question arises whether the term "God" from the Christian tradition is comparable with the term *sunyata* from the Buddhist tradition. The latter stands for emptiness and is considered the highest reality within certain sections of Buddhism. Another example of such a question is the Christian term *agape* (love), comparable with the Buddhist term *karuna* (compassion). This form of interreligious dialogue is often practised by religious specialists, who are well-versed in their own traditions and then continue to acquire knowledge of another religion. They study important books of the other tradition and confer with its representatives, usually fellow religious specialists at conferences. These religious specialists are by and large males.

I myself was especially involved with this particular type of interreligious dialogue and multi-religiousness during my work on my Ph.D thesis. I compared the views on death of a modern Christian scholar, Wolfgang Pannenberg (*1928), with the modern Buddhist scholar Keiji Nishitani (1900-1990). I analysed various difficult concepts and tried to compare them as well as possible. With the study of several years of theology behind me and, therefore, some knowledge of the Christian tradition, I was especially attracted to the intellectual exploration of Buddhism and saw it as an exciting adventure. A completely new world was revealed to me with a different vision of life and death. An important finding in my thesis is that both the Buddhist and the Christian ways of thinking have their own distinctiveness and cannot be reduced to a common form.[1]

A question that remained was: "Do I have to choose between these two modes?" I found that a tough question, as I felt attracted to both. I even wanted them both! This desire prompted me to try another one of the travel guides, but firstly some advantages and disadvantages of the philosophical-theological travel guide for interreligious dialogue and multi-spirituality.

A great advantage for users of this method is that he/she is forced to enter the tradition at a deep level. An important proof of this is that any reflections must be recognisable for members of the other tradition, demanding an in-depth knowledge. My experience of being deeply involved in another tradition brings a sense of great enrichment.

---

[1] Christa Anbeek, *Denken over de dood: De boeddhist Nishitani en de christen Pannenberg vergeleken* (Kok: Kampen 1994).

A disadvantage of this method is that only a small percentage of women participate. This may be due to the fact that it has been the custom for both Buddhism and Christianity to exclude women from higher religious functions, therefore discouraging them intellectually from becoming religious specialists. The lack of female participants is reflected in the choice of the subject-matter which is considered important for interreligious dialogue.

A second disadvantage is the limitation of the intellectual approach. Even though one may be knowledgeable about another tradition, one can fail to know how to live such a tradition. Buddhism, or any other religious tradition for that matter, is not only about insights but rather about a life based on these insights. Therefore every tradition has spiritual exercises and directions for life itself.

These two disadvantages spurred to me to look for yet another travel guide. This was not difficult as there are many on offer. "If you really want to learn to know us" said the Buddhists I encountered, "you must not only learn to know our books but also our spiritual practices". So I followed their advice.

Experiences with the practical-spiritual travel guide

Prior to the writing of any travel guides there are pioneers who go out on their own to explore paths without any form of navigation. Hugo Enomiya-Lasalle (1898-1990) was such a pioneer in the domain of Buddhist and Christian dialogue. He worked as a missionary in Japan and participated for the first time in a Buddhist meditation week in 1943. His motive for doing this was to become acquainted with the richness of Buddhism. Soon he noticed that meditation had a profound influence on his own spirituality. Throughout his life he wrote prolifically about Buddhist and Christian spirituality and supervised numerous meditation courses.

Inspired by pioneers such as Lasalle and others, many people were willing to explore the path of multi-spirituality. One of the initiatives that has been taken in this area is the Monastic Interreligious Dialogue. This is an exchange programme for Buddhist and Christian monks and nuns which has existed since 1979. Participants stay in the monastery of the other tradition for a number of weeks and participate as much as possible in aspects of that tradition such as religious ceremonies, daily chores and prayers and meditation.

An exchange program also started in the United States of America offering in particular the possible exchange of religious from Tibet. The Trappist monk Thomas Merton, a learned author of works on contemplative spirituality and the Dalai Lama, were involved in this exchange programme. These exchanges are on-going up to the present day.

Thema
Theme
Tema

My own encounter with practical-spiritual exchange was through my work at the Tiltenberg centre. At this centre Buddhist meditation courses were given by various Zen masters from both my own country and abroad. Here I was given the responsibility of co-ordinating the Zen programmes and it was part of my duty to be present at the meditations when possible. Hours, days and weeks on end I meditated in an upright position with my face to the wall and heard lectures from masters from Japan, India, America, France, Sweden, England and the Netherlands. Besides the meditation weeks, we also organised conferences in which we reflected on what the Buddhist and the Christian paths have to offer each other.

A great advantage of this travel guide compared with the intellectual form of dialogue, is that the whole body participates (thus) leading to even greater discoveries. Many monks and nuns who participated indicated that they had discovered through Buddhist meditation how important the body and the breath are for experiencing spirituality. Through the body a dimension opens up which goes beyond thinking and channels one into a deep stillness. In this state of stillness a reality can be observed about which, for instance, the Desert Fathers have written. The heart of Buddhist and Christian spirituality seems to lead to the same source.[2]

A disadvantage of this path is that it often causes tension within Christian communities. Many Christians are not interested as their own tradition offers enough guidance on how to live their lives. Others consider it risky to get too intensively involved. Will you lose your own faith? What do I need besides Christ? Dealing with these questions is not always easy. The Monastic Interreligious Dialogue in the Netherlands, for instance, has lead a number of pioneers to leave their monastic communities. Discovering the deep unity between Buddhists and Christians may therefore have a boomerang effect. How then can we cope with these problems within our own communities? How can we understand and appreciate each other amidst vast differences? In this context I became acquainted with another travel guide in a very different setting.

Experience with the inter-human travel guide

For the past nine years I have been working as a pastoral carer in a psychiatric institution. There I have to deal with people from totally different religious

---

[2] Christa Anbeek, *Zin in zen. De aantrekkingskracht van het zenboeddhisme in België en Nederland* (Asoka: Rotterdam 2003).

backgrounds and also cope with diverse forms of illness, educational levels, social backgrounds and family histories. They all share the experience that life at times stagnates. Unexpected problems can arise that place life in a different perspective.

I have noticed how important it is for people to be able to talk about their lives. Not only about current difficulties but also about their pasts, their work, their education, about what they consider really important and valuable, about problems they had encountered and how they resolved them. And also about their futures: what they would like to take up again, new ventures they hope for despite the definitive change of their lives. Group discussions show that people like to listen to one another's stories. It is inspiring to discover that each life history has known highs and lows and then to observe how people move on despite difficulties. The sharing of joy and sorrow can create bonds despite differences in personal histories. It struck me that when people are asked about important events in their lives, they seldom talk about their religion. They talk about their childhood, a sick mother, meeting the ideal partner even if it failed to work out, about their children, about work that gave their lives meaning. Some only mention religion when asked about life supports. When this happens, everyone in the group – religious or not – understands what they mean. The reason for this is that they do not mention dogmas or practices which others might fail to understand, but rather talk about the way faith has developed in their lives. About the comfort it has given them, the doubts, the questions and sometimes resignation to the fact that faith and life itself remain incomprehensible.

These insights have led to an awareness which I now refer to as the narrative interreligious dialogue. Primary questions here are: "Who are you?" "What have you been through?" and then "How have you coped with all that crossed your path", and finally "What has been your source of strength?" The diverse answers to the last question can only be understood in relation to the answers to the previous questions. Insight into a person's religious history and choices can only be attained by understanding his or her life story.[3]

The inter-human travel guide has the advantage that the many answers to the question "What has supported you" is not a weakness but a strength. A huge

---

[3] Christa Anbeek, *Mimi and Akiko* (Asoka: Rotterdam 2005); Manuela Kalsky / Ida Overdijk / Inez van der Spek (eds), *Moderne devoties: Vrouwen over geloven* (De Prom: Amsterdam / Antwerpen 2005).

Thema
Theme
Tema

diversity of creativity and inspiration of equal value is revealed. Behind religious and spiritual differences is the shared adventure of being human, in which sooner or later everyone is confronted with joy and sorrow, health and illness, birth and death – together with the challenge of coping strategies. The ten thousand blooming flowers of spirituality and vitality that have been revealed to me in psychiatry have prompted my awareness of the last travel guide.

Experience with the ecosophical travel guide

This travel guide has been in existence longer than it seems as many of its aspects are familiar from books read in the past. There are several thinkers and activists that have paved the way for this guide. One example is the Norwegian Arne Naess (*1912), an academic philosopher, mountaineer and activist. An important aim of his is to inspire actions that foster the growth of diversity of life on earth. Another writer in this guide is Joanna Macy (*1929), eco-philosopher, Buddhist scientist and social activist. Inspired by her Buddhist belief she works on the liberation of all suffering in this world, not only that of humans but also of plants, animals, polluted rivers and air. Many other individuals and organisations base their reflection on Christian, Buddhist, Confucianist, Islamic, Hinduist, Jewish or humanistic inspiration, and also make a practical contribution towards the maintenance of our earth. In particular I would like to mention the *Forum on Religion and Ecology* in Harvard.[4]

Ecosophy stresses the diversity and richness of cultures and life forms. Furthermore, it encourages people to open their eyes to the fact that amidst this diversity we form one global community which is extremely vulnerable. Ecosophy seeks unity amidst diversity and finds this in our common responsibility for a viable global society which is based on respect for nature, universal human rights, economic justice and a culture of peace. Important principles for building a justified, sustainable and peaceful global society are specified in the declaration *Earth Charter*, in which thousands of organisations worldwide have cooperated, together representing millions of individuals. The document contains fifteen principles, divided into four chapters: 1. respect and care for all living forms. 2. ecological integrity. 3. social and economic justice and 4. democracy, non-violence and peace. *Earth Charter* has, moreover, developed

---

[4] Cf. http://environment.harvard.edu/religion/main.html.

a programme concerning religion and sustainability, and hopes to assemble and strengthen various initiatives and the work of several institutions.[5]

During the international Grail conference I was in a position to experience some of the potential of the ecosophical travel guide for multi-religiousness. Originally the Grail movement was a Catholic international womens' movement, founded in the Netherlands in the second decade of the twentieth century.[6] After the Second World War the movement spread across the world to eighteen countries and broadened its content as well. It opened its doors to Protestant women and women who felt more at home in Buddhism or nature spirituality. The great diversity of Grail women has for a long time raised the question: "Is there a common spirituality that connects us?" That became the theme of the summer conference in 2007.

At this conference all the travel guides for multi-religiousness discussed above were present. There were also theological contributions and, although they were meant to create common premises, they rather served to make the differences clearer. A Catholic woman in Tanzania may consider other departure points more important than a Buddhist Grail woman from the Netherlands. Various forms of spirituality were put into practice. For instance, there was a Lutheran and a Catholic Eucharistic celebration, a purification ritual from the womens' movement and a meditation in stillness. Everyone participated in the various celebrations which undoubtedly created solidarity and respect but also feelings of strangeness and alienation. During the meals and tea breaks there was ample opportunity to experiment with the narrative approach to multi-religiousness. Many participants regretted that these were not part of the official program. Yet listening to each others stories created bonds even between those living at opposite ends of the earth. The greatest mutual concern became apparent during the two workshops on ecospirituality. The first of these was about human suffering in the world, the second about the suffering of nature. Brazilian women are daily confronted with other forms of suffering – poverty, pollution – than women in Africa – war violence, aids, genetic manipulation – or in Western European countries – alienation, suicides, lack of community spirit, violence in the home. Yet there was unanimity in the desire to act by helping to prevent this suffering. The workshop on the suffering of nature enlarged and deepened the unity of the group. Our footsteps, whether they be in Africa, Brazil or Western Europe touch the same

---

[5] Cf. www.earthcharter.org and www.earthcharterinaction.org/religion.
[6] Cf. www.degraalbeweging.nl.

earth. We are all dependent on clean water and clear air. We share a caring which transcends our differences and which we can work on together from different inspirations. The enthusiasm and the togetherness during these two workshops prompt me to further explore the inter- and multi-religious adventure using the ecosophical travel guide in the coming years.

Finally

In the introduction to this paper I indicated that the travel guides which I have used can be characterised by a growing feministic perspective. My criticism of the philosophical / theological travel guide is that by the excluding-mechanisms inherent in religious traditions the majority of the participants in this form of dialogue are male. This fact is reflected in what choice of subject-matter is considered important and in the manner in which the dialogue is conducted. The practical / spiritual travel guide does have some room for female participants. Moreover, the practical approach of this type of dialogue stimulates reflection which is more specifically directed to the practice of spiritual life as it appears in the publications that emerge from this exchange.[7] Yet this type of dialogue also suffers from the excluding mechanisms for women inherent in the Buddhist and Christian traditions whereby consequently the majority of publications are from male participants whence, in the main, female experience remains concealed.

This is not the case with the third and fourth travel guides. The starting point of the third travel guide is the individual narratives of suffering and hope, in which both female and male voices are heard, each with their own sound and colour. The fourth travel guide is not only concerned with the experiences and hopes of men and women but also with that of all living creatures with a view to decreasing all suffering. As far as I am concerned the latter is the core and the concern of a feminist approach to interreligious dialogue.

En este artículo son presentados cuatro guías de turistas del diálogo budista-cristiano. Los diferentes guías reflejan el viaje de veinte años de la autora por el diálogo interreligioso y son presentados en el orden cronológico de sus descubrimientos. El

---

[7] They deal, for instance, with prayer and meditation, growth and development on the spiritual path, community and supervision, spirituality and society, cf. Donald W. Mitchell / James Wiseman (eds), *The Gethsemani Encounter: A Dialogue on the Spritual Life by Buddhist and Christian Monastics* (Continuum: New York 1997); Donald W. Mitchell / James Wiseman (eds), *Transforming Suffering. Reflections on Finding Peace in Troubled Times* (Random House: New York 2003).

primer guía se caracteriza por la perspectiva filosófico-teológica; la segunda es antes bien práctica o espiritual; la tercera perspectiva es narrativa, llamada guía de turista interhumano, y la cuarta es el guía ecosófico del diágolo budista-cristiano. Se debaten las ventajas y los problemas de cada guía, así como la perspectiva cada vez más feminista. Queda claro que cada planteamiento tiene mucho de valioso que ofrecer, pero en las conclusiones la perspectiva interhumana y la ecosófica pasan a primer plano al describirse como las perspectivas del diálogo interreligioso más prometedoras desde la perspectiva feminista.

In diesem Beitrag werden vier Reiseführer zum buddhistisch-christlichen Dialog vorgestellt. Diese Führer spiegeln die Reisen der Autorin durch zwanzig Jahre im interreligiösen Dialog wieder, und sie werden in chronologischer Ordnung ihrer Entdeckung dargestellt. Der erste Führer ist durch einen philosophisch-theologischen Zugang gekennzeichnet, der zweite ist eher praktisch oder spirituell, im dritten wird ein narrativer Zugang oder auch eine zwischenmenschliche Landkarte vorgeführt, und im vierten Reiseführer geht es um einen ökosophischen Zugang zum buddhistisch-christlichen Dialog. Es werden jeweils die Vor- und Nachteile der jeweiligen Zugänge diskutiert sowie ihre zunehmend feministische Perspektive aufgezeigt. Dabei wird deutlich, dass jeder Zugang besondere Vorzüge besitzt, doch in der Schlussfolgerung stellen sich der zwischenmenschliche und der ökosophische Reiseführer als diejenigen heraus, die im interreligiösen Dialog aus feministischer Sicht den besten Erfolg versprechen.

Christa Anbeek (*1961), PhD, theaches religious studies at the University of Tilburg and existential philosophy at the University of Humanistics in Utrecht. During the last ten years she also worked as a chaplain in a mental hospital.

Annette Esser

Salir en busca de espiritualidad feminista en el diálogo interreligioso

En el diálogo interreligioso nos encontramos por doquier con el concepto de "espiritualidad" – lo emplean tanto los representantes de las diferentes religiones como sus miembros, tanto hombres como mujeres. Pareciera que se expresa así la necesidad de algo a lo que no se le ha podido dar otro nombre. La pregunta que de ello resulta es que si después de casi 40 años de teología feminista existen planteamientos y formas de espiritualidad feminista en el diálogo interreligioso, y en caso afirmativo qué importancia tienen para las mujeres de las diferentes religiones y qué importancia tienen en el diálogo interreligioso. Analizaré estas cuestiones ante el trasfondo de la experiencia directa que tengo con la teología y la espiritualidad feministas, que he estudiado muchos años, en especial también dentro de la ESWTR.[1] De este trabajo nació en el año 2007 mi tesis doctoral sobre espiritualidad feminista.[2] Por otro lado buscaré respuestas teniendo en cuenta la experiencia directa que tengo con el diálogo interreligioso, en especial con la ONG acreditada por Naciones Unidas "Religions for Peace", RfP, (conocida también como "World Conference on Religion and Peace", WCRP) en la cual trabajo desde principios de los años 90.

Mi experiencia en la ONG "Religions for Peace" ha sido muy enriquecedora por un lado, pero también decepcionante por el otro. Enriquecedora ha

---

[1] Desde 1987 he venido participando con regularidad en las conferencias de la ESWTR, y fui algún tiempo la mujer de contacto de Alemania y vicesecretaria. En 1999 edité junto con Luise Schottroff el primer anuario de la ESWTR sobre *"Feminist Theology in a European Context"* ; en 2001 junto con Susan Roll y Brigitte Enzner-Probst el tomo sobre *"Women, Ritual and Liturgy"*. En 1993 edité junto con Susan Roll y Anne Hunt Overzee el libro *"Re-Visioning Our Sources: Women's Spiritualities in European Perspectives"*.

[2] Annette Esser, *Interkontexte feministischer Spiritualität. Eine enzyklopädische Studie zum Begriff der religiösen Erfahrung von Frauen in ökumenischer Perspektive* (Theologische Frauenforschung in Europa 23; LIT: Münster 2007).

Thema
Theme
Tema

---

sido la labor voluntaria que he venido desempeñando como directora del grupo Köln-Bonn, y como miembro del comité ejecutivo alemán ("German Executive Committee") y también del "European Governing Board" al igual que la función nueva que desempeño ahora como "Regional Officer" de la red que se acaba de crear "European Women's Network of Faith" (EWNF). Ha sido decepcionante para mí ver que en este contexto interreligioso oficial las mujeres que son las que sustentan este diálogo casi siempre son relegadas a segundo plano por los altos representantes religiosos. En las "mesas redondas de las religiones", p.ej. o también en el "European Council of Religious Leaders" (ECRL) se reúnen casi sólo hombres o al menos la mayoría siempre son hombres. También fue una decepción para mí ver que en esta ONG las decisiones, como es usual en Naciones Unidas, no se toman democráticamente, sino que supuestamente se busca el consenso, pero de hecho los asuntos son decididos por unas cuantas personas 'desde arriba'. "Religions for Peace" tiene efectivamente tanto a nivel internacional como a nivel continental un programa especial para mujeres ("Womeńs Program") y es cierto también que muchas mujeres se dedican con mucho empeño a defender sus asuntos en el contexto interreligioso e intercultural y se interesan por la espiritualidad. Sin embargo, en este ámbito, en el que son una minoría las mujeres que han cursado estudios de teología, casi no hay mujeres que en la práctica se dediquen al diálogo interreligioso feminista-teológico y a la reflexión teórica sobre el mismo.

Por ello, al salir en busca de espiritualidad feminista en el diálogo interreligioso partiré en un primer planteamiento de mis experiencias personales. Siendo cristiana alemana y teóloga feminista saldré en busca de huellas, de algo que no es sobrentendido en el contexto interreligioso. A lo largo de esta busca iré juntando los diferentes elementos que componen la espiritualidad feminista, que a mi manera de ver ya existen en el diálogo interreligioso o que podrían cobrar importancia en el futuro.

Emplearé los conceptos de "feminismo", "espiritualidad" y "diálogo" conscientemente de forma muy abierta. Ya en mi tesis doctoral me había negado por razones de principio a definir estos conceptos, p.ej. porque en ningún momento podemos hablar de "espiritualidad feminista" (en singular), sino que siempre habrá de usarse el término en plural (!) "espiritualidades feministas" de mujeres. Aparte de ello también tengo la impresión de que las mujeres que buscan espiritualidad feminista no usan el término feminismo como una categoría analítica, sino que lo emplean para designar la propia conciencia en el proceso de busca personal de identidad como mujeres. De igual forma casi no se puede definir lo que es la "espiritualidad", sino que se puede entender como expresión cultural de la busca de experiencia y sentido religiosos en la sociedad secular postmoderna. Partiendo de esta interpretación, que es el resultado de la reflexión tanto de mi experiencia personal como de la de otras mujeres en busca de espiritualidad feminista, empero, he llegado a enunciar seis características conceptuales de la espiritualidad feminista en vez de presentar una definición:

(1) el carácter narrativo de la referencia de la vivencia de la espiritualidad feminista
(2) la contextualidad e intercontextualidad básica del teologizar
(3) la percepción de la referencia de la autovivencia y vivencia de la trascendencia
(4) la importancia que tiene la vivencia del cuerpo femenino en la espiritualidad feminista integral
(5) entender la espiritualidad feminista como práctica constructiva de una teología feminista
(6) el primado de la crítica de la modernidad sobre la crítica del patriarcado en la concepción feminista-espiritual

Estas seis características conceptuales servirán de guía en lo que sigue en la busca de espiritualidad feminista en el diálogo interreligioso.

El interés de las mujeres por la espiritualidad y por otras religiones

Es casi imposible determinar si el interés de las mujeres por la espiritualidad hizo surgir el interés por otras religiones o si no fue antes bien al revés. Por lo que he podido ver pareciera existir una interdependencia. Así, p.ej. las mujeres que se interesan por la espiritualidad, se topan automáticamente con prácticas como yoga o zazen, que tienen sus raíces en las religiones asiáticas del hinduísmo o del budismo. Al buscar una práctica espiritual más profunda es necesario entonces estudiar más a fondo las 'otras religiones'. Y viceversa, el interés que demuestran muchas mujeres por otras religiones no es en primer lugar un interés intelectual o teológico, sino que estudiar otras religiones resulta de estar buscando la propia espiritualidad (y a veces también práctica espiritual).

Para comprobar lo anterior, me referiré a experiencias que he venido juntando a lo largo de los últimos 30 años en los grupos de espiritualidad de la 'Sociedad europea de mujeres investigadoras en teología' (ESWTR). En la tercera conferencia de la ESWTR que tuvo lugar en Helvoirt en 1987, no fue sino por la gran demanda que se instauró el 'Subject Group Spirituality', a diferencia de lo que estaba planeado originalmente, pues la 'espiritualidad' no se consideraba como 'materia' entre las materias que deben estudiarse en teología.[3] Me alegré mucho de que se formara este grupo de espiritualidad. Para mí, el intercambio y las divergencias de opinión con mujeres que se dedican a la investigación y que parten de diferentes planteamientos y cuestiones – psicología profunda, mística, práctica meditativa de otras religiones, liturgia feminista, elaboración de un idioma de oraciones inclusivo – fue algo sumamente interesante y fructífero. Sin embargo, por ser tan diferentes los planteamientos, en la siguiente conferencia de la ESWTR de Arnoldshain de 1989 se decidió sustituir el grupo de espiritualidad por distintos grupos temáticos: 'Misticismo femenino', 'Espiritualidad de las mujeres de hoy', 'La gran diosa india', 'Liturgia'. Sin embargo, la existencia de tantos grupos diferentes fue algo que la mayoría percibió en la conferencia como algo muy insatisfactorio. La consecuencia fue que algunos grupos se disolvieron y que muchas mujeres iban de un grupo a otro. Pienso que esto se produjo debido a que muchas de las asistentes de la conferencia no querían tener que decidirse por *un solo* tema de la espiritualidad, porque antes bien estaban en busca del 'todo'. Siendo que pasan de un lado a otro de las fronteras de los distintos ámbitos de la espiritualidad, p.ej. van del misticismo cristiano a la meditación oriental y viceversa, no estaban buscando profundizar intelectualmente en *sólo un* ámbito determinado de la espiritualidad, por el que se tenían que decidir de antemano (como decidirse por una confesión determinada o una tradición determinada), sino que antes bien estaban buscando una perspectiva integradora, es decir, una espiritualidad integral que permitiera integrar tradiciones y religiones que en un primer momento pudieran percibirse como algo diferente e incluso contradictorio. Debido a esta circunstancia se decidió que en la siguiente conferencia de Bristol de 1991 ya sólo iba a haber otra vez *un* grupo de espiritualidad. Dicho grupo lo describí más tarde como sigue:

> Cuando entré en el grupo, éramos unas 30 mujeres. Nunca antes un grupo de espiritualidad había sido tan grande. Casi todo el tiempo se nos fue en presentarnos. Casi no hubo tiempo de entrar en un debate académico. Sin embargo, ¡las mujeres mismas eran algo tan interesante con tantos trasfondos tan diferentes! A cada instante

---

[3] La conferencia de Helvoirt, Países Bajos (1987) fue después de la conferencia fundacional de Boldern, Suiza (1985) y de la primera conferencia de Magliaso, Suiza (1986) según cómo se haga la cuenta la segunda o la tercera conferencia de la ESWTR.

> se vivían momentos de revelación y sorpresa al ver qué motivos tan distintos habían movido a las mujeres a participar en ese grupo. Había mujeres que se ocupaban con la 'diosa celta' no sólo en grupos rituales, sino también en sus trabajos de investigación; había mujeres que practicaban el yoga, zazen o la meditación sufi; mujeres que trabajaban de terapeutas de mujeres y niñas abusadas sexualmente; mujeres que trabajaban con métodos de la psicología profunda; mujeres que condenaban explícitamente el planteamiento junguiano de los arquetipos, en especial la concepción de ánima y ánimus; había mujeres que contaban de forma muy personal su experiencia pastoral en un contexto determinado y otras que estaban luchando por la ordenación en sus iglesias; y por último había mujeres que se sentían inspiradas por el pensamiento antroposófico y esotérico. Fue sumamente interesante escucharlas a todas, pero en el diálogo de grupo apenas avanzamos. ¿Había algún camino que pudiéramos y quisiéramos recorrer juntas? ¿Existía una base de experiencias comunes que nos pudiera servir de punto de partida? Algunas lo dudaban. Otras se ponían a jugar con las ideas que habían surgido en el grupo al hablar de 'espiritualidad'. Hubo quienes propusieran convertir este grupo en un grupo de investigación sobre mística. No lográbamos avanzar. No había propuesta que fuera un verdadero avance. Nos habíamos atascado. Parecía no haber forma clara de hacer converger los diferentes intereses. ¡El diálogo parecía ser un comienzo nada más, una introducción![4]

El hecho de reconocer que por un lado existía el interés común y que todas estábamos buscando algo y que ello había llevado a que nos encontráramos unidas en el grupo de 'espiritualidad' y que sin embargo por el otro lado las diferencias fueran tan grandes que no lográbamos ponernos de acuerdo sobre cómo llevar el debate científico y encontrar una definición de la palabra 'espiritualidad' hizo que me pusiera a analizar la *cuestión básica* de cómo explicar la heterogeneidad de los planteamientos: ¿Esta heterogeneidad es sencillamente algo relacionado con la pluralidad postmoderna o tiene algún denominador común? ¿Existe algo que pudiera llamarse vivencia común de espiritualidad (feminista) o debemos rechazarla categóricamente?

Yo misma encontré en un sueño lo que había en común. Soñé con un jacuzzi en el que la energía salpicaba como agua por los aires pasando de una mujer a otra.

> Anoche soñé con un jacuzzi enorme lleno de agua, en el que se formaban energías que luego seguían fluyendo cual fuente eterna. Alguien también me tocó con esta energía y volé y le pasé esta energía a la siguiente persona. Desperté sorprendida.[5]

---

[4] Esser, *Interkontexte feministischer Spiritualität*, 48 ss.
[5] Ibid., 49.

Para mí, esto quería decir que lo que había en común no podía ser una definición común p.ej. de la palabra espiritualidad, sino que lo que había en común estaba en la energía común que nos había reunido y en la busca común. Al interpretar este sueño me puse a pensar también en la imagen de la fuente de la Morada Cuarta de Santa Teresa de Jesús, en la que Santa Teresa distingue dos formas de oración: una que nace de todo lo que traemos con los pensamientos de afuera, y una que fluye desde el interior muy profundo, y que es la oración de quietud.

> Estos dos pilones se hinchen de agua de differentes maneras: el uno viene de más lejos por muchos arcaduces y artificio; el otro está hecho en elmesmo nacimineto del agua, y vase hinchendo sin nengún ruido... Es la differencia que la que viene por arcaduces es, a mi parecer, los contentos que tengo docho ques se sacan con la meditación; porque traemos con los pensamientos, ayudándonos de las criaturas en la meditación y cansando el entenimiento ... Estotra fuente viene el agua de su mesom nacimiento, que es Dios, y ansí como Su Majestad quiere, cuando es servido, hacer alguna merced sobrenatural, produce con grandísima paz y quietud y suavidad, de lo muy interior de nosotors mesmos, y no sé hacia dónde ni como, ni aquel contento y deleite se siente como los de acá en el corazón ... vase revertiendo este agua por todas las moraday y potencias, hasta llegar al cuerpo, que por eso dije que comienza de Dios y acaba and nuestros, que cierto, como verá quien lo hubiere probado, todo el hombre esterior goza de este gusto y suavidad.[6]

Ambas imágenes – cuando soñé con el jacuzzi y la imagen de la fuente de Santa Teresa – pueden interpretarse teniendo en cuenta lo que hay en común como también teniendo en cuenta las diferentes espiritualidades que puede haber. Así, el agua es símbolo de la energía espiritual, que se puede vivir ya sea por aparte o en grupo y que según Santa Teresa es fuerza divina. En la imagen del jacuzzi las diferentes vivencias – resultantes de las tradiciones religiosas – se pueden interpretar como salpicaduras de agua que van y vienen, representando la variedad de pensamientos e ideas que hay en el grupo; pueden por un lado regalar energía e impulsar nuevos pensamientos, pero igualmente pueden impedir ver el fondo común y percibirlo en calma. En la imagen de Santa Teresa la diferencia reside en cómo fluye el agua, o sea como una fuerza espiritual generada casi artificialmente o como una fuente divina que fluye con naturalidad; la idea de la fuente tranquila que nunca se seca equivale a la profundidad de la vivencia de Dios de cada individuo (en la oración de quietud).

---

[6] Teresa de Jesús, *Las Moradas* (Espasa-Calpe: Madrid 1982), 53-54.

La imagen de la fuente y del jacuzzi son en parte la clave para entender que hay una relación directa entre la base de la espiritualidad individual o colectiva por un lado y la variedad de corrientes espirituales por el otro. Después de haber visto cómo el hecho de profundizar consciente y seriamente en distintas tradiciones espirituales y otras religiones supuso una dura prueba para las mujeres, no podemos calificar sencillamente de superficial o sincretista la busca y la necesidad de una espiritualidad integral, sino que sirve para descubrir el valor especial que poseen los nuevos planteamientos constructivos de la espiritualidad (feminista), con los que las mujeres no sólo han empezado a unir y a integrar diferentes proposiciones, sino que con los que han buscado una base común. Equivale a lo que en la tradición de la mística cristiana es la 'unio mystica', la vivencia de la unión mística por muy diferentes que pudieran ser las formas de manifestación y grandes las divergencias. Aquí podemos ver claramente también que lo que atrae a las mujeres cristianas de otras religiones no es en un primer plano la doctrina, el dogma y todos los conceptos diferentes que tienen esas religiones, sino que una doctrina diferente de la propia es interesante en la medida que sirve para encontrar respuesta a las propias dudas religiosas, y porque ayuda a encontrar una espiritualidad integral – e incluso talvez también una práctica expresamente feminista.

No son pocas las mujeres en busca de espiritualidad feminista – y yo me cuento entre ellas – que por ello trabajan activamente en el diálogo interreligioso y que han podido constatar que efectivamente existe un gran interés por la espiritualidad.

La importancia de la espiritualidad en el diálogo interreligioso

Aquí se ve por qué no podemos prescindir del término 'espiritualidad', por muy inexacto que sea, y es porque no va unido a una religión o creencia concretas. Justamente lo que pareciera ser la desventaja del término, o sea, la discrecionalidad y la pluralidad, es una ventaja. Porque lo que lo hace importante para los distintos contextos y prácticas ecuménicos e interreligiosos no es el hecho de que se pueda definir de forma inequívoca, sino el hecho de que sea un concepto abierto, que es también la clave para comprenderlo. Hoy en día no podemos prescindir de hablar de espiritualidad en el momento en que se juntan individuos con trasfondos diferentes (religión, ideología, cultura, contexto) para tematizar sus experiencias religiosas partiendo del menor denominador común o buscando el mayor consenso posible, y para encontrar una práctica común (p.ej. en la labor mundial por la paz). Pero si la función del término reside justamente en que sirve para resaltar lo que tienen en común las diferentes experiencias religiosas y no para acentuar las diferencias, entonces

Thema
Theme
Tema

vemos por qué no podemos prescindir del mismo, y por qué no podemos sencillamente volver a empezar a hablar de 'religiosidad', 'adoración', 'devoción' o 'recogimiento'. Estos conceptos antiguos no equivalen a lo que significa 'espiritualidad', y en el contexto ecuménico se podrían entender antes bien como señal de que grupos conservadores desean dejar claras las diferencias.

Si partimos entonces de que en el contexto ecuménico y en el diálogo interreligioso se reconoce que todos están buscando la espiritualidad, cabe preguntarse qué se hace concretamente en la práctica para satisfacer esta necesidad.

Una forma importante de hacerlo son las llamadas 'oraciones de las religiones'. Allí no rezan juntos los representantes de varias religiones, sino es estar juntos para rezar. Ello nació de las Jornadas de Oración por la Paz en el Mundo en Asís, a las que el Papa Juan Pablo II invitó en 1989 a todos los líderes de religiones occidentales y orientales. Las diferentes religiones o bien los diferentes grupos religiosos escogen de sus respectivas tradiciones plegarias y meditaciones acerca de un tema, que por lo general ha sido determinado de antemano, p.ej. la paz. A pesar de que los textos casi siempre son textos buenos y significativos, resulta cansador escuchar tantos textos seguidos, y por mucho que haya música entre medio, los oyentes no pueden poner atención todo el tiempo. Lo que un individuo piensa, siente y cree, no debe manifestarse, de ser posible. 'Rezar en presencia del otro' es testimonio de cada uno frente al otro, que sigue siendo otro y que debe seguir siendo otro y diferente. Es decir que esta forma de orar lo que busca no es orar juntos, sino que incluso resalta las diferencias que existen entre las religiones y las tradiciones y quiere evitar cualquier forma de mezcla o sincretismo de las religiones. Una persona *es* budista, la otra *es* católica, y así debe seguir siendo, cada una con su identidad. Es justamente la distancia entre las diferentes religiones lo que forma la base para que haya un 'verdadero diálogo', en el que todos puedan quedarse con su identidad.

En la reunión anual de 'Religiones por la Paz' de Alemania de 2006, que trató el tema de la espiritualidad, propuse una forma diferente de espiritualidad feminista después de haber escuchado la ponencia sobre mi tesis doctoral con el tema 'Intercontextos de espiritualidad feminista'. Primero presenté elementos de liturgia feminista a partir de Diann Neu[7], a quien conocí en 1991,

---

[7] A Diann Neu, quien dirige junto con su compañera Mary Hunt el centro feminista-teológico WATER ("Women's Alliance for Theology, Ethics, and Ritual") en Estados Unidos, la conocí en 1991 en una conferencia en De Tiltenberg (Países Bajos). Ella presentó oralmente estos elementos en esa conferencia. Y es únicamente sobre esta base que los he usado en numerosos seminarios-taller.

e invité a preparar juntos la liturgia, siguiendo un tema que habíamos escogido juntos. El proceso, según el cual los grupos se formaban no por tener todos la misma religión sino por tener los mismos intereses y así, como grupo con diferentes religiones, formular textos, escoger canciones y diseñar actos simbólicos, había llevado a delinear juntos una liturgia. A pesar de que la reacción de los hombres y de las mujeres presentes fue positiva, ni esta forma ni otra similar se volvió a poner en práctica desde esa vez en la sección alemana de 'Religiones por la Paz'. En parte ello se debe a circunstancias externas, pero debido al amplio rechazo que existe de probar liturgias interreligiosas, cabe presumir que tiene que ver también con la cercanía al sincretismo. Las dudas que hay o incluso el rechazo explícito de las llamadas 'celebraciones interreligiosas' por parte de la Iglesia protestante y la católica, pero también de las comunidades musulmanas, que incluso cuestionan el rezar juntos[8], ha puesto en grandes problemas a las escuelas e instituciones que lo venían practicando más después del 11 de septiembre de 2001.

La pregunta de cómo se puede practicar la espiritualidad en el diálogo interreligioso, si sustituyendo p.ej. las 'oraciones de las religiones' por 'celebraciones interreligiosas' o 'liturgias comunes' no solamente tiene que ver con las jerarquías religiosas o eclesiásticas, sino que nos atañe a todas y todos. Una mujer musulmana que participa activamente en el ámbito interreligioso me decía que al estar rezando en un grupo interreligioso se preguntaba que qué podía rezar y qué no; dónde es que se sentía mal y dónde se sentía a gusto, aunque otros musulmanes pensaran diferente. La cuestión de la oración y la liturgia es por ello antes bien algo más profundo, es la cuestión de cuán arraigado se siente el individuo en su propia religión y cuál es su identidad religiosa. Y de ello resulta la pregunta dirigida a nuestra autoconsciencia (feminista): ¿puedo yo (siendo mujer) rezar cualquier forma de plegaria o no? Incluso personas con mucha experiencia viven en un contexto interreligioso momentos de confusión y creen estar saliéndose de los límites permitidos. A mí misma me pasó con un dhikr musulmán y en un ritual vudú en una capilla cristiana. Además, las mujeres implicadas en el diálogo interreligioso se preguntan si no talvez las contradicciones y los conocimientos de la teología y espiritualidad

---

[8] El hecho de tener que cuestionar hoy todavía el tema '¿Rezar juntos?' también en el ámbito interreligioso se ve también en que el libro de Franz Brendle, presidente de 'Religions for Peace Deutschland' lleva el mismo título: Franz Brendle (ed.), Runder Tisch der Religionen in Deutschland, *Gemeinsam beten? Interreligiöse Feiern mit anderen Religionen* (EB-Verlag: Hamburgo 2007).

feministas podrían servir de ayuda a la hora de valorar estas diferentes formas de expresión religiosa, ayudar a saber qué hacer con los límites y a buscar una identidad espiritual, política y feminista en el diálogo interreligioso.

El problema con la teología feminista en el diálogo interreligioso

A pesar de que la teología y espiritualidad feministas tienen sus raíces desde los años 60 no sólo en el cristianismo sino también en el judaísmo[9], y a pesar de que explícitamente también se conocen en el budismo[10], muchas mujeres (representantes de iglesias y religiones) implicadas en el diálogo interreligioso eluden hablar de feminismo o teología feminista. Por lo que he podido observar, no se trata de rechazar simplemente el feminismo, sino que es justamente al unir feminismo con teología que resulta el problema. En la conferencia internacional de mujeres de 'Religiones por la Paz', que tuvo lugar en Amán, Jordania, en 1999, p.ej., muchas mujeres de religiones y culturas asiáticas manifestaron que tenían relación con el movimiento feminista político de sus países, pero que les causaba problema la reflexión feminista-teológica de sus tradiciones religiosas y espirituales. Si bien en esa conferencia se ofrecieron meditaciones, oraciones y rituales comunes, que habían resultado de la práctica de muchas mujeres de todo el mundo, muchas mujeres no querían establecer una relación entre ello y la 'espiritualidad feminista', probablemente debido a que este término se entiende como algo que las separa negativamente de los hombres y como algo que va dirigido 'contra los hombres', por lo que es rechazado por las mujeres en busca de espiritualidad integral. Al finalizar la conferencia, lo resumí como sigue:

> Lo que me pareció interesante fue que nosotras, en tanto cristianas, después de una historia muy larga ahora hablemos de 'misión' de forma crítica y que prefiramos hablar de diálogo; que en apoyo de otras religiones veamos la cuestión de la creación y de la protección de los recursos naturales como algo importante; y que reconozcamos que la teología feminista, que se ha ido desarrollando a lo largo de los últimos 30 años es la contribución en especial de mujeres cristianas y judías.

---

[9] Como 'Starting point' (punto de partida) de la teología feminista he escogido aquí el libro de Mary Daly, *The Church and the Second Sex* (Harper & Row: Nueva York 1968); y de espiritualidad feminista la obra de Carol Christ y Judith Plaskow, *Womanspirit Rising* (Harper: San Francisco 1979).

[10] Cf. p.ej. Rita Gross, "Buddhism After Patriarchy?", en: Paula M. Cooey et al., *After Patriarchy: Feminist Transformations of the World Religions* (Orbis Books: Maryknoll, Nueva York 1991), 65-86.

Lamentablemente esta observación – no de la teología feminista sino solo de la importancia de la investigación teológica hecha por mujeres – no se incluyó en el documento final, que es antes bien un documento político; ello se debió a que se quiso tener consideración con las religiones asiáticas y las religiones naturales y a cómo entienden ellas la espiritualidad.[11]

Estas dudas frente a cuestiones feministas-teológicas las conocíamos ya de Europa y Estados Unidos[12], y sabíamos que venían ya de mucho antes. Incluso yo misma no me consideré feminista por mucho tiempo. Fue a través de descubrir y estudiar a fondo la tradición mística de mujeres (Santa Teresa de Avila, Hildegarda de Bingen, entre otras) que encontré el camino a la teología y espiritualidad feministas. Esto tiene que ver con la busca de una vivencia que fuera más allá del fastidioso nivel de la crítica (feminista) de la iglesia y de la teología, asunto que analicé y describí en mi tesis doctoral al tratar la práctica vivencial en intercontextos.

Espiritualidad feminista como práctica vivencial en intercontextos

Ya se ha reflexionado mucho sobre la interdependencia que existe entre la teología y la espiritualidad feministas (p.ej. en planteamientos que parten de la teología de la liberación o en el trabajo feminista-espiritual de Chung Hyun Kyung). Si bien al principio los términos teología feminista y espiritualidad feminista eran casi sinónimos, con el tiempo las mujeres que buscaban antes bien lo espiritual sintieron que era insatisfactorio dedicarse sólo a la deconstrucción feminista de la religión y teología tradicionales y manifestaron el interés que sentían por la psicoterapia, las artes y otras materias que podrían contribuir a la reconstrucción de la práctica religiosa de mujeres en espacios vivenciales nuevos. El hecho que las mujeres hayan logrado crear nuevas tradiciones de mujeres en espacios vivenciales nuevos (p.ej. la reconstrucción de liturgias feministas) está relacionado con las características de la frontera. La frontera es el lugar del conocimiento[13], porque es un lugar en el que

---

[11] "Die Frauenversammlung der 'Weltkonferenz der Religionen für den Frieden'", en: WCRP-Informationen 55 (2000), 16-21, 20.
[12] Desde 1989 estoy afiliada a la Sociedad europea de mujeres investigadoras en teología; he participado en las conferencias organizadas por dicha sociedad; pertenecí a la presidencia, y soy coeditora de dos de los anuarios (1993 y 2001). De 1994 a 1998 estudié en el Union Theological Seminary de Nueva York.
[13] Cfr. Paul Tillich, *Auf der Grenze. Aus dem Lebenswerk Paul Tillichs* (Evangelisches Verlagswerk: Stuttgart 1962), 13.

tradicionalmente se hacen delimitaciones y se cultivan (p.ej. entre el cristianismo y otras religiones) y porque por el otro lado es el sitio donde tienen lugar encuentros (fronterizos) y debates con otras tradiciones, culturas, ideologías y movimientos. Pensamos que cinco campos fronterizos fueron especialmente relevantes y decisivos cuando se fue formando la espiritualidad feminista. Las mujeres en busca de espiritualidad que conocí en los últimos 20 años se mueven sobre todo

– entre feminismo y teología
– entre la propia tradición religiosa y otras religiones
– entre espiritualidad y psicoterapia
– entre mística y política
– entre las artes y el ritual

Estos espacios intermedios, en los que se solapan las vivencias de diferentes contextos y en los que tienen lugar debates entre los distintos conceptos son los que denominamos 'intercontextos'. Entendemos por ello no sólo una situación en la que las mujeres 'no saben a dónde pertenecen realmente' (como lo dijo una vez Dorothee Sölle al pasar de un lado a otro de la teología, la literatura y la política) y sufren por ello, sino que antes bien relacionamos con ello ciertas experiencias que pueden llevar a nuevos conocimientos.

De esta forma los sujetos pueden alentarse mutuamente a denominar su realidad y su verdadera creencia y hacer lo que Nelle Morton llamó una vez "hearing each other into speech".[14] Es decir que en vez de resignarse o de sentirse solamente apartados, pueden autovivenciarse juntos en un proceso de conscienciación común, al referirse explícitamente a más de un solo contexto (o tradición), que para ese sujeto es (o fue) determinante, desafiante y dador de identidad. En la práctica espiritual en intercontextos también pueden crear y probar nuevos rituales y liturgias, sin que ello tenga que tener la forma de una tradición en especial, por ejemplo tener que ser una misa cristiana. Pero siendo los intercontextos espacios en los que de forma muy especial es posible el diálogo, en los que se puede experimentar con nuevas acciones, p.ej. en la liturgia y en los rituales, y en los que mujeres (y hombres) pueden encontrar y aceptar una nueva identidad, podemos calificarlos de espacios de diálogo, espacios de acciones, espacios de adquisición de identidad.

---

[14] Citado en Carol Christ / Judith Plaskow, *Womanspirit Rising*, loc.cit. vii.

Aquí vemos claramente que los conocimientos y la práctica de espiritualidad feminista pueden desempeñar un papel importante en el futuro del diálogo interreligioso porque son experiencias que se han obtenido en intercontextos. Es aquí justamente donde podemos analizar ahora más a fondo que por qué debe llamársele feminista a lo que he descrito.

Espiritualidad feminista en el diálogo interreligioso

Una de las características de la espiritualidad feminista desarrollada por mujeres de Occidente, es que adoptó por un lado la crítica feminista del patriarcado, y por el otro reconoció la importancia de la variedad postmoderna. La referencia a tradiciones de mujeres diferentes de las judeocristianas fue importante en el momento en que las mujeres cristianas no se sentían a gusto con su religión y práctica de culto y empezaron a buscar otras opciones acordes con la espiritualidad feminista. Sobre todo el empeño de crear nuevas tradiciones de mujeres en espacios nuevos llevó a que despertara el interés por conocer otras tradiciones e impulsó el diálogo con mujeres de otras culturas. A diferencia de como había procedido la teología feminista original, que hacía hincapié en delimitar las corrientes éticas y estéticas, que distinguía claramente las teólogas feministas radicales de las que tendían más a las reformas, la espiritualidad feminista quería antes bien combinar, entrelazar y unir de forma creativa diferentes tradiciones y ritos. Mientras que al comienzo las mujeres con espiritualidad feminista de Occidente buscaban su identidad rechazando sus propias tradiciones religiosas, para poder ser totalmente diferentes, más tarde fueron describiendo la nueva identidad feminista-espiritual haciendo referencia a varias tradiciones religiosas y culturales, admitiendo de forma constructiva 'multiple religious identities'.[15]

Pero justamente la apertura frente a otras tradiciones espirituales conllevó – casi de forma inesperada – el diálogo feminista-interreligioso, así por ejemplo, al adoptar a menudo las mujeres con socialización cristiana occidental (incluso las feministas) en el proceso de busca de espiritualidad, sin reflexionar casi, formas de meditación oriental, porque les parecían en un primer momento más integrales que las formas tradicionales de espiritualidad cristiana. La experiencia de que también la práctica oriental de meditación cuando

---

[15] Tomé el concepto que emplea Gabriella Lettini. Cfr. Gabriella Lettini, *The "allergy to the other": Christian Theology and Its 'Others' in Modern Western Discourses* (Union Theological Seminary: Nueva York 2003).

se ejerce de forma demasiado estricta puede a la larga no dar el resultado que la mujer (consciente de su feminismo) en busca de identidad quiere obtener, hizo que se pusiera atención a las voces que criticaban el patriarcado en estas religiones. La teóloga católica Elisabeth Gössman, que casi todo el tiempo que pasó investigando en Japón, dio clases, constata que el budismo es más patriarcal que el cristianismo.[16] Y la maestra de meditación budista Rita Gross, cuyo artículo "Buddhism After Patriarchy"[17] puede tomarse a la vez como programa, explicó de forma original en un retiro en Nueva York que seguía perteneciendo al budismo porque: *"Buddhism is too good to leave it to the patriarchs!"* [18] Su intento de enseñar el budismo de forma tal que haga justicia a su consciencia de ser mujer, significa no solamente una contribución a la transformación (feminista) del budismo, sino que también ha de entenderse como una contribución al diálogo interreligioso (de mujeres). Ello quiere decir que justamente porque ella se interesa por la espiritualidad oriental, las mujeres de Occidente, sobre todo las que tienen una socialización cristiana, han encontrado un diálogo nuevo e interesante con protagonistas feministas de otras religiones.

Como decíamos anteriormente, la mayoría de las mujeres implicadas de una u otra forma en el diálogo interreligioso no piensan que son feministas o teólogas feministas. Por ello es necesario referirse aquí al ejemplo de las 'indigenous women', que participaron en la conferencia mencionada de Amán y cuyo interés demostrado por la espiritualidad fue la explicación oficial de que no se incluyera en el documento final la palabra 'teología feminista'. Estas son las mujeres a las que se refiere Helene Egnell al hablar en su artículo de que aparte de la gran tradición, esto es la religión tal y como se debe practicar, siempre ha habido una tradición pequeña (la de las mujeres), o sea la religión que se practica efectivamente con los rituales diarios. Si entendemos la espiritualidad feminista como práctica constructiva de mujeres (marginadas), tendríamos en estas pequeñas tradiciones de mujeres en principio ya una práctica feminista-espiritual. Esta práctica es la que tiene en mente Chung Hyun

---

[16] Esta tesis la pronunció ella en una conferencia de la sección alemana de la ESWTR en Gelnhausen en 2004.

[17] Rita Gross, "Buddhism After Patriarchy?", en: Paula M. Cooey et al., *After Patriarchy. Feminist Transformations of the World Religions* (Orbis Books: Maryknoll, Nueva York 1991), 65-86.

[18] Participé en este retiro al que nos invitó Chung Hyun Kyung en octubre de 2008 y que tuvo lugar en el Union Theological Seminary in Nueva York.

Kyung, quien se autodenomina feminista, cristiana, budista y chamana[19] al hablar de su visión de una teología de mujeres asiáticas:

> My fourth and last hope for the future direction of Asian women's theology is that it moves away from the doctrinal purity of Christian theology and risks *the survival centered syncretism*. In their struggle for survival and liberation in this unjust, women-hating world, poor Asian women have approached many different religious sources for sustenance and empowerment. What matters for them is not doctrinal orthodoxy. Male leaders of the institutional church always seem preoccupied with the doctrinal purity of their religions. What matters for Asian women is survival and the liberation of themselves and their communities. What matters for them is not Jesus, Sakyamumi, Mohammed, Confucius, Kwan In, or Ina, but rather the life-force which empowers them to claim their humanity. Asian women selectively have chosen life-giving elements of their culture and have woven new patterns of religious meaning.[20]

Lo que Chung enfoca aquí como visión de la espiritualidad feminista, empero, es algo que en el contexto cristiano tradicional siempre ha sido rechazado por ser sincretista. Un ejemplo famoso es Santa Teresa de Avila, quien se vio obligada a distanciarse claramente de los 'alumbrados', judíos y protestantes, sólo porque la Inquisición exigió que entregara su autobiografía *(Vida)* 'hasta no saberse qué iba a ser de la mujer esa'. También en el diálogo interreligioso las mujeres sienten que tienen que distanciarse claramente de las otras tradiciones y religiones para manifestar así su lealtad frente a su propia tradición religiosa. A diferencia de ello, 'la' espíritu de la obra de Chung es 'otra'. Esta/este otra/otro espíritu de espiritualidad feminista resulta básicamente de tres cosas: primero, de la necesidad de *superar fronteras* y unir diferentes contextos en vez de establecer fronteras; segundo de la necesidad de crear una *contracultura alternativa* en el espacio fronterizo, en vez de tacharla de 'sincretista' e incluso de 'sectaria'; y tercero de la necesidad de *reafirmar y alentar a las mujeres* a construir desde su propia situación de vida una práctica religiosa en vez de tener que atenerse a una doctrina ortodoxa dictada por la jerarquía eclesiástica/religiosa 'desde arriba'.

La última cuestión que debemos abordar ahora es la de la importancia que tiene en el diálogo interreligioso la espiritualidad feminista, tal y como la

---

[19] Para el debate sobre ritual y sincretismo de Chung Hyun Kyung véase Annette Esser, *Interkontexte feministischer Spiritualität*, 336-348.

[20] Chung Hyun Kyung, *Struggle to be the Sun Again. Introducing Asian Women's Theology* (Orbis Books: Maryknoll, Nueva York 1990), 113.

hemos descrito. ¿Acaso una espiritualidad feminista que combina distintas tradiciones y que concede ser sincretista positivamente puede y debe ser la base del diálogo interreligioso? De ser así ¿qué tipo de diálogo interreligioso sería? ¿De qué forma la espiritualidad feminista puede servir de eslabón entre la teología feminista y el diálogo interreligioso?

Si tomamos la espiritualidad feminista como práctica vivencial de mujeres en intercontextos, p.ej. entre teología y autovivencia psicológica, o entre experiencias en diferentes religiones, o entre la busca de autoexpresión creativa y el diseño de liturgias y rituales religiosos, entonces lo que la estaría caracterizando sería justamente la busca de lo común, del diálogo y de la práctica en el espacio fronterizo. Aquí resulta interesante ver que al percibir los intercontextos expresamente como espacios de una contracultura alternativa, lo que hasta ahora se encontraba al margen desde el punto de vista de la tradición, pasa de la periferia al centro de la atención. Es decir que la posición individual al margen (de la iglesia, p.ej.) se convierte en el propio centro aceptado explícitamente, y que la posición de la teología y espiritualidad feministas que hasta ahora estaba al margen de la iglesia, ahora en la sociedad secular se convierten en el espacio que hace que el momento religioso esté presente en la cultura pública. Aunque la teología y espiritualidad feministas todavía sean vistas por las instituciones religiosas como algo periférico, sus planteamientos ya forman parte del discurso público y de esta forma (aunque tomando un rodeo) han llegado a ser un tema central también para las instituciones eclesiásticas y religiosas. Ahora bien, si el debate sobre las tradiciones conservadas (por instituciones religiosas y eclesiásticas) ya no tiene lugar sólo en la frontera, sino que los intercontextos mismos, tales como el diálogo interreligioso llegan a estar en el centro de atención (de la religión/iglesia), entonces esto significa que también el debate (intrarreligioso/intereclesiástico) entre el centro tradicional (patriarcal) y los que hasta ese momento habían estado en la frontera de sus religiones/iglesias adquiere más importancia. Todo ello significa que la importancia de la teología y espiritualidad feministas para el diálogo interreligioso reside en que reflexionó conscientemente sobre la relación que existe entre periferia y centro, es decir, sobre espacios fronterizos, que se convirtieron en nuevos centros y los analizó. Significa asimismo que los temas de la teología feminista se convirtieron en temas centrales del diálogo interreligioso, como

(1) la busca espiritual de las mujeres de Occidente moviéndose entre las diferentes religiones, que hasta ese momento se rechazaba por sincretista;
(2) el sendero espiritual de feministas budistas o islamistas, que hasta esa fecha eran consideradas mujeres apartadas;

(3) las prácticas rituales de mujeres marginadas del Asia, a las que la religión oficial no les daba importancia.

Si no se toman en cuenta las vivencias de estas mujeres, el diálogo interreligioso – si es que tiene lugar sólo entre representantes de las religiones a nivel oficial – perderá la base subjetiva y con ello toda importancia. El hecho de haber llevado estos temas al diálogo interreligioso y de velar por que sigan existiendo en la consciencia, es un mérito de la espiritualidad feminista.

Conclusiones

Para finalizar, quisiera resumir cuál es el resultado de la busca de espiritualidad feminista en el diálogo interreligioso. En primer lugar es constatar sencillamente que efectivamente existe esta espiritualidad – aunque no siempre se califique explícitamente de 'feminista'. Existe ya sólo por los *sujetos*, o sea, por las mujeres que se mueven y participan en los diferentes contextos e intercontextos, es decir, espacios de diálogo. Segundo, también existe debido a la *cercanía temática* que hay entre espiritualidad y diálogo interreligioso. Tal y como traté de explicar al usar la metáfora del 'jacuzzi' y de la 'fuente', el diálogo interreligioso siempre busca una dimensión que va más allá de la disputa de términos, y es la realidad espiritual. El carácter abierto de la espiritualidad no para ante barreras fronterizas o 'tuberías de agua' puestas por las diferentes religiones, y justamente en ello reside su fuerza, con la que puede superar incluso grandes obstáculos. Y tercero, ello significa, empero, que el diálogo interreligioso movido por la espiritualidad siempre se encontrará cerca del *sincretismo*. Las protagonistas de las espiritualidades feministas tienen mucha y muy variada experiencia en no tacharlo de peligro, sino en tratarlo en su práctica de forma constructiva. La creciente importancia de la espiritualidad feminista en el diálogo interreligioso reside en gran parte en incluir activamente estas experiencias en el diálogo interreligioso y sus temas, actuando como mujeres autoconscientes y no sólo como 'auxiliares de reuniones de hombres'.

Übersetzung aus dem Deutschen: Gisela Boehm

Als feministische Theologin, die sich seit den 1990er Jahren im interreligiösen Bereich engagiert hat, begibt sich die Autorin auf Spurensuche nach Elementen feministischer Spiritualität im interreligiösen Dialog. Obwohl sich dort allerorten die Rede von „Spiritualität" findet und diese so etwas wie einen gemeinsamen Nenner darstellt, wenn religiöse Erfahrungspraxis der verschiedenen Traditionen und Kul-

Thema
Theme
Tema

turen thematisiert werden soll, und obwohl es auch einen starken Bezug interreligiöser Organisationen zu politischen und religiösen Frauenorganisationen weltweit gibt, ist in diesem Dialogkontext die Rede von feministischer Theologie und Spiritualität immer noch eher suspekt. Denn gerade da, wo Abgrenzungen als notwendig erachtet und klare Identitäten („man' *ist* katholisch oder buddhistisch...) als Voraussetzungen des Dialogs gefordert werden, stellt die konstruktive Bejahung religiös-kultureller Vielfalt seitens feministischer Spiritualität eine Provokation dar. Die Autorin findet nun Elemente feministischer Spiritualitäten (1) in den spirituellen Suchbewegungen westlicher Frauen ‚zwischen den Religionen', die bis dato als synkretistisch abgelehnt werden; (2) im spirituellen Weg buddhistischer oder islamischer Feministinnen, die bis dato als Einzelgängerinnen galten; und (3) in den rituellen Praktiken von marginalisierten Frauen Asiens und anderer Kontinente, die von Seiten der offiziellen Weltreligionen als irrelevant betrachtet werden. Die Gemeinsamkeit in der Verschiedenheit feministischer Spiritualitäten hat sie dabei selbst im Traumbild des Whirlpools und im mystischen Bild der Quelle von Teresa von Avila visioniert. Nicht zuletzt diese Vision ermutigt die Autorin dazu, in einem Klima, in dem Synkretismus ein stetes Verdachtsmoment darstellt, zu behaupten, dass in Zukunft das feministisch-spirituelle Unterfangen, Grenzen zu überwinden, eine alternative Kultur im Grenzraum zu schaffen und Frauen am Rande zu bestätigen und zu ermutigen, nicht mehr bloß ein peripheres oder beliebiges Thema feministischer Theologie darstellt, sondern zum zentralen Thema des interreligiösen Dialogs selbst werden wird.

As a feminist theologian engaged in an inter-religious organisation since the 1990s, the author is searching for elements of feminist spirituality in inter-religious dialogue. In this context, even though "spirituality" is a favourite term that seems to serve as a mutual notion when a name is given to practical religious experience in the various traditions and cultures, and even though there is a strong relationship between inter-religious organisations and both political and religious women's organisations worldwide, any talk about feminist theology and spirituality is still regarded as suspect. At precisely the point where boundaries are regarded as necessary and where clear-cut identities (one *is* Catholic or one *is* Buddhist) are postulated as basic conditions for dialogue, any kind of constructive affirmation of religious-cultural plurality from the side of feminist spirituality is felt to be provocative. The author finds elements of feminist spirituality (1) among Western women in their movements of spiritual quest 'between the religions' that have been considered syncretistic to date; (2) in the spiritual approaches of Buddhist or Muslim women who have so far been seen merely as individual searchers; and (3) in the ritual practices of marginalized women in Asia and other continents which – from the viewpoint of official world religions – have so far been looked at as irrelevant. Furthermore, she envisions a mutuality within the differences of feminist spiritualities in her own dream-image of the whirlpool and in the mystical image of the fountain used by Teresa of Avila. Not least, it is this vision that encourages the author to claim that, in a climate where syncretism is always suspected, for the future, the feminist-spiritual enterprise of transcending boundaries, of creating an alternative culture at the borderline and of affirming and encouraging women on the margins will no longer constitute a merely peripheral theme, but will become the central issue for inter-religious dialogue itself.

Annette Esser (*1957), estudió teología católica y protestante, bellas artes y geografía en Colonia, Münster y Nueva York. Cursos de perfeccionamiento profesional de terapia de arte, bibliodrama y psicodrama. Profesora de escuela y de universidad. Trabaja desde hace muchos años con la *ESWTR* (desde 1987) y en la ONG acreditada por la ONU *Religions for Peace* (desde 1990). Tesis doctoral *Interkontexte feministischer Spiritualität*, Universidad de Nijmegen, Países Bajos (2007). Coeditora de los anuarios de la ESWTR *Feminist Theology in a European Context* (1993) y *Women, Ritual and Liturgy* (2001); además de *Re-Visioning Our Sources. Women's Spirituality in European Perspectives* (1997) y *Kinder haben – Kind sein – Geboren sein. Philosophische und theologische Beiträge zu Kindheit und Geburt* (2008).

Nadja Furlan

Women in Interreligious Dialogue
Transformation of Negative Gender and Religious Stereotypes

The European Union and the growing need for interreligious tolerance
Within the contemporary social transformations in the post-industrial age, one of the important issues in a 'united Europe' is the growing need for intercultural and interreligious tolerance. The European Union has defined itself as a system of values and actions based on the basic principles of freedom and democracy, as well as recognition of human rights, fundamental liberties and the rule of law. Freedom of thought, conscience and religion form an integral part of these basic rights, as does the respect afforded by the Union to cultural and religious diversity. Behind the principles and the political and civil rights of the Union lies the assumption that its member states have a constitution that recognizes and guarantees both the autonomy of church and state, and freedom of religion and conscience. Even though all European Union member states are formally secular and recognize freedom of religion, they do not always remain neutral towards different religions and religious denominations. For example, some members have a state church and others do not. Even where there is no state church, one denomination may in practice be privileged above others. On the other hand, recognizing a state church does not necessarily exclude equal treatment of other churches. Each member state has its own history of the relationship between church, state, politics and society, which has resulted in specific arrangements. Thus, on the question of the separation of church and state there is no single European model.

Europe, where there are so many different varieties of religious expression, has some societies that are overwhelmingly Protestant, some overwhelmingly Catholic, and some a combination of both. In addition, the presence of Jews and Muslims varies from one country to another. Europe, in short, is not only religiously diverse; it is diverse in its approach to religion. Many official religious organizations insist on the importance of interreligious tolerance in the face of religious diversity. But such appeals will mean little unless ordinary people themselves are tolerant of those whose faith is different from their own.

At this point the role of feminist theology and active participation of women in interreligious dialogue is of great importance. A necessity, indeed a pronounced significance, the contribution and vantage of women's interreligious dialogue and feminist theology as "the missing dimension in the interreligious dialogue,"[1] as Ursula King has pointed out, will fundamentally contribute to a more concrete and direct transfer of the results of interreligious dialogue into life. An active participation by feminist theologians or the women's voice in interreligious dialogue is, in the first place, the introduction of women's issues into interreligious dialogue and, consequently, the recognition and ascertainment of the presence of negative gender and religious stereotypes and prejudices. This, as a result, enables a more expansive and concrete learning about and recognition of the diversity and specialty of the "other," as well as the uncovering of many negative stereotypes and prejudices that are deeply rooted in our cultural collective awareness stemming from ignorance about the other – in this sense mostly the female. This brings the other, the different, closer. In this sense, the female dimension of interreligious dialogue concretises the fields of diversity and dissension, as it faces the challenges and issues concerning the concrete personal experiences and stories of women, which 'liven up' through interreligious dialogue. It is precisely this 'live dialogism' that is of the utmost importance in getting to know the diversity and particularities of determinate religious manifestations and women's religious experiences. In the words of Maura O'Neill: "We need to learn about these religions not just from books but by meeting and dialoguing with their practitioners, for only personal conversation can place an ideology in its human context."[2]

Feminist theology in search of interreligious tolerance

Feminist theology has become a worldwide and omni-religious movement, emerging as a response to women's experience of discrimination and patriarchal dominance, which regulated and defined their religious and secular lives. Just as individual Christian women's experiences differ and shape the particular efforts within Christianity, so women's religious experiences within other world religions vary widely. Despite enormous variations, all women share the experience of discrimination and fear of patriarchal violence. Although

---

[1] Ursula King, "Feminism: the Missing Dimension in the Dialogue of Religions", in: John D'Arg May (ed.), *Pluralism and the Religions: The Theological and Political Dimensions* (Cassell: London 1998), 40.

[2] Maura O'Neill, *Mending a Torn World, Women in Interreligious Dialogue* (Orbis Books: New York 2007), 3.

discrimination and patriarchality can be defined differently in individual cultural-religious spheres, the desire and need to "talk about the female experience" and to awaken women's voices are universal. In this sense we can say that feminist theology and religious feminism have together become intercultural and interreligious phenomena. They connect women and empower activism for liberation against oppression and religious patriarchal violence similar to the struggles against slavery, racial discrimination and genocidal ethnic violence. Rooted in women's religious experience, feminist theology is pluralist and diverse as it strives for liberation and greater respect for the female principle of action and greater gender harmony.

As a genuine intercultural phenomenon, feminist theology faces new challenges for cooperation and dialogue within different branches of Christian feminist theology as well as with feminist theologies emerging from other religions. As a special philosophy of religions[3] and theology of religions[4], feminist theology contributes the variety of women's experience of past and present discrimination to interreligious dialogue and raises concrete questions and challenges connected therewith. In *Mending a Torn World: Women in Interreligious Dialogue*, Maura O'Neill suggests the following topics and issues for women's interreligious dialogue: women's spirituality, sexuality and gender roles, the relationship of the past to the present and the nature of religious authority.[5] A further, very important topic of women's interreligious dialogue is the issue of ecofeminism, as the importance of environmental solidarity emerges in today's nature-unfriendly and discriminatory world. Sally McFague proceeds from the fact that the entire world and nature should be looked upon

---

[3] The possibility of *feminist theology as a philosophy of religion* was noted by Pamela Sue Anderson, who saw feminist theology as a new form of philosophy of religions. For details see: Pamela Sue Anderson, "Feminist Theology as Philosophy of Religions", in: Susan Frank Parsons, *The Cambridge Companion to Feminist Theology* (Cambridge University Press: Cambridge 2002), 40-57.

[4] *Feminist theology as a theology of religions* is a relatively new expression, which in the opinion of Rita Gross denotes the awareness that in the background of religious plurality and diversity there exists a key common to all religions. In the case of feminist theology it is thus about the common key of women's experience of patriarchal subordination and discrimination of women by all religions. Gross appeals to all feminist theologians to try to develop the right approach for women's participation in interreligious dialogue to truly come alive. See: Rita M. Gross, "Feminist Theology as Theology of Religions", in: Susan Frank Parsons, *The Cambridge Companion to Feminist Theology*, ibid., 61.

[5] O'Neill, *Mending a Torn World*, 114-122.

as "God's body", which can be polluted and thus desecrated by improper behaviour and treatment. Joining this view is Aruna Gnanadason, who calls on Indian women to strive for a holistic environmental and spiritual theological vision, which should be gracious both to nature as well as to all the oppressed.[6]

Faced with cultural and religious plurality, feminist theology is trying to develop a suitable key, a methodology for understanding the other that can facilitate solidarity, interreligious tolerance and respect in light of interreligious dialogue. In the process it tries to find critical categories that can improve the treatment of gender, racial, cultural and religious diversity within feminist theory and theology. Ursula King points out the importance and necessity of developing a critical approach and methodology that would enable feminist theology to truly face religious pluralism.[7]

Towards a methodology of women's interreligious dialogue

A good dialogue recognises and breaks up negative stereotyped notions and prejudices, elevates the level of tolerance and strengthens mutual understanding. The incorporation of women's voices into interreligious dialogue and women's interreligious dialogue tend to be essentially practical and personal. These two characteristics positively affect the development of tolerance and the quality of dialogue. In order to reach the characteristics of openness, respect, tolerance, directness, honesty, acceptance, regard, listening that are associated with the concept of dialogue and dialogism in Western thought, practical and personal experience is crucial. Exchanging and learning from personal experience is able to overcome the first obstacle precluding a good dialogue, namely the covert presence of negative stereotypes and prejudices, i.e. a stereotyped evaluation of the others.

The danger of stereotyping others is classified as one of the main obstacles on the road towards a quality dialogue by Maura O'Neill who also warns of the danger of selective information and the fear of identity loss.[8] To avoid these obstacles O'Neill suggests the following methodology:

1. Clarifying the primary purpose of coming together as dialogue and not persuasion or imposition of one's own belief on others.

---

[6] Kwok Pui-lan, "Feminist theology as intercultural discourse", in: Susan Frank Parsons, *The Cambridge Companion to Feminist Theology*, 23-37.
[7] King, "Feminism: the Missing Dimension in the Dialogue of Religions", 40.
[8] O'Neill, *Mending a Torn World*, 104.

2. Using personal stories as a method to break the ice of formality, to stimulate trust, remove distrust and to confront the fear of identity loss.
3. Active listening without preconceived interpretations, but creatively and with an openness to unexpected and unfamiliar experiences. [9] When this listening is not done, when women believe that their view of women's rights is universal, much damage can occur in intercultural and interreligious situations.

To these three points of O'Neill's proposed methodology I would like to add a fourth: clarification of terminology (including basic value systems, the meaning of womanhood and the concept of feminism). This is important because value systems may differ radically and there is tremendous diversity among feminists concerning the meaning of womanhood. Furthermore, our very definitions of feminism may vary. Therefore, by defining our terms we enhance our ability to understand each other across cultural contexts and we improve our ability to deal with the diversity among the world's oppressed.[10]

In addition to these four elements of the proposed methodology for women's interreligious dialogue, we must remain ever vigilant about the covert and pernicious character of negative stereotypes and prejudices that may be present in our mental perceptions. Therefore, let us briefly review the character of prejudices and stereotypes.

Stereotypes and prejudices

The term prejudice was first used by the American journalist, Walter Lippmann, who was also the first to describe a stereotype as a "mental picture" drawn by the individual about himself and others. It is characteristic of a stereotype to be based on unverified facts and reports about a certain event, person, object, etc. Prejudices, for Lippmann, were emotionally charged negative or positive stereotypes. Negative prejudices are typically ascribed by the dominant group to subjected groups, while positive prejudices are only reserved for members of the superior group. It is in the interests of ruling groups to turn such prejudices into objects of a coherent ideology and to accept such prejudices as plain truth.[11]

---

[9] O'Neill, *Mending a Torn World*, 106-111.
[10] Maura O'Neill, *Women Speaking, Women Listening* (Orbis Books: New York 1990), 56-60.
[11] Mirjana Nastran-Ule, *Temelji socialne psihologije* (*Fundamentals of Social Psychology*; Znanstveno in publicistično središče: Ljubljana 1994), 103.

Forum
Fórum

According to the Slovenian sociologist Mirjana Nastran-Ule, a member of the "superior group" in the European context is a "heterosexual white male, member of the western urban culture, professing affiliation to liberal Christianity and belonging to the middle or higher social class".[12] As members of the dominant gender, men have formed numerous stereotypes about women's inferiority throughout history. And women have often accepted these gender stereotypes about themselves since negative prejudices are often received and subscribed to by members of the very group to which these prejudices refer.

In contemporary Slovene society, phrases, such as: *"men don't cry"* and *"woman – a hen"* (the woman is as brainless and confused as a hen) are quite widespread. These are two very common prejudices denoting characteristics that are supposed to be typical of the male or female genders. Since prejudices are uncritically adopted opinions that are not based on logically and empirically founded judgements, both these phrases qualify since they are based on stereotyped, generalised notions that are extremely simplified and categorical. Let me mention a few more examples of prejudices that are not all gender related, but also mark racial, class and religious determinateness or denotation: *"black people are stupid," "all capitalists are exploitative," "Islam is a religion of violence,"* and *"Muslim women suffer the greatest gender discrimination."* Although they are unfounded, prejudices and stereotypes catch on easily and persist due to their simplicity and clear character. They assert themselves easily in groups, especially when they perform an important psychological function – enabling easier distinction between groups, helping to create an atmosphere of cohesiveness and greater value for the members of a group, etc. Prejudices are thus based on stereotyped, simplified judgements. They differ from common erroneous judgements in that they are extremely resistant. One does not give them up easily, even when confronted with well-founded arguments about their erroneousness.[13]

The basic standpoints on which prejudices are based are gender, ethnic and racial affiliation, religion and social status. Prejudices are most often manifested in disrespectful, intolerant or contemptuous attitudes towards members of different groups.

---

[12] Mirjana Nastran-Ule (ed.), *Predsodki in diskriminacije, izbrane socialno-psihološke študije* (*Prejudices and Discrimination: Select Sociopsychological Studies*; Znanstveno in publicistično središče: Ljubljana 1999), 299-300.

[13] Janek Musek, *Psihološki portret Slovencev* (*A Psychological Portrait of the Slovenes*; Znanstveno in publicistično središče: Ljubljana 1994), 27.

It is the primary task of interreligious dialogue to uncover and break up such negative stereotypes and prejudices as well as to raise awareness about the true face of diversity. This is the key "medicine" for greater tolerance and better communication, as the unchecked spread of negative stereotypes leads to discrimination and violence.

Women transcending boundaries: a call for women's interreligious dialogue and the healing of "Balkan war wounds"

Feminist theology in Slovenia is still in its infancy, where it should find an exciting space between Catholic, Protestant, Orthodox and Muslim religious communities in the new cultural and political setting of a modern European state. Geographically and economically speaking, Slovenia is a bridge between the West and the East, between the "European Union" and "the Balkans" or former Yugoslav republics. It was the first state to secede from Yugoslavia in 1991. Its religious structure comprises members of all major religions of the individual former Yugoslav republics preceding 1991. The differences in ideologies, religious and ethnic affiliation, the different languages, customs and traditions of the inhabitants of Yugoslavia before 1991 were, in addition to different political and economic agendas, the factors that caused the disintegration of the former Yugoslav state. The wounds, which only deepened with the secession of individual former Yugoslav republics from the kin state, were left at the mercy of the winds of a collapsing state economy, capitalist globalisation and time. I would argue that a women's conference in the framework of interreligious dialogue could be of extraordinary importance in "healing the wounds of the Balkans." Women's interreligious dialogue in the territory of former Yugoslavia could overcome many of the present obstacles. There are many practical problems troubling women in different religious spheres of the individual states of the former Yugoslav geographical area. Seeing that feminist theology is still in its early stages in these post-socialist states, women's interreligious dialogue in this area could also contribute to the strengthening of feminist theology and religious feminism.

As Maura O'Neill pointed out, "ideological issues become secondary when women join forces to work out solutions to practical problems."[14] In first-world countries, on the local level, women of all religions and religious perspectives come together to improve the quality of their children's education and

---

[14] O'Neill, *Mending a Torn World*, 99.

the safety of their neighbourhoods. On a broader, more global scale, women are working together to address problems that affect all sides of economic or geographical boundaries: domestic violence, sexual exploitation of women and children, lack of clean air and water, and religious and ethnic intolerance. Women who are members of these groups are forming bonds that transcend religious or political differences.

Conclusion
Facing and getting to know diversity and the particularities of individual women's religious experiences enlivens women's interreligious dialogue. Women's participation and cooperation through interreligious dialogue erases geographical, political, religious and other ideological dependencies. By breaking up negative stereotypes and prejudices such dialogue transcends the limits of personal and collective blindness and strengthens the awareness of interpersonal and interreligious tolerance. A more active integration and promotion of women's interreligious dialogue in the areas of the European Union and the Balkans is an urgent issue for the women's ethic of care of Europe and around the globe, which can be understood as the next step in the evolution of humankind.[15]

> Dieser Artikel beschreibt die Bedeutung des interreligiösen Dialogs unter Frauen als global relevantes und gegenwärtiges Phänomen. Er unterstreicht die Wichtigkeit und Dringlichkeit eines aktiveren und häufigeren interreligiösen Dialogs unter Frauen innerhalb der Grenzen der Europäischen Union, um größere interreligiöse Toleranz zu schaffen. Der Beitrag stellt zentrale Charakteristika des interreligiösen Dialogs unter Frauen vor und zeigt bedeutende Schritte auf, um Hindernisse besser zu erkennen und mögliche Methoden für solche Dialoge zu entwickeln. Da negative Stereotypen eine ständige Gefahr für Dialogprozesse darstellen, beschreibt der Artikel den Charakter solcher Stereotypen und Vorurteile. Schließlich ruft der Beitrag die Frauen auf „dem Balkan" dazu auf, „die Wunden der Balkankriege zu heilen", indem sie sich am interreligiösen Dialog beteiligen.

> En este artículo se describe la importancia del diálogo interreligioso de mujeres en tanto que fenómeno actual de importancia global. Se subraya que es importante y

---

[15] For further consideration cf. also Philip Leroy Culbertson (ed.)., *The Spirituality of Men* (Fortress Press: Minneapolis 2002); Ann Cathrin Jarl, *In Justice: Women and Global Economics* (Fortress Press: Minneapolis 2003); Rosemary Radford Ruether, *Integrating Ecofeminism, Globalization, and World Religions* (Rowman & Littlefield Publishers: New York 2005).

urgente que el diálogo interreligioso de mujeres sea más activo y frecuente en la Unión Europea, para generar de esta manera más tolerancia interreligiosa. Se presentan las características principales del diálogo interreligioso de mujeres; se indica cuáles pueden ser pasos importantes para detectar obstáculos y posibles métodos del diálogo interreligioso de mujeres. Teniendo en cuenta el peligro de que constantemente están presentes en el diálogo interreligioso estereotipos negativos, en el artículo se describe brevemente el carácter de estos estereotipos y prejuicios. Finalmente, en el artículo se hace un llamado a las mujeres de los "países Balcánicos" a comenzar a sanar "las heridas que dejó la guerra en los Balcánicos" participando en el diálogo interreligioso de mujeres.

Nadja Furlan (*1974), Research Assistant at the Science and Research Centre of Koper, University of Primorska, Slovenia, holds a PhD in theology and women religious studies (Faculty of Theology, University of Ljubljana). In order to accomplish her research project *Inculturation of the Christian Marriage into Zambian Culture*, she worked six months in three different missions in Zambia. During the war in Kosovo, she worked for two months as a volunteer in a refugee centre in Drac, Albania. She has published two scientific books: *Manjkajoče rebro: ženska, religija in spolni stereotipi* (*The Missing Rib: Woman, Religion and Gender Stereotypes*; Koper 2006) and *Iz poligamije v monogamijo* (*From Polygamy to Monogamy: Inculturation of the Christian Marriage into Zambian Culture*; Ljubljana 2008). She edited a special issue of the journal *Poligrafi*, *Ženske in religija* (*Women and Religion*; Nova Revija: Ljubljana 2007). Currently she is a Fulbright Visiting Scholar at the University of Berkeley.

Humera Khan

Exploring Women's Rights in Islam through Interfaith Dialogue

It was by chance that I became involved in interfaith dialogue back in 1987. At the age of 27 I had only two years previously re-connected with my Islamic faith having up to that time been a product of secular multi-cultural Britain (also known as not very interested in religion)! A friend of mine was involved in a Jewish, Christian and Muslim (JCM) interfaith residential conference in Bendorf, Germany[1] – she offered me a free place if I was interested in participating.

The experience of the Bendorf conferences

Dialogue was, and to some extent still remains for me a strange phenomenon. Growing up as I did in a community where the 'social norm' was daily interaction with people of so many different cultures, races, languages and religions, I was intrigued to know what new experiences a 'formal' dialogue conference would offer. So I went, naïve, but interested.

What followed was surreal – being one of only a few people of colour (all of whom were from the Muslim group) I suddenly felt as if I was in a test tube experiment being ogled to see what I would do and say next by individuals who were filled with stereotypes and most probably prejudices about Islam, Muslims and in particular Muslim women.

But that was the fun bit – getting to know new people from other faiths, being challenged and challenging back in return – I loved getting my teeth into complex and difficult issues, trying to unravel our views and experiences towards some kind of a shared consensus. Not always possible but by the end of each encounter the mysteries and misunderstandings always appeared a little less enormous.

---

[1] See www.bendorferforum.de

Forum
Fórum

The experience that surprised me more at this conference was the intra-faith experience within the Muslim group. Being smaller in number than the other faiths and generally much less experienced in such dialogues, the group was an eclectic group of people cautiously getting to know each other. Not used to meeting in such a way even in our own back home situations it was inevitable that conversation ended up heated or in conflicting disagreements about issues to do with Islam, our objectives in interfaith, purpose existence and so on. Actually we differed almost about everything but by the end of the week we started to work things out and developed a respect for our differences as well as our similarities. It was a real learning experience and I was smitten with dialogue!

The JCM conferences were special partly because they were coming from the shared Abrahamic tradition meaning fewer complexities and operating within a shared historical and spiritual frame of reference. What was also fascinating was that these conferences operated at many different levels. There were key note addresses, discussion groups, text based workshops, project groups, shared meditations, sharing of religious services and a range of other spontaneous activities – mind, body and soul experience! In the early years the conferences were held twice a year – in the spring was the mixed conference and in the autumn was the women's conference. It was at the women's conference that I first became interested in the role of women in theological thinking.

Struggling with the issue of women in Islam

I really struggled with the issue of women when I first started to re-think Islam. Endless discussions and questions on the 'what's, why's and why not's' were asked to whoever came into my line of fire. By the time I started engaging in interfaith I had come to terms with my most elemental questions but it was meeting women from Christian and Jewish backgrounds who were digging deep to redress inequalities on the issue of gender within their faith traditions that fascinated me and became a mirror to some of my own thinking.

The books I had read up to this point about women in Islam were not extensive as the availability of interesting books was very limited. There were two key messages that the available literature and scholars presented – firstly, how the Quran gave equal rights to women in the eyes of God and secondly, the differential roles of men and women in our earthly lives, men as protectors and women as mothers and homemakers. The Quranic perspective was not so complicated – though I read it in English it was clear to see that God doesn't differentiate between men and women in our relationship to Him even though some Muslims do! Despite my acceptance of this and willingness to continue on my Islamic journey there were other difficult verses that were interpreted in a way that was not so easy to accept unconditionally such as the so-called verses on beating of wives, polygamy and segregation. But, I was a new comer to religion so was willing to see what would unfold.

As well as trying to come to terms with issues within theology I was concerned about the obvious difficulties Muslim women faced in their everyday lives caused to a great extent by the segregated and very gender differentiated roles that they lived. Being a second generation British Muslim I still had my feet rooted in my 'cultural traditions'. But as time went by, and to my families great distress, my aspirations were increasingly shaped by the western, secular society I was growing up in which questioned the fundamentals of everything including what was for me the 'norms' is my everyday life. The traditional gender norms in my culture were seen as antiquated and oppressive and I spent many years struggling within myself where I stood on this. If I accepted what secular liberal thinkers were saying then I would have to go against my family. If I accepted my family's position I would feel that I was maintaining the status quo and not being true to myself. The emotional pendulum swung back and forward and it was many years before I was able to work things out for myself. This in the end meant finding a place within my own faith and culture but working within it to transform it.

Struggling with the 'Eve story' – and seeking gender enlightenment

This is where I was in my life when I first encountered Christian and Jewish women who were not prepared to accept the status quo and the first subject matter that seemed to come up again and again was the 'Eve' story and the question of 'original sin'. I came across passionate women who were presenting papers and having discussions on their own investigations and interpretations of the 'Eve story'. The recurring theme was the question of male interpretation of divine scripture – wow! I had never previously thought that there could be a 'male interpretation' – after all, wasn't there only one?

Listening to these women evoked various emotions within me. At first I must admit I couldn't understand why they were so obsessed with addressing the issue of 'original sin'. Though born and brought up as a Muslim I was never taught the Quranic stories in any depth – I knew that we believed in Adam and Eve but that was it. In fact my understanding of this story was

Forum
Fórum

shaped more by Christian interpretations as this was more accessible. Listening to de-constructions of this story I did sometimes think some of it was a little paranoid especially when it came to the concept that the word 'Evil' coming from 'Eve' as she was the person responsible for the 'original sin' – I am still unclear about the authenticity of this perspective today but it is a discussion that left a massive impression in my mind!

Because some of this discussion was led by women who possibly took things to extremes it was easy to step back from it and maybe not take it too seriously. But once out of the polemics I came across women who looked at the issues more pragmatically. These discussions were usually more scripturally and historically based identifying how women had become exploited and marginalised in religious and cultural life. It was these discussions that made me question my own thinking.

The Eve story though interesting, was not controversial for me because the Quran clearly gives responsibility to both Adam and Eve for their disobedience of God's command. It was issues such as women's role in society, in particular public life that concerned me. The case for women staying at home was already strongly made but do we have a role in life other than being wives and mothers? In the 1980's it was difficult to find literature or scholars who defended the right of Muslim women to take leading role in public life or even more controversially, in theological life. As I heard Jewish and Christian women investigate, scrutinise and reinterpret their theological traditions I found myself questioning my own thinking and searching even harder for relevant information. Some of the discussions that came up included: women's authority, creativity and perspectives, women's role in scriptural stories, the value of their role and contribution in scripture, culture and society, women in religious leadership.

Asking similar questions within a Muslim framework wasn't easy because you inevitably were labelled as a 'feminist' which as in other communities at this time was seen as a derogatory statement! But questions needed to be asked and men needed to me made accountable and I guess someone had to do it!

Thus began the journey to seek gender enlightenment. Over the years as I have gained access to great scholars and more thought provoking literature and my understanding of some of these questions have deepened from the Islamic perspective. Issues that endlessly troubled me continue to be worked through though how to implement them into society remains challenging to say the least! It is on this question that I feel I differ in some of the debates within

Judaism and Christianity today. While Muslim women today have greater ability to choose their own path for gender equality and to be taken seriously, personally I am not so interested in the 50/50 equality debate whether that is in the home or outside of it. I do think that we need more women in religious leadership but I am not really interested in competing with or working within religious hierarchies. I don't want to play men at their own game nor do I want to live in a world where I can no longer get on with them. I quite like some of the traditional roles women play and I like living in a family centred world.

New perspectives

After years of engaging with the gender debate amongst women of other faiths I began to loose some interest as I felt the thinking eventually became too insular. Though many Jewish and Christian women I knew during these years certainly achieved much and were pioneers in changing attitudes I somehow felt that the price that was paid was to some extent a certain amount of isolation. My own journey now takes me to contemplate more the Prophetic saying 'The more you know yourself the more you know your Lord'. I want to discover my own spiritual depths without having to constantly defend myself or be reactionary. I think women who are at peace within themselves and able to deal with inequalities and injustices through this inner strength are more awe inspiring than women constantly on red alert to attack. I know because I have been one.

> En este artículo, en el que se estudian los derechos de la mujer en el islamismo a través del diálogo interreligioso, se relata a nivel muy personal cómo se pueden compartir ideas, pensamientos y experiencias con mujeres de otras religiones. Se intenta demostrar que no todos los encuentros tienen que tener lugar a un nivel teológico o académico muy alto, y que algunas experiencias muy poderosas pueden recibirse a través de la simple reflexión e interacción. Este aspecto resalta en particular la importancia que tiene el entorno en el diálogo, señalándose en especial la experiencia sin igual de Bendorf en donde se logró crear un espacio seguro y sano para aprender, olvidar y volver a aprender. El artículo es finalmente la experiencia de una mujer musulmana que desea reevaluarse en la época en la que vive.

> Dieser Beitrag, der sich mit der Erkundung von Frauenrechten im Islam mittels des interreligiösen Dialogs befasst, erzählt auf persönliche Weise über das Aufeinandertreffen und Teilen von Ideen, Gedanken und Erfahrungen von Frauen unterschiedlicher Religionen. Er versucht zu zeigen, dass nicht alle Begegnungen auf einem hohen theologischen oder akademischen Niveau stattfinden müssen, und dass

Forum
Fórum

äußerst kraftvolle Erfahrungen über einfaches Nachdenken und über Interaktion gemacht werden können. Vor allem dieser Aspekt hebt die Bedeutung der Umgebung für den Dialog hervor. Speziell wird dabei auf die einzigartige Erfahrung von Bendorf verwiesen, wo es gelungen ist, einen sicheren und heilsamen Raum für Menschen zu schaffen, zum Lernen, Verlernen und Wieder-erlernen. Der Beitrag reflektiert schließlich auch die Erfahrungen einer Muslima, die versucht, sich selbst neu zu finden in den Zeiten, in denen sie lebt.

Humera Khan (*1960) is a founding member of the pioneering An-Nisa Society, an organization working for the welfare of Muslim families. She has been an activist and educator for over 20 years, working in race and gender equality, the voluntary sector and social services. She is also a commentator, contributing regularly to mainstream and independent media, as well an author of a series of books on Islam and sexual health, Muslim fatherhood and recently completed a 12month project working with Muslim boys and young men. Other work includes involvement in various interfaith activities, co-facilitates a Jewish-Muslim dialogue group and is the Family specialist member for the Archbishop of Canterbury's Christian Muslim Forum.

Alice Schumann

Experiences of Inter-religious Dialogue as a German Hindu Woman

I am writing this article from the perspective of a German woman who grew up in a Christian church context and has been initiated into Hinduism for 27 years. However, I am neither a theologian nor an Indologist and have only studied comparative religion for a few semesters. As a social educationalist now writing a thesis on "Pro-sociality in Hinduism"[1], and also as the director of the Hindu charitable organisation "Food for Life"[2], I am nevertheless not simply an ordinary run-of-the-mill woman. On the contrary, precisely as an academic and a practising Hindu, I have been in demand over the past 15 years from church bodies with increasing frequency and have presented Hinduism in many different dialogue situations; this has been the case despite many years of commitment to ISKCON[3], a movement of Vaishnava Hinduism which is still described as a "sect" in church documents.[4] Against the background of these experiences, I should therefore like to describe my experiences of inter-religious dialogue in what follows.

In this dialogue, what I usually encounter first is the basic question of how "you" can be a Hindu as a German. Many orthodox Hindus from India would claim that it is not possible at all to "convert" to Hinduism without having been brought up as a Hindu. And for many Western people whom I meet, this process is a contradiction in itself: how is it possible to switch from such a

---

[1] Dissertation at the University of Cologne under Prof. Hansjosef Buchkremer. Subject: *Pro-sociality in Hinduism – the ideal and the reality*.

[2] Food for Life Deutschland e.V. was established officially in Germany in 1994 and has since been directed and administered by Alice Schumann.

[3] ISKCON (International Society for Krishna Consciousness), founded in 1970 by an Indian, A.C. De Bhaktivedanta Swami Prabhupada, who came to the West in 1969. It is a further development of the Vishnuitic Bhakti (loving devotion to God) movement, Brahma Madhva Gandija – discipleship of followers – which is linked with the Holy Reformer Chaitanya (1486-1533) – also known popularly in Germany as the "Hare Krishna" movement.

[4] e.g. IDEA-Spektrum No.4, 28 January 2001, p.18. (Source: Ev. Zentrale für Weltanschauungsfragen) Idea e.V., Evangelical News Agency.

liberal, Christian, democratic society to that discriminatory, caste-ridden, Hindu religion and to do so as a woman who seemed to be keen on "emancipation" even in their youth?

In view of this fundamental questioning, the subject of this book on feminist approaches to inter-religious dialogue initially put me on the defensive. My spontaneous answer was that I am not a feminist and I understood the invitation as a request once again to give an account of the position of women in Hinduism. In such a situation where I have to defend Hinduism I should like to begin with the following quotation from Walter Kerber:

> "In (inter-religious) debates of that kind, there is a widespread false assumption that one can compare the ideal picture of one's own religion or worldview with the reality in other religions and worldviews which leads one to conclude: we are obviously better than all the others. One can avoid this ethnocentric prejudice by comparing reality with reality and the ideal with the ideal."[5]

The distinction between the ideal and the reality of each religion seems to me to be of fundamental importance. With regard to Hinduism, I should like to take account of both components in my contribution: the philosophical religious ideal as it is presented in the "holy" scriptures of Hinduism and the reality of Hinduism determined by socialisation and tradition as it appears to me as a woman. Although my description is certainly based on biographical experiences and less on objective facts and observations, this is not merely because I can only approach the subject in this subjective way as a result of my own socialisation, my own character and my own psyche; I believe, in addition, that witness to one's personal experiences and conclusions is the most important basis for a genuine dialogue.

Since I have been asked about my experiences as a German Hindu woman, I shall therefore also respond as a woman for whom – almost in contradiction to her spontaneous rejection of the concept of feminism – the question of reconciling her spiritual path with her sense of emancipation has always remained an issue, even though she has given it low priority at certain times. For me, this has been evident above all in intra-religious disputes within the Hindu community in which I have been active for longest in Germany and in which the question of power and leadership by men and women arose and had to be resolved increasingly. Parallel to these intra-religious processes, I have then been in demand in

---

[5] Walter Kerber (ed.), *Religion und prosoziales Verhalten* (*Religion and pro-social behaviour*; Kindt Verlag: Munich 1995), 121.

inter-religious dialogue precisely as a woman. Hence the questions of feminist theology, with which I have been confronted by the editors of this annual review, have always played an important part in my conscientisation process.

This initial reflection has already touched on the way that dialogue takes place on three levels which I should now like to discuss in greater detail:

1. *Inner-religious dialogue*, i.e. my personal quest for self-fulfilment and the dialogue within myself as well as the quest for God and dialogue with God;
2. *Intra-religious dialogue*, i.e. my real perceptions and practical experiences within the Hindu groups that I have encountered in the course of my quest;
3. *Inter-religious dialogue*, i.e. the encounters that I as a Hindu woman have had within my "native", traditionally Christian society and the interchange with "people of other faiths" in religious organisations and at inter-religious conferences.

When going on to reflect on my experiences at these three levels, I shall particularly concentrate on the feminist theme of this book while paying less attention to other important issues of Hinduism which I consider equally relevant for religion and philosophy.

The inner-religious dialogue

To start by reflecting on inner-religious dialogue as the first level of dialogue, I should like to describe my own search for self-fulfilment which was geared, on the one hand, to a specific *ideal* and how, on the other hand, it took shape within a particular *reality*, namely that of my German and originally Christian socialisation. It also seems to me that a personal quest for self-fulfilment in the form of an inner dialogue – not only with myself but with God – is the basic requirement both for my own process of conscientisation and for every additional dialogue with other people.

As the granddaughter of an "apostate" Lutheran missionary[6] and the daughter of an "apostate" Catholic doctor, who resolved to leave the Roman Catholic

---

[6] Friedrich Schroeder, *Aus dem Leben eines Abtrünnigen oder vom Orthodoxismus zum Liberalismus* (*About the Life of an Apostate or From Orthodoxy to Liberalism*; A. Martini & Grüttefien GmbH: Elberfeld 1912). Schroeder was sent out as a young, new missionary of the Rhenish Missionary Society to Gibeon, South West Africa, and served there from 1886 to 1899.

Church following the prohibition of the pill[7] by Pope Paul VI, I was exposed early in life to the ambiguities of the Christian churches. This was all the more so when – in my constant search for the meaning of life and an answer about what happens after death – I "bombarded" the teacher of religious studies with questions and unfortunately received no answers that satisfied me. In this situation, I came across a book of yoga exercises that my mother had and I discovered my father's copy of Hermann Hesse's "Siddharta"; in this way my path to Hinduism was really marked out naturally "from the cradle". But what I was looking for was not an "India trip" or a "Guru trend". Although I was engaged in an intense quest, I had no wish to associate myself with the "Bhagwan movement" (later "Osho") that was spreading at that time, despite the fact that a number of my acquaintances were drawn to it in those days. I had no desire to dress in red, nor did I find the answers of the "Bhagwan followers" to my philosophical questions satisfying. "Just ask Bhagwan!" That answer was not enough for me.

During the following period I then came across the TM practice of *Maharishi Yogi*.[8] After hesitating for quite some time, I asked the local TM teacher to give me a "mantra" for which I had to pay. Although meditation with the mantra gave me strength, I had problems about the role of the "teacher" who gave me strict instructions about how long I should meditate each day. Nevertheless, I wondered where the strong energy came from that I sensed during the meditation. It was not that the meditation was like a drug; it was something other-worldly or transcendental. In my innermost heart I had not forgotten my quest for the "cause of all causes" or the search for God. But there was never any talk about "God", only about self-fulfilment and self-perfection. Later I learnt that this was more a matter of the non-personality path (monism) within Hinduism. However, that was not what I had been looking for. I had always sought, conceived of and seen God as a person. Perhaps this was an effect of my Christian upbringing because, even as a child, I had always prayed to God and tried to have a dialogue with God. For me, even today God is still the same God as always. Precisely because I cannot speak with "nothingness", I have never been interested in Buddhism, which was described to me in religious instruction as the "doctrine of nothingness", despite its popularity here in the West. Today I know that Hinduism embraces all the different approaches

---

[7] Encyclical *Humanae Vitae* (in: Acta Apostolicae Sedis 60, 481-503) of 25.07.1968.
[8] TM = transcendental meditation.

– polytheism, monotheism and monism – which in some way complement each other. So through TM I had only experienced the force of divine radiation. The unquestionably positive yoga technique of deep meditation helped me to balance out my deficits of order, discipline, purity, concentration of the mind and correct behaviour in society. But I felt the lack of a dialogue with and about God. Especially at the weekend seminars, it struck me that each of the participants was interested only in their personal progress and less in interpersonal relationships.

In addition, my teacher did not consider it his task to answer my philosophical questions. So the following questions remained open for me: why should a mantra like this cost anything? Why is it secret? Why must I observe strict time limits for meditation (no more than 20 minutes morning and evening)? Where does God fit into this path? Where is there any interchange or dialogue? What makes up the role of the teacher?

Despite receiving instructions to the contrary, I experimented by engaging in unlimited meditation several times. And in this way I experienced a "vision", the memory of which is deeply imprinted on my consciousness even today. A little bit ahead of me I saw a figure meditating. For me, it was clear that this must be "God". It was only later, referring to descriptions in ancient Hindu scriptures, that it became clear to me that it had been an incarnation of Vishnu. Other people may claim that I could have imagined it, but for me this was an experience of a "knowledge of God" or "vision". For the time being I pursued this no further. I had come upon something, something permanent and authentic, the cause of everything. And it was something quite personal that no one could take away from me. I could also continue happily to pray to the same God as before; for me, God had remained unchanged. After that, I did in fact abandon the contact with TM but continued with the meditation technique for myself personally.

Years later, when I had long since settled into a quite normal student life in Berlin and spirituality appeared to play no more part at all in my context, through an old acquaintance I came across another Hindu movement which practices the way of Bhakti yoga. In the days that followed I discussed philosophical issues, vegetarianism, reincarnation, karma, etc. with my acquaintance. Although I had difficulties about his rigorous sense of mission, I felt that his inner conviction was genuine and his philosophical arguments were unbeatable. He initiated me into the chanting of the "Hare Krishna mantra". That is a meditation based on sound and speech which was unfamiliar to me at first because, on the one hand, it is meditation but, on the other, also prayer, i.e. dialogue with God. Very soon I had the inner sense that this way was authentic and right – and my way. From that time onwards, I stopped eating meat, fish or eggs, drank no alcohol or coffee and devoted myself enthusiastically to studying the Vedas. These have been translated in detail from Sanskrit into English by *Swami Prabhupada*, the founder of this Hindu organisation.[9] Although the descriptions in these ancient scriptures explained my divine vision, it struck me already at that time that the androcentricity in the author's commentary and his ideal image of women did not fit the philosophy as I had understood it and were certainly inappropriate in a German society. He described women in certain passages as less intelligent or compared them with children. But the predominant, spiritual force and authenticity of these writings led me to take these passages lightly. Indeed, in general I found many satisfactory answers to my questions about reincarnation, karma and meditation. This and the intense spiritual atmosphere as a result of jointly practising Bhakti yoga (yoga of loving devotion to God) produced a special strength and also an exaltation to a spiritual, transcendent level.

So my personal quest for self-fulfilment and the dialogue with myself and with God finally led to my being able to identify with this form of Bhakti yoga. I accordingly had myself initiated and attempted as a *brahmacarini* (nun) to do "mission" for Hinduism in this society with its Christian background.

The intra-religious dialogue

I should now like to go on to describe how my practical search for fulfilment within the Hindu community increasingly gave rise to intra-religious dialogue in the course of time and how this finally led me to an awareness of the necessary inculturation and reform of this Hindu community in Germany.

The community and the give-and-take within the organisation were essential for me really to enter deeply into the spiritual practice. But precisely my experiences in the spiritual community made me more aware of issues which had appeared secondary to me at the beginning of my quest. Although I had already been disturbed about paying for the mantra and sticking to rigid regulations about prayer, what struck me more and more in the ISKCON was the

---

[9] Abay Caran De Bhaktivedanta Swami Prabhupada (1896-1977), also known as Shrila Prabhupada. Founder of ISKCON and of the publishers Bhaktivedanta Book Trust (BBT); author of 80 books including numerous translations of ancient Indian and Vedantic documents.

allocation of roles according to gender combined with the automatic assumption of the predominance of the men. In fact, I had already felt very ambiguous about my first visits to the temples in the early 1980s. On the one side, the atmosphere radiated an authentic, pure spirituality even more strongly than the books described, and the people seemed to be very satisfied and treated me in a very friendly and personal way; but, on the other, the Indian dress made a strange impression in most cases. The shaven heads of the men and the women's heads covered by saris looked to me like something which did not fit the philosophy at all as I had understood it.

Indeed, according to the philosophy and religion of Hinduism, it is only the embodied souls which are subject to the duality of the sexes; the soul itself is spiritual by nature and thus transcends these temporary dualities. On the spiritual level, only God is male (here as Krishna) and the souls are female. And even in this male form Krishna always appears with his female partner Radha; the two are one as a divine couple. Moreover, in addition to numerous goddesses, Hinduism also has many female saints.

However, as time went on I observed – as far as discrimination against women was concerned – that neither the social reality of Hindu India nor that of the temples in Germany corresponded to this philosophical ideal. I began to realise that the strong emphasis on different gender roles and positions in the reality of the temples was out-of-date for Western society. At that time, the women always sat and stood behind the men and only received their food after the men. At the joint devotional ceremonies, the men did the chanting and the readings were done exclusively by men. All the Gurus were men as well.[10] This androcentricity which often caused readings to degenerate into deprecation of women went against my grain. Because in my female body I sometimes had the feeling it would be better to make myself invisible when encountering men. It was extremely strange and unpleasant for me that men were trained not to look at women when talking to them.

I later learnt that this training did not really have anything to do with women as such, but that an attraction to the other sex was considered an obstacle for one's spiritual life. It is not without reason that there are ashrams for men or for women as well as monasteries and nunneries. I also learnt that women had to cover their hair in all religions so that men will not be distracted from their

---

[10] Guru in Sanskrit means "heavy weight" so Gurus are those who are heavily laden with wisdom or "wise" teachers.

Forum
Fórum

religious path or confused by sexual desires. So the Bhagavad Gita states in one verse that desire is the greatest enemy on the way to self-realisation.[11] I have some doubt as to whether these measures really help and whether women are more protected in this way. But it was quite clear to me that, as "objects of desire", they were negated, discriminated and seen as evil in themselves. According to my experiences in an ashram and also in inter-religious dialogue, sexual restraint was considerably more difficult for men than for women. And, in fact, women as such are by no means as "desiring" as men may imagine them to be. However, because of this indoctrinated conception, women minimise themselves and are in danger of losing their self-respect. In a social setting, this tends to be at the back of people's minds.

I found myself facing a growing dilemma in my Hindu community. On the one hand, I knew that Bhakti yoga was the way for me but, on the other, this clear distinction between the roles of the different sexes bothered me. For this reason, I was also only able initially to bear temple life for a short time and took refuge in the kitchen instead of participating in the novices' programme (mantra meditation, veneration of deities[12] and reading) which was very much geared to the men. The woman cook, a long term pupil of the founder, enabled me to observe devoted service to God in practice and I also learnt Indian cooking. I sensed that this kind of "Bhakti yoga" was my religious path. And, in spite of all my criticism of the discrimination, I recognised the spiritual force and devotion to God which radiated from this path and also from the people who followed it.

Equally as important as my experiences with the cook in this connection was the fact that I undertook several pilgrimages to India during my years as a "Brahmacarini". In contrast to Germany, there I felt very much at ease in a sari. And I was never bothered by Indian men. Whether I covered my head or not made no difference. From this I concluded that men in India pay more attention to their duty to control their senses themselves instead of making this an exaggerated burden for the women by avoiding them, disguising them or declaring them the sex with greater desires. Moreover, in the Indian temples and for the distribution of meals, the women more frequently stood at the front rather than the back. And in my daily dealings with "renouncers" (monks) I was naturally respected and never experienced their not looking at me when

---

[11] BG 3.37ff.
[12] Deity means a figure or an image of God.

they were speaking to me. On the contrary, they addressed me as "mataji" (mother) as a sign of respect. The background to this is the advice from the scriptures that men should consider all women – except their own wives – as mothers.[13] I in no way wish to minimise the many forms of discrimination against women in India which also contradict the Hindu ideal, but am only referring here to the difference in relation to morality as I experienced it in daily life. In some way, this confirmed the critical view I mentioned before of the unpleasant and unnatural contact with men in the German temples. It was only during my later studies that I learnt that the poetry of the Bhakti tradition was written in the 15th century almost exclusively by Indian women of the lower castes. The most famous woman poet even today is Mirabai.[14] Just as Buddhism provided a way out of the rigidity of the caste society, the Bhakti movement offered women an escape from their position of discrimination within this system.[15]

I then found my first way out of the dilemma of roles being assigned according to gender in what is known as "Sankirtana" (singing together) that was described by the founder of ISKCON as a form of mission on the street. This meant that we travelled in groups of three or four women from one town to another and tried to offer translations from the Vedas to people on the street. The positive side-effect connected with the intra-religious approach was that I developed a respect for women which I had lost to a large extent because of their acceptance or toleration of being discriminated in their role in the temple community but also because of the competitive philosophy which is current in our society. On our missionary journeys it was no longer important whether you were a woman or a man. This situation is reinforced by the philosophy of reincarnation, i.e. that our bodies are temporal while our souls are eternal and spiritual. Moreover, at that time missionary service was the most respected position for women. This meant I enjoyed special appreciation so that I no longer felt my female body to be an obstacle in this community.

---

[13] Manusamhita, Chap. 4 and 6.

[14] Mirabai (about 1498-1546), Indian mystic and poet. Her quite personal ecstatic love and lament songs have remained alive throughout the centuries and are still famous in India among Hindus, Sikhs, Christians and Muslims. There are many books and CDs with these songs. Her life has been filmed on many occasions and her verses form part of world literature alongside the poet-mystics Hafis, Rumi, Kabis and Hildegard von Bingen.

[15] cf. Sarah Hughes, *Women in World History* (M. E. Sharpe: New York 1997), 54; cf. also: Alice Schumann, "Wege und Umwege zur Bhakti" ("Ways direct and indirect to Bhakti"), in: *RIG (Religionen im Gespräch)* 8, Nachrodt 2004, 114-122.

After that, living together in the temple for a time made sense to me again. Although the way was my personal one and I had always refused close followers, the community with like-minded people was important because, on my own, I should never have found the strength and courage to follow this path so consistently here in the Western society which is so materialistic. But, unfortunately, with regard to gender nothing had changed in the temples. All the responsible positions such as gurus, swamis or temple directors were occupied by men. And even the National Council was a purely male gathering. I continued to be dissatisfied about the contrast between our active missionary work and the *ideal image* of a Hindu woman who is chaste, subservient to her husband, devoted and reticent.

As a result of a historical development, I then found a second way out of the dilemma of the roles assigned to me as a woman. When the frontiers with the GDR opened up, this coincided with my need to combine my missionary activities with more responsibility and to pursue my organisational inclinations. An enormous number of books were distributed in the East after the wall came down which led us to conclude that a centre was needed there as well. Since, at that time, no male members were able or wanted to undertake this responsibility, I was allowed to attempt to open a centre there. So I set out alone, equipped only with a bag and a small car, for Weimar, found a place to rent and – initially on my own – organised weekly programmes with cooking, music and introductory lectures. It soon became clear that the East German interest was purely in buying cheap literature which had previously been prohibited. As a result of their "Socialist socialisation", the people were almost exclusively atheists who, for the time being, did not want to hear anything about doctrines of whatever kind. But the advantage was that the women there exercised their rights quite naturally. It was unknown for them that women should need to fight for their rights like in the West. This suited me very well because I did not need to introduce any "reforms" for women and so made no distinction between men and women from the very beginning. The repeated criticism about my bad "standard" in the temple, voiced by male "authorities" from the West who visited the centre to give lectures, was something I put up with. It was more important to me to protect the women from discrimination.

At the same time, two women had taken over the running of temples in West Germany as well which meant the National Council could no longer avoid also admitting women. That was where the difficult but worthwhile reforms in the intra-religious realm finally began. We were granted the right to vote. With some other strong women, we also set up a National Women's

Council. And bit by bit we demanded more rights for the women. In the centres run by women, and later in other centres as well, the women no longer stood behind but beside the men. They also gave lectures and became cantors during the programmes. However, many men including swamis and gurus found it hard to accept the new reforms. In this situation, I observed that Western men, who had converted to Hinduism, had problems especially about having to share their positions with women, whereas their Indian counterparts tended more to have difficulties about giving up long established roles and traditions. But there were also women who did not want to support these reforms for fear of getting a bad reputation as "heavy women", as they started calling us, and for this reason not finding a husband. Nevertheless, they also benefitted (silently) from our reforms.

My life was now full of dialogue. My "inner-religious dialogue" with God, in the form of God's name which is not different from God, took place during my morning meditation, during the day and by praying before the deities. The "intra-religious dialogue" took place in singing together, philosophising and discussing with like-minded people – the women missionaries and temple dwellers. And the "inter-religious dialogue" with Christians, followers of other religions and so-called atheists took place for me initially on the street and then also in my own centre.

Inter-religious dialogue

My inter-religious dialogue really started with my missionary activities. In the process, I met more than a hundred people each day, spoke to them, communicated with them, gave them books and proclaimed and defended my religion and philosophy. It was only recently that I became aware that, through my activities as a Hindu missionary on the streets of Germany, I had basically been following in the footsteps of my grandfather who, after his work as a Christian missionary in South West Africa, had also been a missionary in Cologne.[16] If this activity had not become so discredited today, because our main religions, the churches in Germany, no longer need this kind of mission owing to the established church tax system, an inter-religious dialogue on the horizontal level – rather than on the verticle level as a present – would be much more natural.

What I learnt from the encounters and dialogue with people on the street, to whom this approach was totally foreign and who were sometimes friendly,

---

[16] cf. Schroeder, *Aus dem Leben eines Abtrünnigen*, 63ff.

Forum
Fórum

sometimes unfriendly and occasionally even aggressive, was humility, tolerance and taking firm refuge in God. It was a success each time someone took a book away with them, especially the Bhagavad Gita.[17] I saw myself in the process merely as the deliverer of a spiritual treasure. What the person in question then did with the book was not my business. Despite the limitations, deprivations, discipline and sometimes an inner struggle with myself, this uncompromising, full-time spiritual life gave me a joy, a happiness, a religious conviction and, at the same time, a freedom such as I had never known or experienced before. Naturally, I also wanted to share this happiness with everyone and that included my family and my friends. With this stronger sense of a missionary calling, I unfortunately frequently lacked diplomacy. But at least I managed to convince my mother and sister to become vegetarians.

However, it was not easy week after week, month after month and year after year to keep this joy going in Germany with its Christian and atheistic towns. Because, despite all its virtues, spirituality and mission, ISKCON was considered a sect. One reason for this was that the church had introduced the newly established profession of "commissioner for sects" who devoted themselves energetically to discrediting all the groups and movements outside of the church and also did so through the media. But among the followers of my Hindu movement there was also a feeling of superiority over people who thought differently which sometimes made it impossible to exchange ideas on an equal footing.

After the street mission, the time in East Germany was for me also the end of a closed group existence, because merely distributing books and then moving on to the next person required no lengthy discussions with people of different views. What mattered in Weimar was to continue to live with the local people in a cooperative way. So I became more involved in the dialogue with the media and with the local church representatives. In this context, it was not appropriate to preach or do mission, nor to defend oneself; it required a friendly exchange of opinions which then developed into a fruitful interreligious dialogue. However, then the commissioners for sects from the West started their "mission" in the media. Suddenly, numerous reports on us were published in the local daily papers. The worst and most decisive article appeared in Weimar's largest daily paper. It was an enormous article with photos of our centre under the heading, "When the ego is on the edge of an abyss". After that, the dialogue was broken off and our neighbours who had previously

---

[17] The Bhagavad Gita ("Song of the Highest"), also known as the "Hindu Bible", sets out the philosphical essence of the Vedic writings and was Gandhi's favourite reading matter.

been kindly disposed, as well as the local population, turned against us. Even the food distribution project, which I had built up for local needy people, got a bad name.

We became some kind of "outlaws" for many East Germans who had preserved some sort of nationalistic, racist thinking subconsciously under the Socialist regime, and this then was expressed in public in the form of skinheads. And then, when some new members came to Weimar from the West and from other eastern countries, because the organisation had always been international anyway, we were subjected to innumerable attacks on our cars, the new centre and even physically. Once I myself was the victim of such an attack when a skinhead tried to stab me one evening in a telephone box with an enormous knife. The people living nearby just observed this in silence from behind their curtains. During this period of threats and discrimination by the local people (despite the former concentration camp, Buchenwald, being only 10 km away), I could sometimes well imagine how a Jew must have felt during the Third Reich. In the context of this continuing background of threats, I finally returned to the West after four years.

That was the end of my organisational task and my "position" as a temple director. But I soon received a new and much more influential "position" through the inter-religious dialogue, and that was also, in a sense, my third step out of my dilemma as a German Hindu woman. The numerous challenges and experiences I had had in my encounters with people of other convictions while on mission and with the East German population had stimulated an urge in me to become more actively involved in inter-religious dialogue. Indeed, only by means of direct communication with representatives of politics and other religions was there a chance to enable others to understand, respect and accept my religion and philosophy in a comprehensible way. And so this area became my main task in addition to managing Food for Life Deutschland e.V. I attended inter-religious seminars and events, organised inter-religious conferences myself and had in the meantime become the public relations woman and later the chairwoman of the organisation in Germany as well. I also established contact with the people behind the inflammatory propaganda, with the commissioners for sects, with representatives of politics and the media and I set up a "Communication Team".

The inter-religious debate was and still is of mutual benefit today: church institutions like to "flaunt" the merit of also seeing Hinduism represented at their inter-religious meetings, and I myself have gained acceptance and recognition in academic circles. As a result of my presence, I have been able to counteract numerous hair-raising clichés about Hinduism with which I have

Forum
Fórum

been confronted among "educated" church representatives and followers of other religions. For example, on one occasion, a Protestant mission director claimed that the Hindus needed Jesus because they otherwise had no possibility of breaking out of the circle of birth and death. And the reverse was also true: thanks to the inter-religious exchange of views, I had my own long-standing clichés about Islam corrected e.g. by Muslim women representatives.[18]

For the dialogue, the discussions with ISKCON representatives from England was also helpful. Because of its different colonial history and the many Hindus who live in England, the organisation enjoys the same acceptance there as the other religious communities. Its followers started early on describing themselves explicitly as "representatives of Hinduism" – and not as representatives of a "new religious movement" (or even a "sect" as in Germany). They also deliberately joined up with the Indian Hindus and formed a "Hindu Council". This enabled them to engage in activities in educational institutions as well and they were able to be employed by schools and universities. In the meantime, representatives of this organisation have become lecturers at various universities and have founded the "Oxford Centre for Hindu Studies"[19]; in the near future, a state university will also be established under its leadership. It seems to me that it is only on this level of mutual acceptance that partners in inter-religious dialogue can really meet eye to eye, and not when one claims that the other belongs to a "sect" or to something that is not a "true" religion.

But in Germany the conditions were quite different. Indeed, in 1997 under pressure from the churches, the German Bundestag (parliament) appointed a commission of enquiry with the title "So-called sects and psycho-groups". As the commissioner for dialogue, I established close contact at that time with the experts (psychologists, sociologists and commissioners for sects) and the members of parliament on this commission and put forward the view internally that ISKCON should be more open to society and admit the past errors of the organisation. In order to create transparency, it was also possible to convince the conservative authorities of our organisation that reforms were necessary and to overcome the social deficits which still existed. After all, one cannot simply claim that liberality or openness constitute reforms without being liberal

---

[18] E.g. Women on the staff of ZIF (Zentrum islamischer Frauenforschung – Centre for Islamic women's research, Cologne).

[19] The University of Wales, Lampeter, provides a course entitled "Vaishnava Theology" in cooperation with ISKCON; the teaching takes place at the "Bhaktivedanta College", an institution belonging to the organisation in the Ardennes in Belgium.

and introducing reforms in one's own ranks. Since in the meantime, as a result of the inter-religious dialogue, some well-intentioned contacts had been established with representatives of the Protestant and Catholic churches and with other academics, and these had been helpful for this "inquiry"[20], the experts also recognised the deeper significance and serious spirituality and philosophy of the organisation and its Hindu authenticity. The result of the commission of inquiry was that the organisation was not a "sect".[21] Thanks to this outcome we were able to counteract many prejudices as well and finally the public was also compelled to listen to us and not simply to write us off. Nevertheless, there are still certain individuals or institutions which continue to try to ignore the result even today.

It was then possible for me myself to adopt a quite different stand in the inter-religious context; I felt I had been authorised to be a representative of Hinduism. My contacts in the inter-religious dialogue led to my being invited with increasing frequency to provide information in schools about ISKCON, on the one hand, and, on the other, to give lectures and presentations about Hinduism in general in secondary schools, academies and universities. In order to be on the same academic level in inter-religious dialogue, i.e. to be able to pass on my knowledge of Hinduism in a well-founded way, I started to study comparative religion. I also studied over two years for my diploma as a social educationalist in order to be qualified as director of the charitable association Food for Life.

In my dissertation, I am trying to use my studies and experiences to uncover the ethics in the ideal and the reality of Hinduism and to point to possibilities for counteracting discrimination on the basis of Hindu ethics.

Conclusion

The exchanges I have had with people in inter-religious dialogue have led me to the following conclusions:

- Inter-religious dialogue is only possible if the partners in the dialogue are consciously on the same level (this applies both to men and women).

---

[20] *Inter alia* EZW (ev. Zentrale für Weltanschauungsfragen, Berlin), Refidi (Referat für Interreligiösen Dialog, Cologne); membership of INTRA° (Interreligiöser Arbeitskreis, Iserlohn), RfP (Religions for Peace, Cologne-Bonn), DIG (Deutsch-Indische Gesellschaft, Frankfurt).

[21] Cf. Final report of the Commission of Inquiry of the German parliament "Sogenannte Sekten und Psychogruppen", 1998, 169f; cf. also Interview with Alice Schumann in "Special Report", an appendix to this report.

- In order to reach the same level, any sense or form of mission is inappropriate and an obstacle to inter-religious dialogue.
- No inter-religious dialogue is possible without tolerance and respect for other confessions of faith.
- Inter-religious dialogue is possible only if one can stand up for one's own convictions.
- If I am unable to stand up for my religious community in its ideal and/or real form, I must firstly become aware of my own points of criticism and then also state them frankly.
- In the process, there should be no fear about possibly also changing one's religion. Even though the representatives of certain religions see this as a danger in inter-religious dialogue and call for clear lines of distinction, it also constitutes an opportunity.[22]
- Through inter-religious dialogue the problem e.g. of discrimination against women becomes more or less visible in all religions and societies. This implies that no one can point a finger at the others; "people who live in glass houses should not throw stones."
- Through inter-religious dialogue, the female partners become aware of existing discrimination and are able to state and change things in their own community through mutual support and solidarity.
- As a result of inner-religious, intra-religious and inter-religious dialogue, one of my essential benefits is the recognition that knowledge is the only means of counteracting discrimination (including one's own).

Om tat sat

Translation from the German: Margaret A. Pater

Dieser Artikel greift mehrere Thematiken auf: Zunächst wird die innere Entwicklung einer im deutsch-christlichen Kontext aufgewachsenen Frau, die sich einer völlig „fremden" Religion, dem Hinduismus, anschließt, aus ihrer eigenen Sicht beschrieben. Wie es zu diesem religiösen Bekenntnis und den damit verbundenen Selbsterfahrungen und -verwirklichungen gekommen ist, fasst sie als *inner-religiösen Dialog* zusammen. Als *intra-religiösen Dialog* bezeichnet sie ihre Erfahrungen im Austausch mit Glaubensschwestern und -brüdern innerhalb hinduistischer Gemeinschaften, unter besonderer Berücksichtigung geschlechtsspezifischer Rollenverteilungen. Die dritte Kategorie, der *inter-religiöse Dialog*, handelt von

---

[22] Many famous persons from the Hindu tradition tried out other religions without any fear of contact and were also open to the possibility of changing (e.g. Ramakrishna and Gandhi).

ihren Begegnungen mit (meist christlichen) Andersgläubigen in der deutschen Gesellschaft, vorwiegend im Rahmen interreligiöser Veranstaltungen, Seminare und Organisationen. Bei ihren Schlussfolgerungen und Konsequenzen, die sie aus ihren persönlichen Erfahrungen im interreligiösen Dialog gezogen hat, betont sie besonders, das philosophisch-religiöse Ideal der einen Religion, wie es in ihrer jeweiligen „heiligen" Schrift dargelegt ist und in ihren Grundsätzen besteht, nicht mit der sozialisations- und traditionsbedingten Realität einer anderen Religion zu vergleichen.

En este artículo se tratan diferentes temas: primero se describe la evolución de una mujer que creció en el entorno alemán-cristiano y que luego se convirtió a una religión totalmente "ajena", al hinduísmo. Ella habla de *diálogo religioso interno* cuando describe cómo fue que encontró esta fe, la autovivencia y la autorrealización que la llevaron al hinduísmo. El *diálogo intrareligioso* es para ella la interacción con sus hermanas y hermanos en la fe, dentro de las comunidades hinduistas, teniendo en cuenta especialmente el reparto de roles por sexos. La tercera categoría es el *diálogo interreligioso*, o sea, sus encuentros con personas de otra fe (en su mayoría cristianas) en la sociedad alemana, sobre todo en actividades interreligiosas, talleres y organizaciones. Al sacar las conclusiones de sus experiencias personales con el diálogo interreligioso la autora subraya sobre todo que el ideal filosófico-religioso de una religión, tal y como queda plasmado en las respectivas "sagradas escrituras" y en los fundamentos de dicha religión no debe compararse con la realidad de otra religión, resultado de la socialización y de la tradición.

Alice Schumann (*1959), Study of Philosophy in Cologne (1979-1981), Studies of Spanish, German philology, journalism and religious studies (1981-1985), Study of the Vedas, Hinduism, pilgrimage and development aid in India (1985-1999); since 1994 director of the Hindu charitable organisation "Food for Life" in Germany; 2000 Diploma in social education; finishing a thesis in paedagogy at Cologne University on "Pro-sociality in Hinduism".

Uta Blohm

Women Ministers and Rabbis in London
Intra- and Inter-Faith Relations

The Research

This article is based on research conducted between 1998 and 2000 among Jewish and Christian women in roles of religious leadership mainly based in London.[1] I will reflect especially on inter- and intra-faith relations among women in religious leadership positions and argue that current theological and political issues can be more divisive than established denominational differences or even traditional boundaries between different faith communities. In addition I will show that interviewees showed a surprising willingness to build relations across traditional boundaries and despite conflicting theological and political convictions. The article discusses the findings regarding intra-faith relations first referring to issues within the Christian or the Jewish community (intra-faith relations). This is followed by reflections on relations across the religious divide of a faith community (inter-faith relations). This section will argue that clergy are prepared to build relations with people of other faith despite theological convictions that might have deterred them. It will highlight the theological difficulties arising in a Christian context and how they are resolved by Christian clergy in practice. Data explicitly referring to questions of gender and inter-faith relations will be discussed separately. The final passage points to the importance of building relations within today's divided and conflicted world.

The sample reflects the reality of the two faith communities in Britain and is limited to groups where women have reached a formal status of equality (with the exception of Anglicans).[2] The sample included 17 rabbis from

---

[1] Uta Blohm, *Religious Traditions and Personal Stories. Women Working as Priests, Ministers and Rabbis* (Studies in the Intercultural History of Christianity 137; Peter Lang: Frankfurt a. M. 2005).
[2] See next paragraph.

Reform or Liberal background, 16 Anglicans, 10 Methodist presbyters, three Baptist ministers, three Congregational and one United Reformed minister. The qualitative interviews focused on women's relationship with their diverse traditions. How do women define themselves in a context that to some extent questions the legitimacy of what they are doing? It proved fruitful to use a story based approach in order to ascertain women's sense of identity. The interviews were semi-structured but left space for material that emerged during the interviews as important to the interviewees but had not previously been considered by the researcher. The fact that many interviewees discussed questions of ecumenical (intra-faith) and inter-faith relations, often without being prompted, indicates the relative importance of this inter-religious reality in the daily work of religious leaders. This is especially true in the diversity of the urban context in which most of these women were working.

The Diversity of the Religious World in Britain

Unlike other European countries the Christian scene in England is very diverse and includes Anglicans, Methodists, Free Churches, Roman Catholics and others. A growing number of people from non-Christian religious backgrounds are living in England. The historic churches, other than Pentecostal or those of non-European origins, are in decline. Christians are by no means the majority in many London areas. Since the 1970's ecumenical relations among Christian churches have improved and on a local level formal arrangements of collaboration (covenants) exist. Since some Christian congregations can be very small, different churches have decided to work together more closely by sharing ministers or buildings. Sometimes church buildings have been sold to serve other purposes (such as supermarkets or pubs). In other cases, congregations have been alert and directed that their ecclesiastical buildings should be transformed more imaginatively into community centres with an ethical purpose (e.g. space for refugee centres, charities) or into a smaller (sometimes neutral) worship space. Public space is scarce in London and many churches let their premises to local groups.

The Church of England presents by far the biggest Christian denomination in England. For many people in the general public, the reality of Christian life is represented by Anglicans. The role of women in this church is therefore of particular significance. Currently, the ordination of women as bishops is being discussed hotly. Should this come to pass, a mile stone in a fight for women in roles of religious leadership would have been passed. In fact, women bishops have become a distinct possibility in the Church of England. The last General Synod (July 2008) decided to proceed with legislation allowing women to become bishops. This development occurred more than ten years after the first women had been ordained priests (1994). But when this happens eventually, it will be about hundred years since women had started pressing for ordination. In 1913 Ursula Roberts, the wife of a clergy man, had suggested a conference on women's ordination but the 1920 Lambeth conference rejected the idea of women in the priesthood.[3] When the first women were ordained as priests in the Church of England in 1994 many people thought that these were the first ordained women. But this is far from the truth.[4] Constance Coltman was the first congregational minister to be ordained to the ministry of "word and sacrament" in 1917. Maude Royden, disillusioned with the Church of England, became a pastor of a congregational church in London. She later founded her own inter-denominational church attracting huge crowds. In 1918 the first Baptist woman Edith Gates was called to take pastoral charge. But due to the strong emphasis on the independence of congregations and a tendency towards scriptural literalism women's roles remain a contested issue in Baptist congregations.

Within Methodism women had been very active as preachers at the beginning of the movement.[5] After a lot of soul searching John Wesley had advocated the concept of a special vocation given to some women for preaching. But later, when the movement had become more established, divisions arose that reflected differences of social class as well as conflicts over the roles of women. The founder of the Primitive Methodists, for example, had been expelled from Wesleyan Methodists after writing a pamphlet in favour of women's preaching. The Methodist church as it exists today ordained the first women as ministers in 1972.

The Methodist and the Church of England have tried to find common ground to unify as long as the Methodists indicate a willingness to formally accept the Episcopacy. Some Methodist interviewees were not prepared to further relations with Anglicans unless women were also allowed to become Bishops within the Church of England and expressed concern over ecumenical dialogues that did not consider issues of gender within the churches.

---

[3] Sean Gill, *Women and the Church of England. From the Eighteenth Century to the Present* (SPCK: London 1994).

[4] For example, Elaine Kaye / Janet Lees / Kirsty Thorpe, *Daughters of Dissent* (The United Reformed Church: London 2004).

[5] Jacqueline Field-Bibb, *Women towards Ordination. Ministerial Politics and Feminist Praxis* (Cambridge University Press: Cambridge 1991).

Forum
Fórum

The Jewish community in its non-traditional part is divided into a Reform and a Liberal wing in Britain. Both movements train their rabbis jointly at Leo Baeck College and maintain close links. Jacqueline Tabick was the first woman to be ordained in 1975.[6] Student numbers are almost even at this point and in 2000 75 women had graduated from Leo Baeck College.[7] Interviewees felt equally treated at the college while still facing difficulties when working in the community. During the debate for women's ordination in the Church of England women rabbis had on occasion been invited to speak about their experiences.

Intra-Faith Relations

Some of the data shed light on relations between the Jewish and Christian faith communities but primarily also those within the Christian world. Even though the Christian world is divided along denominational lines some evidence suggests that theological and political differences may be increasingly more divisive than denominational identities. Two quotations will be discussed that exemplify this. One Baptist and one Methodist interviewee emphasized their good relationship with the local Anglican woman vicar based on shared theological convictions.

The Baptist woman who describes herself as "evangelical" discusses her good relationship with an Anglican vicar with whom she works locally. The term evangelical is used to describe her views on mission and ethics. A commitment to a personal relationship with Jesus is important to her. Ethically she would uphold the importance of marriage as opposed to e.g. raising children in a committed relationship.

> My allegiance is very much as a Christian first and I meet to pray with a woman who is the vicar of what was an ecumenical church plant. It's now just become Anglican in the last year and I meet with her and pray and we share a very similar spirituality and values (…) we acknowledge there are different ways in certain things that we do (…) but we can certainly pray together and share values and get excited and share in one another's ministries without the denomination being a barrier at all.[8]

She works with the local Anglican vicar based on their shared evangelical spirituality despite the traditional Episcopal versus Free Church disagreements on

---

[6] Several interviewees pointed out that they found the term "ordination" inaccurate in a Jewish context but continued to use it in an English speaking context for want of a better word: Blohm, *Religious Traditions*, 143-146.
[7] Leo Baeck College. Annual Report 2000.
[8] This and all the following quotations are unpublished material from my dissertation.

e.g. the structure of church governance and worship style. The Baptist interviewee is engaged in building a church in a newly established residential area supported by her husband and Christians who happen to live locally. Her example illustrates how a shared evangelical conviction can overcome denominational differences. The following case exemplifies how liberal convictions are equally binding.

The Methodist minister is part of an ecumenical network that includes Pentecostal churches, house churches and "protestant" (low) Anglican churches. Some of the churches are of non-European origin. She finds it very difficult to relate to clergy from churches who tend to be evangelical as described above. To her such differences present the real boundary as opposed to denominational distinctions. She finds it easier to be part of a network with more like minded members. She also has a good relationship with the local Anglican vicar who is a woman. They support each other in their ministry and work well together because of their gender and shared theological convictions.

> I am the highest church as a Methodist, believe it or not, and also often the most liberal member of the clergy meeting and I actually, when we have our joint services, I often think this is just not what I believe. It isn't Christianity that I would want be part of and yet at the same time, I hold very, very strongly to ecumenism, so it is how you stay in and maintain any kind of integrity and good relationships.

She would accurately be defined as a liberal Methodist theologian because she questions e.g. the idea of eternal salvation ("heaven"). From her perspective Jesus is someone who came to preach the kingdom of God to an oppressed group of people. Politically she would consider herself left leaning. The term "high church" describes a commitment to a formal liturgy rather than to a plainer Protestant style of worship.

Although she is committed to serious ecumenical commitment at a local level, present theological disputes in the Christian world seem to make cooperation more difficult than denominational differences in the past.

Both examples indicate that women support each other in their ministry even across denominational boundaries. This will be discussed in the third section.

Issues of intra-faith relations were occasionally also discussed by Jewish interviewees. Whereas denominational divisions in the Christian world date back to pre-modern times the Jewish world is divided between more traditional and more modern wings. Modernity has pointed to the historicity of supposedly timeless, divine revelations. This challenge is dividing Christians within one denomination whereas the Jewish community has been divided institutionally along these lines. Jewish interviewees felt a need to work towards better relations within their own faith community. One interviewee in particular stressed the importance to build relations within the Jewish community between more liberal and more traditional (orthodox) Jews. Relations between these factions can be difficult but there was evidence as well that they may in practise be better than presented in public by the *Jewish Chronicle*, a weekly paper serving the Jewish community. One interviewee in particular felt comfortable in all parts of the community. Others took issue with problems in their own liberal community.

Inter-Faith Relations

Interviewees discussed issues of inter-faith relations without being asked which indicates the importance these have in a city where people with very diverse religious affiliations live. Rabbis and Christian ministers/priests described how they deal with people from other faiths on a practical level.

A Baptist interviewee who describes herself as "open evangelical" discusses her willingness to work with people from all faith backgrounds although she points out that she does not share their religious values. She distinguishes between social justice projects and religious commitments. She is prepared to run community projects with people who identify as secular. As the ecumenical dean of the main churches in the area she works with people from other faiths on issues of social concern, such as housing provision and health care provision. She is quick to point out her own limitations when dealing with more religious issues:

> I would not want to work on shared worship. I think that that is a real issue. Or I mean any Muslim I know who is a committed Muslim would not want to work on shared worship and any committed Christian I know would find it just as difficult. I'm very keen personally to dialogue and co-operate wherever possible on issues of common humanity; but I personally still hold the position of the uniqueness of Christ. So I would want dialogue and also evangelise people of other faiths but with respect and dignity and maybe agreeing to differ. (…) But I am very happy and would want to work wherever possible with Muslims, Buddhists whatever.

Her clarity of position as a committed Christian allows other people of faith to judge whether they feel comfortable with her commitment to evangelism and missionary activities. Given her work as a teacher in a local school, which is predominantly Muslim, her position surprisingly seems to generate respect and trust.

More liberal Christians, such as the following (Anglo-catholic) interviewee, would disagree on the centrality of Christian mission. In her interview, this clergywoman positions herself differently regarding inter-faith relations. She disavows the need for evangelism, which shows the extent to which Christian perspectives are influenced by Christological convictions:

> I mean, if I turned my back on Christianity I know I would personally be objecting to something which I'd been opened up as it were, but it doesn't mean to say that I would have sleepless nights of guilt because I can't go out and tell my neighbours, who are Muslims that they ought to be Christians and I wouldn't dream of doing so. I do know that there are certain values and things that are common to both of us (…). We all have a spiritual dimension. And at the heart of that is God by whatever name we call him and as a Christian I believe utterly that Jesus simply came to show us God, not to stand himself in the centre and say: "Look at me." But everything he says, says: "through me you will see God".

Her understanding of the role of Jesus in salvation shapes her perspective on inter-faith relations in a Christian context. Her interpretation of Jesus' role as someone who gives a perspective on God enables her to relate to people from other faiths on an equal footing.

Another (Anglican) interviewee explicitly repudiates Christological exclusivity as a form of imperialism. She maintains that the disregard for other cultures is rooted in disregard of other religions. Given this perspective she also thinks that people from other faiths can be (and are) genuinely in contact with God:

> Even if they're not your faith journey, anybody who is seriously serious about their spirituality is worth listening to because they may have something to teach me about my God that I have not seen.

This politically and theologically liberal theological position contrasts with the view of a Methodist woman who emigrated from a country where Christianity is in a minority position and under constant threat from the majority religion. She would argue in favour of connecting Christianity with other cultures while still holding onto the idea of the uniqueness of Christ. This position is similar to the Baptist woman quoted at the beginning of this section who was prepared to work on issues of social justice but not on more explicitly religious issues. This Baptist minister would aim for her congregation to be more inclusive of Christians with other cultural backgrounds while holding onto key doctrinal concepts. A criticism of colonialism from the perspective of this Methodist preacher does not involve a new reconsideration of other religious teachings and faith traditions.

> Oh well, as a Christian I would say the only salvation is through Jesus. That doesn't mean that I do not have dealings with people from other faiths. Because they feel they believe they are right and we believe we are right (...). A lot of other faiths would say they believe in God – God is God – but the uniqueness of Jesus really compared to say like Islam where he was just another prophet.

Her perspective also reflects a particular type of Christianity (Protestantism) that emphasises human dependency on Christ in salvation and foregrounds being saved by grace over religious rituals.

For the Jewish interviewees such preoccupation with salvation appears somewhat secondary. Their concern with ethical and *halakhic* questions of everyday life shape their commitment to inter-faith work on a local level. Jewish leaders interviewed reflected on their practice of giving talks at inter-faith meetings and involvement in religious networks on a local level. All the rabbis have been engaged in inter-faith work as part of their training. Only one rabbi described her commitment to her own traditions as a potential problem in inter-faith encounters:

> There's a bit of me I suppose that gets a bit triumphalist and thinks: "well, how can anybody not believe in Judaism?"

She feels she has to be careful how to approach Christians at inter-faith conferences in order not to offend people as she finds central aspect of Christian doctrine very problematic.

Although evangelical Christians and orthodox Jews are very different in their world views because of the differences between Jewish and Christian traditions they may both be offering similar responses to modernity. Even across the religious divide the distinction between a liberal and more traditional commitment to faith impacts relations among religious leaders. One rabbi ventured that liberal Jews and Christians may find it easier to build relations with each other rather than with people within their own communities:

> ... liberal Judaism and liberal Christianity, I know it sounds funny, have in many ways more in common in terms of their openness than liberal Judaism and ultra-orthodox Judaism and liberal Christianity and evangelical Christianity.

Although the non-traditional part of the Jewish world has also considered historical questions and rejected some historic decisions on a traditional life style, those religious leaders who embraced historical-critical considerations relate to colleagues from other faiths on those grounds.

But as we have seen inter-faith work is not necessarily limited to clergy who identify as liberal. This section has shown that an increasing number of non-liberal, religiously conservative clergy engage in inter-faith work and thereby raise the prospect of changing inter-faith relationships for the future.

Gender and Inter-/ Intra-Faith Relations

The interviewees were aware that questions of gender and religious leadership were a focus of this study and they discussed their views freely during the course of the interviews. Issues of inclusive language in worship and gender difference emerged frequently.

Gender is the most public and clear marker of the boundary between liberal and non-liberal religions. Modern Christian (protestant) fundamentalism, for example, had its roots in a fight against modern views on gender roles.[9] The Roman Catholic and the orthodox churches, as well as orthodox synagogues do not ordain women. The Church of England, which many in the UK perceive as the main religious body in England, began ordaining women very late. Similarly, only the liberal wings of the Jewish community ordain women to the rabbinate.

The role of women therefore influences ecumenical relations profoundly: Some Christian women from non-Anglican backgrounds viewed official ecumenical dialogues with suspicion and wondered whether women's issues would be sidelined for the sake of Christian unity. On the other hand, the Anglican women were hoping for support from female clergy in other denominations. They considered it especially difficult to find their voice in a fight for justice that would benefit them personally. The Anglican sample showed clearly how divisive and disempowering oppression is to those directly affected. The existence of groups of ecumenical women clergy indicates that some women feel a need for support from their colleagues across denominational boundaries. This, however, was not expressed by the majority in the Anglican sample.

---

[9] Mark Chaves, *Ordaining Women. Culture and Conflict in Religious Organisations* (Harvard University Press: Cambridge, Mass. 1997).

Forum
Fórum

The relations among women in the Church of England exemplify some of the difficulties women experience with each other when confronting misogyny and injustice.[10]

For some women in the Anglican Church the struggle for ordination was fought on political grounds in order to achieve change.[11] This political engagement was rooted in a counter cultural decision to fight for justice against the prevailing Christian ethos of passive prayer and the ideal of righteous suffering. A Christian culture that encourages dependency on God discourages political fighting. Those who espoused such Christian ideals discredited the political fight for justice as selfish. In other instances, the opponents of women's ordination revealed plain misogyny by describing women as strident and accusing them of being un-feminine. The severity of these debates left many Anglican interviewees divided amongst themselves over these political issues. There was a clear distinction between those women who had been confronted with such open hostile opposition and those who were spared. Already the second generation showed little understanding of the pain experienced by those who had gone through these abrasive debates. All Anglican interviewees expressed a strong desire to leave the history behind even though all interviewees had experienced some resistance to their priesthood at some point. It might be interesting to revisit some of these Anglican clergy today in order to test the development of this "lucky" generation.

For many women in this sample, reliance on female colleagues for support was important. Although they did not mention gender as the primary focus of their identification with colleagues, alliances with other women were deemed useful by some in the sample. Shared theological convictions or collaboration on similar issues (such as childcare) were also cited as reasons to build a meaningful relationship with other women clergy.

In addition to the previously discussed two Christian women clergy who support each other in their work, one should also mention the women rabbis, who have formed a support group that has published two books and raised their profile as women in roles of religious leadership.[12]

---

[10] Blohm, *Religious Traditions*, 309-310.
[11] Jean Maylend, *Women Ministering. Change amongst the Churches* (Unpublished paper, Undated).
[12] Sybil Sheridan (ed.), *Hear Our Voice. Women Rabbis Tell their Stories* (SPCK: London 1994); Sybil Sheridan / Sylvia Rothschild (eds), *Taking up the Trinble. The Challenge of Creating Ritual for Jewish Women Today* (SPCK: London 2000).

For others support crosses religious boundaries and is found outside their own immediate religious context. Some Christian interviewees had at some point been part of a local ecumenical (this case Christian) female clergy group. A few rabbis eventually joined these Christian clergy groups in order to collaborate on shared concerns. While these Jewish women found some support in their relationships with Christian clergy, they also encountered classic Christian anti-Jewish teaching. I can confirm the presence of such anti-Jewish stereotypes, for example when some interviewees made disparaging remarks about the so called Old Testament which they considered less inclusive than to the New Testament.

Building Future Relations
The research was limited to interviews with women clergy. It is therefore impossible to draw conclusions about male clergy or to argue that women are more willing (than men) to work on relationship building. We know from the psychological literature that women tend to experience themselves more in relationship whereas men emphasize autonomy and separation from others.[13] While this cannot be argued here, it may be the case that women clergy see themselves especially drawn into relationship building in and between communities.

What has been shown is that women as religious leaders are making a vital contribution to the future shape of communities. The sample of interviewees model different types of relatedness and showed that varying degrees of collaboration can be valuable in themselves. The range was between those willing to work on joined worship to those who insisted on clear boundaries and a sense of identity. Even those who insisted on a clear sense of identity were willing to work with people of other faiths on issues of social inclusion. The impact of these forms of community building cannot be underestimated. Such existing relationships sustain communities during periods of conflict, contain violence and help to rebuild in the aftermath. It is hoped that such relationship building will also permeate traditional boundaries and transform the more fundamentalist movements. The theological encounter with the other may turn out to be an encounter with the divine. I, for one, am hopeful that religious leaders will encounter the divine in the other's image. The greatest challenge

---

[13] My thinking is influenced by Nancy Chodorow, *The Reproduction of Mothering. Psychoanalysis and the Sociology of Gender* (University of California Press: Berkeley / Los Angeles / London 1978; 1999 New Preface) and Carol Gilligan, *In a Different Voice. Psychological Theory and Women's Development* (Harvard University Press: Cambridge, Mass. 1982).

Forum
Fórum

may lie in the frayed relations between liberal and non-liberal clergy within a faith or denomination (in the case of Christians) and not across the religious divide.

Der Artikel beruht auf fünfzig qualitativen Interviews mit Pastorinnen und Rabbinerinnen, die in erster Linie, aber nicht ausschließlich in der Großstadt London arbeiten. Fokus der Interviews waren Fragen der Geschlechter- und religiösen Identität im Amt. Die Interviewpartnerinnen äußerten sich darüber hinaus oft ungefragt zu Themen interreligiöser und ökumenischer Zusammenarbeit. Die Autorin zeigt, dass interreligiöse Zusammenarbeit über die Religionsgrenzen hinweg unproblematischer sein kann als innerhalb der eigenen Religionsgemeinschaft. Eine Herausforderung für die Zukunft wird die Zusammenarbeit innerhalb der eigenen religiösen Gruppen zwischen sogenannten Konservativen und Liberalen sein. Deutlich wird ebenfalls, dass interreligiöse Zusammenarbeit keineswegs auf liberale Amtsträgerinnen beschränkt ist. Die Interviewpartnerinnen berichten von einem überraschend hohen sozialen Engagement über die Religionsgrenzen hinweg, oft mit sehr unterschiedlicher theologischer Begründung.

Este artículo está basado en cincuenta entrevistas cualitativas de pastoras y rabinas, que trabajan prioritaria pero no exclusivamente en Londres. Se enfocaron ante todo cuestiones de identidad de género y religiosa a la hora de desempeñar el cargo. A menudo, las mujeres entrevistadas hablaron, sin que se les preguntara por ello, de temas de cooperación interreligiosa y ecuménica. La autora quiere demostrar que la cooperación interreligiosa puede ser menos problemática al salirse de los límites de la religión que quedándose en la propia comunidad religiosa. En el futuro, uno de los retos será el diálogo dentro de los propios grupos religiosos entre las llamadas conservadoras y las liberales. También se pone de manifiesto que el diálogo interreligioso en ningún momento se limita a mujeres liberales que ocupan algún cargo. Las mujeres entrevistadas cuentan que es sorprendente el enorme compromiso social que existe más allá de los límites religiosos, que muchas veces tiene un fondo teológico muy diferente.

Uta Blohm (*1967), Dr. theol., mother of two daughters (three and five years old), lives together with her family in London. She works voluntarily as a pastor in the United Reformed Church. Her publications deal with women in the ministry and the rabbinate, Jewish-Christian dialogue and motherhood.

Rachel Herweg, Gisela Matthiae und Rabeya Müller

Erfahrungsbericht aus dem Ersten Interreligiösen Feministischen Lehr- und Lernhaus

In unserer säkularen und gleichwohl multireligiösen Gesellschaft interreligiösen Dialog erlernen, erproben und mit anderen Frauen praktizieren: Darauf zielte das Programm einer erstmalig von 2006 bis 2008 in sieben Abschnitten durchgeführten theologischen Fortbildung ab. Dieses erste interreligiöse Lern- und Lehrhaus für Frauen war ein Kooperationsprojekt zwischen dem Frauenstudien- und -bildungszentrum in der EKD in Gelnhausen/Hofgeismar (FSBZ) und dem Zentrum für Islamische Frauenforschung und -förderung (ZIF). Drei Theologinnen aus drei Religionen planten und leiteten das Projekt: Dr. Rachel Herweg sprach für die jüdische Tradition, Dr. Gisela Matthiae repräsentierte die evangelisch-christliche und Rabeya Müller die islamische Religionsgemeinschaft. Unter den Teilnehmerinnen befanden sich entsprechend der mehrheitlichen Verhältnisse in Deutschland weniger Musliminnen und Jüdinnen; dennoch demonstrierte das Projekt, dass es möglich ist zu lernen, interreligiös zu denken und zu arbeiten.

Das Dozentinnenteam stand vor der Herausforderung, einen Mittelweg zwischen wissenschaftlicher Vermittlung von Theologie bzw. feministischer Theologie und der Lebenspraxis aller Teilnehmerinnen zu finden. Zugleich sollten Anregungen und Methoden zum eigenständigen Forschen, sowohl in der eigenen Religion bzw. Ideologie als auch den anderen gegeben werden. Der Titel der Fortbildung war zugleich Konzept und soll hier kurz vorgestellt werden. Das Projekt war erstens *interreligiös,* zweitens *feministisch* und drittens *dem gemeinsamen Lernen und Lehren verpflichtet*:

Das Projekt: Interreligiös – feministisch – dem gemeinsamen Lehren und Lernen verpflichtet

1. Interreligiös

Unsere gegenwärtige gesellschaftliche Situation macht es dringend erforderlich, dass wir religiöse Inhalte, Gesten und Gebräuche aus dem jeweiligen Selbstverständnis ihrer Vertreterinnen und Vertreter verstehen lernen. Das Wiederholen gängiger Klischees, das wir derzeit beobachten, verstärkt gegenseitige

Diffamierungen und verhärtet die Fronten bis hin zur Ablehnung der je anderen Religion aus Unkenntnis und Angst. Das bedarf mehr als der Vermittlung von Kenntnissen; denn Religion wird als gelebte Religion vollzogen und wahrgenommen. Die je eigene Religiosität bildet sich in einem aktiven Aneignungsprozess heraus und besteht aus einem Gemenge aus inkulturierter Religion, überlieferten Traditionen und Lehrmeinungen, sowie der persönlichen Glaubenspraxis. Wer sich auf der Ebene der eigenen Religiosität interreligiös verständigen möchte, muss lernen, die Andere als religiöses Subjekt anzusprechen und bereit sein, einen distanzierten und bisweilen kritischen Blick auf die eigene Religion zu werfen. Ein Dialog zwischen religiösen Subjekten versucht sowohl die Fortschreibung bestehender Unterschiede zwischen den Religionen als auch eine vorschnelle Behauptung von Gemeinsamkeiten zu vermeiden. Stattdessen besteht das Ziel darin, auf der Basis gegenseitigen Respekts und Anerkennung der religiösen Haltung zu Formen gemeinsamen Handelns und einer gleichberechtigten Koexistenz der Religionen zu gelangen.

2. Feministisch

„Uns verbindet die feministische Kritik und Weiterentwicklung unserer religiösen Traditionen und Praxen" – diese im Programm ausgeschriebene Annahme war der Ausgangspunkt und darin ein alle Unterschiedlichkeit übersteigendes gemeinsames Anliegen. Tatsächlich verband uns die Überzeugung, dass der Geschlechterdiskurs in jeder der drei Religionen Diskriminierungen der Frau auf der Basis ganz unterschiedlicher Grundannahmen und Argumentationen hervorgebracht hat. Dabei überraschte zum Beispiel, dass die sogenannte „Rippenstory" aus Genesis 2, die in der gesamten christlichen Anthropologie zur Unterordnung der Frau aufgrund ihres Geschlechts geführt hat, im Qur'an keineswegs vorkommt und dennoch auch das islamische Frauenbild geprägt hat. Mit jüdischer Auslegungskunst wiederum hätten Fehlinterpretationen und Falschübersetzungen dieser Verse längst überwunden sein können. Solche Beispiele zeigen, wie wichtig es ist, sich in der Aufarbeitung theologischer und kultureller Argumentation der Geschlechterverhältnisse gegenseitig zu unterstützen und an gerechten Verhältnissen gemeinsam zu arbeiten.

Verbindend war den religiös geprägten Frauen aller drei Religionsgemeinschaften die Entwicklung feministischer Hermeneutiken, um die eigene religiöse Identität mit dem Bestreben nach Emanzipation zu verknüpfen. Trotzdem zeigte ein Blick in die Geschichte auch die unterschiedlichen Entwicklungen feministischer Theologien: Während Feministinnen in allen drei Religionen an einer kritischen Revision der jeweiligen Schriften arbeiten, zeigten sich gravierende Unterschiede im Frauenbild und Geschlechterverständnis. Während in der christlich-feministischen Theologie Begriffe wie Gleichheit und Differenz sowie der Dekonstruktivismus von Geschlechtsidentitäten prägend geworden sind, erwies sich dieses sozialwissenschaftliche Vokabular moderner und postmoderner Geschlechterforschung weniger hilfreich im Kontext der Schriftauslegung anderer Religionen. Eine religiöse Fundierung von Geschlechtergerechtigkeit mag zwar schwieriger zu erreichen sein, ist aber nachhaltiger und überzeugender, zumal viele Theologinnen der begründeten Überzeugung sind, dass ihre Religion im Grunde jegliche Form von Frauendiskriminierung verabscheut. Dennoch erweist sich der interreligiöse feministische Dialog als eine Quelle gegenseitiger Unterstützung und bereichernder Argumentationshilfen.

Androzentrische Vorstellungen revitalisieren sich häufig genug in anderen ethnischen oder religiösen Gruppierungen. So stellte sich die Frage nach Frauenordination aus vier verschiedenen Perspektiven, jüdisch und evangelisch je nach liberaler Ausrichtung, katholisch durch die bekannte Sichtweise des Vatikans und muslimisch aus der Tatsache heraus, dass es im kirchlich verstandenen Sinn gar keine Ordination (auch nicht für Männer) gibt. Trotzdem müssen alle vier Richtungen um eine geschlechtergerechte Sichtweise kämpfen: So ist in einigen Teilen der evangelischen Kirche die Frauenordination rückläufig, und in muslimischen Gruppierungen, zumindest in der Bundesrepublik, ist es so gut wie ausgeschlossen, dass Frauen eine geistliche Führungsposition übernehmen. Der Blick auf vergangene und gegenwärtige Geschlechterkonflikte kann die Wahrnehmung für Wandlungsprozesse sensibilisieren und gemeinsame Zielsetzungen erkennbar machen. Oft war die Grundtendenz zunächst so, dass die bereits in der eigenen Religionsgemeinschaft erkämpften Positionen und Theorien als Maßstab genommen wurden, während die „anderen" Religionsgruppierungen als „noch nicht so weit" gesehen wurden. Daher war es zentrales Anliegen, über das Erzählen aus der eigenen Religionserfahrung zu gemeinsamen Analysen hinsichtlich weiblicher Perspektiven von Gemeinsamkeiten und Unterschieden zu gelangen.

3. *Lehr- und Lernhaus*
Der Begriff des Lernhauses knüpft an die jüdische Tradition an und wurde um den Begriff des Lehrhauses ergänzt, denn die Vermittlung von Kenntnissen aus den je anderen Religionen war unverzichtbar, um in ein qualifiziertes Gespräch zu kommen. Wie bei allen Lernerfahrungen stellte sich heraus, dass die Wissenslücken immer größer werden, je stärker das Wissen voneinander

und übereinander wächst. Erst wer über die Grundkenntnisse hinaus geht, kann die Fülle der unterschiedlichen Denkschulen und Traditionslinien erkennen. In einem persönlich geführten Lerntagebuch hielten die Teilnehmerinnen ihre Erkenntnisse und Erfahrungen über die je anderen Religionsgemeinschaften fest. Dieses Lerntagebuch war zwar freiwillig und wurde nie von jemand anderem eingesehen, aber nahezu alle Teilnehmerinnen machten von dieser Gedächtnisstütze Gebrauch. Das Lerntagebuch half emotionale Befindlichkeiten auszudrücken und sich in späteren Situationen daran zu erinnern. Gerade dieses „Erinnerungslernen" war eine große Hilfe beim Austausch im Plenum und Kleingruppen. Besonders zeigte sich dieser Effekt auch, wenn eine Frau zum Beispiel argumentativ in eine Situation geriet, die sie vorher aus der „Gegenüberperspektive" wahrgenommen hatte. So waren nicht nur die Rollentheorien, sondern auch eine Art „Rollentausch" Bestandteil des Lern- und Lehrmodells.

Die Module
Gegenstand des gemeinsamen Lernens waren also die Theologien der drei Religionen Judentum, Christentum und Islam in der beschriebenen Form der Auseinandersetzung. Wichtig war dabei, klassische Positionen ebenso zur Sprache zu bringen wie unterschiedliche Traditionslinien und nicht zuletzt auch kritische feministische Perspektiven aufzuzeigen und zu diskutieren. Die sieben Module waren an den klassischen Inhalten orientiert:

1. Bekenntnis / Glaubenszeugnis
2. Gott – Mensch
3. Schriftverständnis
4. Religiöse Ausdrucksformen
5. Feste – Feiern – Rituale
6. (Bio-)Ethik
7. Abschlusskolloquium mit den Praxisprojekten

Über den langfristigen Prozess der sieben Module konnte Vertrauen wachsen und Offenheit und Mut entstehen, auch unbequeme Fragen zu stellen und Befremden zu äußern. Konflikte, die unvermeidlich auftauchten und nicht selten ihren Ort außerhalb des Lehr- und Lernhauses hatten, mussten gemeinsam angegangen werden. Größtmögliche Sensibilität war gefordert im Umgang mit religiösen und somit auch hoch emotional besetzten Themen. Am Ende stand ein gemeinsames Ritual mit Elementen, dem sich alle anschließen

konnten. Und ganz am Ende stand natürlich das Feiern und das gemeinsame Lachen – durchaus auch über die jeweiligen Eigenheiten der verschiedenen Religionen.
Im Folgenden sollen konkrete Erfahrungsberichte einen Eindruck zu den Inhalten liefern:

Das Modul: „Feste – Feiern – Rituale"
Ziel dieser Einheit war es, eine Einführung in jüdische, christliche und muslimische Feste, Feiern und Rituale in vergleichender Auseinandersetzung zu geben. Die Unterschiede und Anknüpfungspunkte der religiösen Praktiken und Ausdrucksformen sollten für den interreligiösen Dialog nutzbar und in praktische Handlungskompetenz umgesetzt werden. Als Veranstaltungsort wählten wir bewusst das multikulturelle und interreligiöse Köln. Hier sollten exemplarisch insbesondere Orte muslimischer (Gemeinde-)Praxis aufgesucht, sinnlich erfahren und in Gesprächen mit Vertretern der jeweiligen religiösen Institution die Möglichkeit gegeben werden, Erfahrungen in konkreten interreligiösen Dialogsituationen zu sammeln und anschließend zu reflektieren. Dabei wurde deutlich, dass die grundsätzlichen Regeln des interreligiösen Dialogs oft in Konflikt mit den folgenden „Problembereichen" geraten:

- Die gesellschaftlichen Gegebenheiten von Mehr- und Minderheiten bedeuten, dass die im Dialoggeschehen immer wieder eingeforderte „gleiche Augenhöhe" nicht vorausgesetzt werden kann.
- Vor dem Dialog steht das kommunikative Kennenlernen, aber in jedem System gelten andere Kommunikationsregeln. Wenn im Dialog das jeweilige Gegenüber aus seinem / ihrem eigenen System heraus „verstanden" werden soll, dann bedingt dies Kenntnisse der jeweils internen Kommunikationsregeln.
- Erfahrungen aus „undialogischen" Situationen können Vertrauen in das aktuelle Gelingen eines Dialogs verhindern.
- Das Hineindrängen eines Gegenübers in Positionen der Rechtfertigung ist unbedingt zu vermeiden.

Die Praxis solcher interreligiöser Dialogsituationen initiiert Lern-, Umlern- und Veränderungsprozesse, die erst noch theoretisch aufgearbeitet werden müssen. Ein Ergebnis dieser Einheit war die Erarbeitung eines *gemeinsamen Rituals*. Dafür wurden Kriterien und Inhalte gesammelt, bei denen sich alle Teilnehmerinnen angesprochen fühlten. Zunächst wurde bewusst auf traditionelle Formen und Inhalte verzichtet; denn die Teilnehmerinnen wollten sich nicht gegenseitig einladen, sondern gemeinsam feiern. In Arbeitsgruppen wurden schließlich einzelne Elemente neu entwickelt. Das abschließende Ritual enthielt die Elemente: Ankommen, Besinnung auf die Nähe Gottes, Texte, Gebete, Lieder, meditative Handlungen, Abschluss.

Das Modul: „Ethik"
Ziel dieser Einheit war es, ethische Entscheidungsfindungen und ihre zugrunde liegenden theologischen Konzepte in den drei Religionen kennen zu lernen und selbst anwenden zu können. Am konkreten *„Streitfall Leben"* – (juristisch-) ethische Positionen zum Status des Embryos, zu Schwangerschaft und Geburt – wurde dies exemplarisch durchgeführt und erprobt. Nach einer einführenden Begriffsklärung zu Moral, Ethos und verschiedenen Formen der Ethik, die für alle Teilnehmerinnen gleichermaßen relevant war, gaben die drei Dozentinnen jeweils einen Überblick über historische und gegenwärtige Positionen ihrer Religionen zu:

- Schwangerschaft
- Verhalten der Mutter
- Status des Embryo
- Beginn des Lebens / Beseelung / Embryonenschutz
- Verhütung
- Schwangerschaftsabbruch
- Künstliche Befruchtung
- Genetische Diagnostik
- Leihmutterschaft
- Klonen

Theologisch relevante Themen waren dabei das Verhältnis von Schöpfung und Geschöpf, Einhauchung des Geistes (islamisch) und Gottebenbildlichkeit (jüdisch-christlich), Menschenwürde. Hierzu wurden verschiedene Lehrmeinungen innerhalb der jeweiligen Religion wiedergegeben, insbesondere offizielle Verlautbarungen und aktuelle Äußerungen in den Medien, unter anderem von Mitgliedern der Ethikkommissionen, von Rabbinern und Genforschern, von islamischen Gelehrten und Stimmen von Interessensverbänden, wie zum Beispiel der Evangelischen Frauenarbeit Deutschland und des ZIF in Köln. Den Teilnehmerinnen wurde so ein differenziertes Spektrum vorhandener Positionen in einem unabgeschlossenen Diskussionsprozess vor Augen geführt und als umfangreiches schriftliches Material ausgehändigt.

Rachel Herweg, Gisela Matthiae und Rabeya Müller
Erfahrungsbericht aus dem Ersten Interreligiösen Feministischen Lehr- und Lernhaus

Im vergleichenden Gespräch ergaben sich interessante Einsichten: Während in Judentum und Islam die Bedeutung des Schöpfers als alle menschliche Möglichkeiten der Gentechnologie übersteigend gilt, wird christlicherseits oft das Argument vorgebracht, der Mensch wolle sich auf eine Stufe mit Gott stellen. Um die Situation der Frauen als Eizellenspenderinnen und als Schwangere in einer embryonenzentrierten Diskussion in den Focus zu bekommen, bedurfte es christlicherseits der expliziten Stimmen von Frauen, während jüdischerseits das Wohl und die Entscheidungsfreiheit der Mutter immer schon im Vordergrund stehen und die Entwicklung des (ungeborenen) Kindes grundsätzlich als abhängig von der Beziehung zur Mutter verstanden wird. Interessant ist zudem die Begründungslogik in den Religionen. Während insbesondere die römisch-katholische Kirche eine ontologische und naturrechtliche Ethik vertritt, tendieren evangelische Christen zu einer Beziehungsethik; im Judentum wird induktiv von Fall zu Fall entschieden, ebenso im Islam, wo die Zuordnung der Seele als der entscheidende Faktor betrachtet wird. Der Zeitpunkt wird allerdings in unterschiedlichen muslimischen Gruppierungen verschieden angesetzt.

Eine weitere wichtige Gesprächsrunde drehte sich um das Verhältnis von Biotechnologie und Ökonomie, um den Körper zwischen Technologie und Biologie, um das Verhältnis von Fortpflanzung und Sexualität, um wertes und unwertes Leben. Deutlich wurde in dieser Diskussion – neben den unterschiedlichen Herangehensweisen in den Religionen –, dass wir selbst immer wieder auf verschiedenen Ebenen diskutieren: auf einer theologischen, einer politischen und einer seelsorgerlichen Ebene bzw. der Ebene des Gewissens. Während christliche Argumentationen oft politisch geführt werden, sind sie muslimischerseits theologisch ausgerichtet. Das führt nicht selten zu dem Vorwurf an den Islam, er sei dogmatisch, doch resultiert dies aus einem mangelnden Respekt vor der Bedeutung der Theologie und wirft ein interessantes Licht auf das jeweilige Verhältnis von Theologie und Politik.

Einen weiteren inhaltlichen Schwerpunkt bildete der *Umgang mit Behinderung* in den drei Religionen. Sehr spannend in diesem Zusammenhang war der Beitrag einer körperlich behinderten Teilnehmerin, einer promovierten, christlichen Theologin mit jüdischem Familienhintergrund, die Behinderung als Versuchung zum Unglauben in Abkehr von traditionell christlichen Erklärungsmustern wie Behinderung als Strafe oder als Erziehungsmaßnahme Gottes oder als zu tragendes Kreuz verstand.

Die Diskussion erbrachte, wie schwierig tatsächlich ein Umdenken in Richtung Inklusion aller in die Gesellschaft ist. Bei diesem Modell muss das traditionelle Hilfehandeln durch Assistenz ersetzt werden. Das erfordert nicht nur

Forum
Fórum

andere technische Möglichkeiten, sondern ein völliges Umdenken. Gerade hier kann der interreligiöse Dialog fruchtbar gemacht werden, wie die Beiträge von Dr. Rachel Herweg und Rabeya Müller deutlich machten. Muslimischerseits gilt ein behinderter Mensch als gleichwertiges Geschöpf Gottes, das des besonderen Schutzes bedarf. Dabei ist es wesentlich, die behinderten Menschen bestmöglich zu fördern und sie, entsprechend ihren Fähigkeiten, in die Gemeinschaft zu integrieren. Halachisch gesehen, haben Bedürftige einen Anspruch auf Unterstützung, die ohne Demütigung und Beschämung zu leisten ist, und auf weitgehende Selbständigkeit.

Das Modul „Praxisprojekte"
In verschiedenen Gruppen hatten die Teilnehmerinnen während der Fortbildung eigene Praxisprojekte entwickelt und durchgeführt oder von ihnen bereits im Vorfeld initiierte (teilweise noch laufende) Praxisprojekte reflektiert und konzeptionell erweitert. Dazu hatten sie einen Leitfaden erhalten. Diese Projekte wurden schriftlich dargestellt, medial aufbereitet und gemeinsam ausgewertet. Da die Projekte im jeweiligen Kontext der Teilnehmerinnen entstanden waren, wurden vor Ort zahlreiche weitere Menschen erreicht: in Schulen, in Kindergärten, in Kirchengemeinden, in Krankenhäusern, in Städten und Gemeinden, sowie über freie Bildungsangebote Interessierte.

Mit diesen vielfältigen Projekten erreichte die Fortbildung „INTERRELIGIÖS – von und miteinander LERNEN – jüdisch-christlich-muslimisch" ihr Ziel. Damit wurde gewonnenes Wissen umgesetzt und weitergegeben, es fand eine wichtige Vernetzung statt und mehr Menschen konnten in den interreligiösen Dialog mit einbezogen werden. Es wurde deutlich, dass Frauen eine besondere Rolle haben, weil sie ihre spezifischen, beruflichen und religiösen Erfahrungen, sowie ihre Alltagserfahrungen einbringen und sich mitunter weniger von bestehenden Strukturen und Denkrichtungen abhängig machen. Besonders allgemeine Diskriminierungserfahrungen, die Frauen in allen Religionen aufgrund ihrer Geschlechtszugehörigkeit gemacht haben, führten zu einer wesentlich intensiveren Bewusstseinsbildung und erhöhten Sensibilisierung füreinander. Gleichzeitig wurde es möglich, dass Frauen ihre theologischen Kompetenzen und ihr kreatives Potential ausschöpfen konnten.

This essay reports on the first "feminist interreligious house of teaching and learning" that took place in Germany. Three feminist theologians from the three Abrahamic religions (Judaism: Rachel Herweg; Islam: Rabeya Müller and

Christianity: Gisela Matthiae) planned this course of seven modules for participants from all three communities. Each module ((1) faith confessions, (2) God and human, (3) scripture, (4) forms of religious expression, (5) festival and rituals; (6) ethics; and (7) practice internships) was intended to convey basic information about each religious tradition along with feminist reinterpretations and allow participants to engage in dialogue. Participants applied their newly acquired knowledge by independently developing and implementing local interreligious projects. In conclusion, the authors are confident that their model succeeded in broadening the knowledge base of participants and creating lasting relationships of trust.

En este artículo se presenta la primera "Casa feminista interreligiosa de enseñanza y aprendizaje" que tuvo lugar en Alemania. Fue planeada para participantes de las tres comunidades religiosas por tres teólogas feministas de las tres religiones abrahámicas (judía: Rachel Herweg; islámica: Rabeya Müller; cristiana: Gisela Matthiae), quienes diseñaron el curso, que consta de siete módulos. Cada uno de ellos ((1) confesión de fe; (2) Dios y el hombre; (3) escrituras; (4) formas de expresión religiosa; (5) fiestas – festividades – rituales; (6) bioética; (7) coloquio final sobre los proyectos de práctica) transmitió informaciones básicas sobre las distintas tradiciones religiosas junto con nuevas interpretaciones feministas, para hacer posible el diálogo entre las participantes. Al desarrollar y llevar a cabo proyectos interreligiosos propios en el lugar mismo fue posible poner en práctica directamente lo que se había aprendido. Las autoras están convencidas básicamente que con ayuda de este modelo lograron divulgar y afianzar conocimientos fundamentales de las participantes y crear relaciones de confianza duraderas.

Rachel Herweg (*1960), Judaistin, promovierte Erziehungswissenschaftlerin, Systemische Therapeutin / Deutsche Gesellschaft für Systemische Therapie und Familientherapie (DGSF) und Supervisorin in eigener Praxis, seit 2006 Direktorin der Masorti-Kindergärten, Berlin. Mitbegründerin der jüdisch-feministischen Fraueninitiative *Bet Debora*, Berlin. Ehemaliges Vorstandsmitglied der Interreligiösen Konferenz europäischer Theologinnen (IKETH), Vorstandsmitglied der Stiftung ZURÜCKGEBEN – Stiftung zur Förderung Jüdischer Frauen in Kunst und Wissenschaft. Autorin diverser Beiträge, vor allem über Judentum, jüdische Exegese und Frauen(geschichte). Buchveröffentlichung: *Die Jüdische Mutter. Das verborgene Matriarchat* (Darmstadt 1994).

Gisela Matthiae (*1959), promovierte evangelische Theologin, Pfarrerin, bis 2007 Studienleiterin am Frauenstudien- und -bildungszentrum der EKD, freiberufliche Referentin in der Erwachsenenbildung, Lehrbeauftragte, Clownin (u.a. auch mit einem interreligiösen Stück), Gelnhausen, www.clownin.de. Veröffentlichungen (Auswahl): *Feministische Theologie. Initiativen, Kirchen, Universitäten – eine*

Erfolgsgeschichte, hg. zusammen mit Renate Jost, Claudia Janssen, Antje Röckemann, Annette Mehlhorn in Verbindung mit Kristin Bergmann, Angelika Fromm, Mieke Korenhof, Anna Karena Müller, Hildburg Wegener, Kathrin Winkler (Gütersloh 2008); Art. „Humor im Alten Testament", in: www.wibilex.de; *Clownin Gott. Eine feministische Dekonstruktion des Göttlichen* (Stuttgart 1999; 2. Auflage 2001).

Rabeya Müller (*1957), Studium der Pädagogik, Islamwissenschaften, Islamischer Theologie, Ethnologie; Leiterin des Instituts für Interreligiöse Pädagogik und Didaktik (IPD Köln). Stellvertretende Vorsitzende des Zentrums für islamische Frauenforschung und Frauenförderung, ehemalige Vorsitzende der Interreligiösen Konferenz europäischer Theologinnen (IKETH), Mitglied der KIRU (Kommission für den islamischen Religionsunterricht), 1. Sprecherin von Interreligiones (Forum für Religiöse Bildung), Mitglied WCRP (World Congress Religions for Peace), Mitglied der EAWRE (European Association For World Religions In Education), Mitglied bei INTRA (Interreligiöse Arbeitsstelle), Beiratsmitglied der Internationalen Friedensschule Köln. Jüngste Veröffentlichungen: *Gemeinsam vor Gott – Gebete aus Judentum, Christentum und Islam*, hg. von Martin Bauschke, Walter Homolka und Rabeya Müller (Gütersloh 2004); *Der Koran für Kinder und Erwachsene*, übersetzt und erläutert von Lamya Kaddor und Rabeya Müller (München 2008); *Saphir, Religionsbuch für junge Musliminnen und Muslime*, hg. von Lamya Kaddor, Rabeya Müller und Harry Harun Behr (München 2008).

Helene Egnell and Annette Esser

European Projects and Initiatives for Women's Interreligious Dialogue

ATE – Asociación de Teólogas Españolas

La Asociación de Teólogas Españolas (ATE) nace en 1992 porque cada vez hay más mujeres que elaboran una teología feminista desde una perspectiva académica y casi todas se unen con el fin de hacer ciencia teológica propia e impulsar también el pensamiento multidisciplinar. La ATE ha sido y es canal de debate y encuentro entre teólogas y entre investigadoras feministas de distintas disciplinas y religiones. Canalizados a través de las Jornadas que la asociación organiza anualmente hemos debatido sobre "Espiritualidad y Empoderamiento" 2005, "Historia, Memoria y Género" 2006, "Mujeres, Salud y Salvación"2007 y "Mujer Palabra y Comunidad Eclesial" 2008, sólo para citar los debates más recientes.

www.asociaciondeteologas.org

Centre for Inter Faith Dialogue, Stockholm

The Centre for Inter Faith Dialogue was established in January 2008, as a resource for praxis and reflection on interfaith encounters. The centre is funded by the diocese of Stockholm together with the national level of the Church of Sweden. The centre wishes to contribute to cooperation and good relations between Christians and people of other faith through

- Providing support for activities in the fields of interfaith encounters within the local parishes of the Church of Sweden, with a focus on the Stockholm area.
- Offering courses, discussion evenings, dialogue groups etc.
- Channelling knowledge, contacts, literature etc.
- Theological reflection on experiences of interfaith encounters.

The centre is run by the Bishop's advisors Rev. Dr. Helene Egnell and Rev. Annika Wirén:

helene.egnell@svenskakyrkan.se
annika.wiren@svenskakyrkan.se

Forum
Fórum

EPIL – European Project for Interreligious Learning

EPIL is a European project for interreligious learning between Christian and Muslim women. It is an educational process to train students to understand and manage religious diversity in order to build equitable and peaceful communities. It focuses on Christian-Muslim relations and on the role of women in creation and culture. The project aims to:

- show how Islam and Christianity are "systems of being in the world",
- explore the nature of religious freedom in the secular and democratic context of European societies,
- build awareness of the historical role of Islam in Europe and the way memories shape today's relationships in everyday life,
- analyse conditions that may lead to a misuse of religion for non-religious purposes and identity ways to avoid it,
- develop a gender perspective, keeping the viewpoint and contributions in focus,
- harness the potential of religion to create an everyday culture of peace and social harmony, and explore the role of women in this process,
- train students in proven methods of dialogue, communication and conflict mediation.

The European Project for Interreligious Learning, Study Course 2007-09 is a co-operation with the *Ecumenical Forum of European Christian Women*.
www.epil.ch
epil.ch@hispeed.ch

EWNF – European Women of Faith Network

On May 22, 2008, a groundbreaking meeting with women from over 13 European Countries was held in Rovereto, Italy, to establish the *Religions for Peace European Women of Faith Network*. The newly created network was officially presented during the European Conference of *Religions for Peace* that took place in Rovereto from 22-24 May 2008, bringing together over 250 delegates from 35 countries in Europe. *Religions for Peace* – accredited as a non-governmental organization (NGO) to the United Nations – is the world's largest multi-religious coalition advancing common action for peace since 1970. The NGO works with women of faith networks, youth networks and 70 affiliated inter-religious councils in six continents of the world. The European Women of Faith Network is one of the four regional women of faith networks within *Religions for Peace Global Women of Faith Network*. The Coordinator of the global network, Mehrezia Labidi-Maiza from France said that "women are core to their faith communities but not necessarily seen as religious leaders. We need to validate the important work that women do and be a force for peace in the world". The co-chairs of the EWFN, Ravinder Kaur Nijjar, from Scotland and Yolande Iliano, from Belgium stated that this network will put into practice the shared human and spiritual values of Faiths in Europe in all aspects of its work and relationships to advance peace and shared security. Thus the European Network will:

- Enhance interfaith networking among women of faith in Europe through practical projects.
- Promote gender equality and women's empowerment in multi-religious collaboration for peace.

In November 2008 the EWFN was invited to introduce itself at the European Union in Brussels during a luncheon. A support of its work was promised by the EU for the future.

Co-Chairs:
Ravinder Kaur Nijjar: rknijjar@hotmail.com
Yolande Iliano: yolande.iliano@wcrp.be
Regional officers:
Dr. Annette Esser: a.esser@gmx.eu
Iris Maci: irismaci@yahoo.com

FACIT – Feministischer Arbeitskreis christlicher und islamischer Theologinnen

Der *feministische Arbeitskreis christlicher und islamischer Theologinnen* hat sich in Köln im Juni 2004 im Anschluss an das Ausstellungsprojekt mit Begleitprogramm *"'Jede hat ihren Glauben, aber es ist ein Gott' – Begegnungen mit Musliminnen aus der Region"* formiert. Zur Präsentation einer Wanderausstellung, die von Theologie-Dozentinnen und Studierenden der RWTH Aachen gemacht worden war[1], fand sich eine interreligiöse Projektgruppe, getragen von der Köln-Bonner Gruppe ‚Religions for Peace' (RfP), vom ‚Zentrum für islamische Frauenforschung und Frauenförderung' (ZIF),

---
[1] Miriam Neubert / Ursula Rudnick (Hg.), *"Jede hat ihren Glauben, aber es ist ein Gott". Begegnungen mit muslimischen Frauen* (Hora-Verlag: Hannover 2003).

Forum
Fórum

von der Evangelischen Arbeitsstelle für Christlich-Muslimische Begegnung, vom Katholischen Stadtdekanat und vom ‚Referat für interreligiösen Dialog des Erzbistums Köln' (Refidi) zusammen, um ein Begleitprogramm mit einem Kabarett, Vortrags- und Gesprächsabenden und einer gemeinsamen Liturgie zu veranstalten.

Die Reflexion dieser Ausstellung führte dazu, dass sich eine Gruppe aus katholischen, evangelischen und muslimische Theologinnen formierte, die sich später den Namen „FACIT" gab. Wie es eine muslimische Teilnehmerin ausdrückten, geht es in diesem Kreis darum, „endlich miteinander Tacheles zu reden", das heißt, über populäre Themen wie die leidige Kopftuchfrage hinaus in einen feministisch-theologisch engagierten interreligiösen Dialog über heiße Themen zu treten, wie Gewalt gegen Frauen, Wahrheit, Monotheismus / Dreifaltigkeit, Jesus in Bibel und Koran, oder Fudamentalismus. Um in geschütztem Raum offen miteinander reden zu können, tagt dieser Kreis nicht öffentlich; doch können auf Anfrage weitere Frauen dazu kommen.

Seinen ersten öffentlichen Auftritt hatte FACIT am 8. Juni 2007 auf dem Evangelischen Kirchentag in Köln, wobei zum Thema „Wahrheit, die ich meine – Wahrheitsanspruch im Gespräch" zunächst außen stehende ZuhörerInnen zu einem „Fisbowl-Gespräch" in den Gesprächskreis eingeladen wurden. Diese Form der Einladung zum interreligiösen Dialog setzt FACIT seitdem in weiteren Veranstaltungen fort. Weitere Aktivitäten, auch über den Kölner Raum hinaus, werden geplant.

Rabeya Müller: ZIFrauenforschung@gmx.net
Pfrn. Dorothea Schaper: schaper@kirche-koeln.de

ICETH – Interreligious Conference of European Women Theologians / Interreligiöse Konferenz Europäischer Theologinnen

ICETH was founded in 2005, after some years as the "Initiative Conference of European Women Theologians". It started as an intiative within the German association of Protestant women theologians, "Konvent Evangelischer Theologinnen in der BRD", for supporting Catholic women's demand for ordination. However, because of the close relationship and cooperation between the German women theologians and Muslim women activists connected to the Centre for research and empowerment of Islamic women in Cologne (ZIF – Zentrum für Islamische Frauenforschung und Frauenförderung), it was soon decided that the initiative was to be interreligious and work for the rights and status of women in all religious communities, especially the Christian, Muslim and Jewish ones.

ICETH has the following goals:

- to discover the spiritual dimension of inter-confessional and inter-religious encounters;
- to reflect on commonalities and differences in hermeneutical positions;
- to form a community of solidarity for the equality of women theologians in all fields and at all levels;
- to connect theological scholarship and ministry at community level in theory and practice;
- to contribute to peace in Europe through furthering interreligious understanding.

In relation to ESWTR, ICETH is more activist, in that it actively promotes women's ordination. It is also more consciously interreligious, in that interreligious cooperation and understanding is one of its explicit aims. Though some of its members work in the academy, it is more geared towards theologically trained women working in religious institutions and in education.

ICETH currently has about 70 Christian, Muslim and Jewish members from 10 European countries. Members meet for an annual conference, and keep in contact through a Newsletter and the homepage.

www.iketh.eu.

Women's Inter Faith Initiatives in the UK

A plethora of women's inter-faith initiatives has arisen in the UK over the last decades. A survey was made by Fatheena Mubarak for the Inter Faith Network for the UK, in which she recorded 42 initiatives.

She found six broad types of women's inter faith initiatives:

- freestanding inter faith initiatives that have been set up by women;
- women's inter faith initiatives that are part of a larger inter faith organization;
- women's inter faith initiatives that are part of a larger single faith organization or initiative;
- women's inter faith initiatives that are part of a secular organization;
- women's initiatives that are not specifically inter faith in their aims;
- inter faith initiatives for girls and young women within secondary or higher education.

The most popular types of activities mentioned in the survey are: shared meals; dialogue; discussion and meetings; and celebrations of special events and days.

Fatheena Mubarak found, not surprising, that most initiatives operate on a very small budget or no budget at all, and that most of the work is done on a voluntary basis.

A few examples of Women's inter faith initiatives in the UK:

- The *Women's Peace Meeting* in Birmingham started during the war in Bosnia 1993, with mainly Christian women who met to pray for peace. They continued to meet after that war, and gradually the group became inter faith. At the meetings, the women share thoughts about their faith, life experiences, social issues etc. Practical outcomes of the meetings have included help for refugees, fundraising and travelling on pilgrimage together.
- *Asian Women's Advisory Service* offers a drop-in centre for Asian women. In a inter faith volunteering project, they trained volunteers, all women, from the Hindu, Muslim and Sikh communities to enable better relations and strengthen the links between faith groups.
- *The Leicester Christian-Muslim Women's Group* was set up in 2002 for women of Christian and Muslim backgrounds to explore aspects of each other's beliefs and practices. It meets approximately once in six weeks and has covered topics such as traditions in Islam, denominations in Christianity, marriage customs and the scriptures.

The report can be downloaded from the website of the Inter Faith network: *www.interfaith.org.uk/publications/womenssurvey06.pdf*

Sarah und Hagar

Sarah und Hagar als Stammmütter der sogenannten „Abrahamitischen Religionen" (Judentum, Christentum und Islam) gaben im Jahr 2001 zwei interreligiösen und überparteilichen Fraueninitiativen den Namen. Sie wurden unabhängig voneinander in Hessen und Berlin ins Leben gerufen. In beiden Fällen arbeiteten Frauen aus Politik und Religion Hand in Hand.

In Berlin wurde die Idee von der Journalistin und Rabbinerin Elisa Klapheck und der evangelischen Pfarrerin Gerdi Nützel entwickelt. Carola von Braun griff die Idee auf und stellte die Verknüpfung zur Überparteilichen Fraueninitiative Berlin (ÜPFI) her. Die Finanzierung übernahm das Bundesministerium für Familie, Senioren, Frauen und Jugend. Die hessische Initiative entstand in enger Kooperation mit dem hessischen Sozialministerium und der Evangelischen Akademie Arnoldshain.

Inzwischen findet sich unter dem Dach dieser Initiativen ein weitmaschiges bundesweites Netzwerk von Frauen aus Politik und Religionswissenschaften. Ziel ist der interreligiöse Austausch über gemeinsame politische Anliegen. Frauen aus Politik und Religion verständigen sich jenseits von Parteiinteressen oder Reglementierungen durch religiöse Institutionen. Sie treffen sich regional, überregional und bundesweit zu Tagungen, Workshops und Kongressen. Für das Jahr 2011, im 10jährigen Bestehen der Initiative, wird ein bundesweiter Kongress geplant, um die Arbeit der letzten Jahre auszuwerten.[2]

Die Initiative findet derzeit Platz unter dem Dach des Bendorfer Forums für ökumenische Begegnung und interreligiösen Dialog: *www.bendorferforum.de* und des EVAngelischen Frauenbegegnungszentrums Frankfurt: *www.evafrauenzentrum.de*

Sophia

Recientemente, entre los pasos que se van dando debemos destacar la experiencia del grupo *Sophia*, que nace a partir de la Cátedra de las Tres Religiones de la Universidad de Valencia. El grupo está integrado por mujeres de diferentes tradiciones religiosas de la Ciudad de Valencia; se trata de una de las pocas iniciativas que no parten de una tradición religiosa particular. La asociación Sophia que vio la luz en Mayo del 2007 está formada por mujeres judías, católicas, musulmanas, bramakhumaris, budistas, etc., y pretende ser un foro abierto a todos y todas las *"que deseen participar en el desarrollo de una conciencia de paz y amor que el mundo de hoy tanto necesita"*.
www.asociaciondeteologas.org

---

[2] Zur weiteren Information: Annette Mehlhorn, „Religion – Politik – Gender. Geschichte und Hintergründe der interreligiösen Initiative ‚Sarah und Hagar'", in: *EPD Dokumentation* 31.1.2006, 6. Die Initiative wurde 2009 mit dem Leonore-Siegele-Wenschkewitz-Preis ausgezeichnet.

Larissza Hrotkó

Ungarische Frauen im Aufbruch zwischen Religion(en) und Politik. Ein Überblick über die Entwicklung der ungarischen Frauenbewegung

Die ersten Frauenvereine in Pest[1]

Dass Pest über eigene gesellschaftliche Verhaltensmuster verfügte, zeigen unter anderem die von einem österreichischen Reisenden um 1840 niedergeschriebenen Zeilen: „Die erwachsenen Töchter in Pesth behaupten einen gewissen Grad Selbständigkeit und haben sich, z. B. den Männern gegenüber mehr emanzipiert, wie dies in anderen Städten der Fall ist, wo das Töchterchen vom Mütterchen sich nie entfernen darf, um mit diesem oder jenem jungen Herrn allein zu sprechen."[2]

Die Pester Frauen wollten mehr als eine Scheinemanzipation, sie strebten Gleichberechtigung sowohl in der Familie als auch in der Gesellschaft an. 1790 protestierten ungarische Mütter gegen familienrechtliche Diskriminierung. Die Abgeordneten des ungarischen Parlaments rieten den Frauen, die unnötigen Aufstandsversuche einzustellen und die natürliche Priorität der Männer gehorsam anzuerkennen.[3]

Mit dem Wachstum der Metropolen wurden die Männer bald dazu gezwungen, die Beteiligung der Frauen an der gemeinschaftlichen Arbeit zu gestatten. Es kam zur Gründung verschiedener Frauenvereine, deren Arbeit jedoch auf die Wohltätigkeit beschränkt wurde. Im „Wegweiser für Fremde und Einheimische durch die königliche ungarische Freystadt Pesth" beschreibt Dorffinger 1827[4] zwei solcher Vereine: Einer befand sich in der Waldzeile, der andere

---

[1] Pest und Buda waren bis 1873 getrennt.
[2] G. S. B., „Eine Pesther Gesellschaft bei Bürgerlichen," in: *Österreichische Daguerreotypen. Bilder aus dem Leben und Treiben der österreichischen Hauptstädte*, 1. Heft (Verlag Philipp Reclam jun.: Leipzig 1841), 4-5.
[3] „Női szörnyetegek," in: *A nő és a társadalom* (1907 I/2), 17-18; Rózsa Bédy-Schwimmer, „A magyar nőmozgalom régi dokumentumai," in: *A nő és a társadalom* (1907 I/4), 51-53.
[4] Andreas Joseph von Dorffinger, *Wegweiser für Fremde und Einheimische durch die Königliche ungarische Freystadt Pesth* (Trattner: Pest 1827), 102.

Women's traditions
Frauentraditionen
Tradiciones de mujeres

in der Allianzgasse der Theresienstadt, des ältesten und zugleich größten Stadtteils vom damaligen Pest. Laut Dorffinger wurden um 1817 zwei christliche Pester Frauenvereine gegründet. Ihre Aufgabe war es, den Notleidenden in der Großstadt Rettung und Hilfe zu verschaffen. Neben der Stiftung von Armenschulen und Wohltätigkeits-Instituten versuchten die Frauenvereine Selbsthilfe-Ketten zum Verkauf der weiblichen Handarbeiten zu organisieren, damit die verarmten Frauen nicht nur von Almosen leben mussten. Ob es wirtschaftlich auch geglückt ist, ist bisher noch nicht erforscht. Die Oberste „Ausschussfrau" (Ehrenvorsitzende) aller Frauenvereine in Theresienstadt war um 1827-1828 die Erzherzogin Marie Prinzessin von Württemberg, die Vorsteherin Frau Gräfin Johanna von Teleky.

Die meisten Jüdinnen und Juden wohnten Anfang des 19. Jahrhunderts in Theresienstadt, einem Stadtteil von Pest. Pests Stadtväter wollten auch die jüdischen Gemeindevorsteher dazu bewegen, eine Frauengruppe ins Leben zu rufen, die sich mit Anfertigung und Verkauf von Handarbeiten beschäftigen sollte. Das weist zumindest eine Eintragung in einem jüdischen Gemeindeprotokoll aus dem Jahr 1828 nach.[5] So entstand die jüdische „Mädchen-Schule", die wahrscheinlich zum Fundament des 1866 gegründeten jüdischen Frauenvereins wurde.

Der jüdische Frauenverein
Auch die Pester jüdische Gemeinde beschränkte den Tätigkeitsbereich der Frauen zunächst auf die Familie. Dennoch beteiligten sich Frauen von Anfang an beruflich am jüdischen Gemeindeleben. So geht aus den Eintragungen des Pester Gemeindeprotokolls hervor, dass schon 1828 „Krankenwächterinnen", „Kindl-Bett Wächterinnen" und Hebammen in der Gemeinde arbeiteten. Die jüdischen Hebammen waren schon wegen der Zwangstaufe für die Gemeinde von existentieller Bedeutung.[6] Allerdings gibt es keine Nachweise, dass die Arbeit der Frauen von der Gemeinde finanziell entlohnt worden wäre. Es kann also noch von keiner gesellschaftlichen Berufstätigkeit der Frauen gesprochen werden.

1866 wurde der erste jüdische Frauenverein gegründet, der nicht nur einige soziale Aufgaben der Gemeinde, sondern auch die der Stadt übernahm. Die

---

[5] Protokoll vom 19. Oktober 1828, 29 (ohne Zeichen, jüdisches Archiv).
[6] Im jüdischen Archiv von Budapest gibt es Taufnachweise von Neugeborenen ohne Einverständnis der Eltern.

Johanna Bischitz 1827-1898

Gründung des Vereins, der nicht mehr ausschließlich innerhalb der Gemeinde funktionieren sollte, stieß zunächst auf Schwierigkeiten. Erst nachdem der Oberrabbiner von Pest für diesen Plan gewonnen worden war, kam die Sache in Gang. So lautete die schriftliche „Lizenz" des Rabbiners an Frau Johanna Bischitz: „Madame Bischitz Johanna, welche die Güte hat, für den zu gründenden Frauenverein hier sich besonders lebhaft zu interessieren, ist hiemit ermächtigt: Beitrittserklärungen bei den hiesigen isr. Damen zu sammeln, und werden die Unterschriften auf diesem Sammelbogen als vollkommen giltige Meldungen betrachtet und referiert werden. Pest, 11 Februar 1866".[7]

Alle zehn Stifterinnen des Vereins kamen aus vermögenden Familien, was dem Verein eine geschäftliche Grundlage ermöglichte. Rechtlich gesehen durften die Frauen allerdings keine selbstständigen Entscheidungen über das Vermögen des Vereins treffen.[8] So sollte der Frauenverein zwar auf wachsende Armut und Not jüdischer Frauen in der Großstadt reagieren, aber die Frauen konnten die Ziele des Vereins im Sinne des Rechtssystems nicht selbstständig bestimmen.

Gemäß der Vereinsstatuten gehörte zur Hauptaufgabe des jüdischen Frauenvereins die „Hilfeleistung den *tugendhaften* weiblichen Armen, insbesondere den Kranken, Erwerbsunfähigen, Schwangeren, Witwen und Waisen." Aber,

---

[7] Ignaz Reich, *Beth-El, Ehrentempel verdienter ungarischer Israeliten*, I-II (Eduard Neumaner: Budapest 1856/1868), 79.
[8] Unter den Revidenten, welche die Finanzen des Vereins beaufsichtigten, gab es natürlich keine einzige Frau. Es handelt sich um die Herren Bernát Stern, József Fleischl, Oppenheim J. S., Miksa Brüll und Imre Ullmann. „Hazai hirek," in: *Egyenlőség* (19. Mai 1889, VIII. Jahrgang / Nr. 19), 8.

so fragt sich sogleich, welche Frauen galten als *tugendhaft?* Zur Zeit der Stiftung gab es in Pest zahlreiche „ledige Mütter". Auch in der jüdischen Gemeinde wurden nach 1840 die unehelichen Kinder, deren Väter meistens anonym blieben, als „nicht gesetzlich" immatrikuliert. Man mag bezweifeln, ob eine berufstätige, traditionstreue ledige Mutter mit ihrem illegalen Kind tugendhaft genug war, um den Verein um Hilfe zu bitten. Aber gerade solche Frauen brauchten ja die Unterstützung, da die meisten ledigen Mütter in der Großstadt ganz auf sich bzw. auf ihre Arbeitgeber angewiesen waren.

1867 wurde das Waiseninstitut für jüdische Mädchen als erste Anstalt des Frauenvereins eröffnet. Das Waiseninstitut sozialisierte die Mädchen in der religiösen Tradition, obwohl die meisten Gründerinnen säkulare Schulen im Ausland absolviert und sogar berufliche Ausbildung erworben haben. So war zum Beispiel die Vereinsvorsitzende Johanna Bischitz gelernte Krankenpflegerin, die für ihr berufliches Engagement während des Bosnien-Krieges (1877) von Kaiser Franz Joseph mit dem Goldehrenkreuz ausgezeichnet und in den Adelsstand erhoben wurde.[9] Die Schülerinnen des Waiseninstituts wurden sowohl auf traditionelles Eheleben als auch auf das berufliche Leben vorbereitet. Unter anderem lernten die Mädchen Haushaltsarbeit, wenn auch die meisten ledigen Mütter gerade aus der beruflichen Gruppe der Dienstmägde stammten. Erst 1889 wurde auf Anregung bzw. großherzige Spende des jüdischen Frauenvereins ein Heim für jüdische Lehrerinnen erbaut, bei deren Eröffnung Großherzogin Marie Dorothee anwesend war. Die Vereinsdamen veranstalteten erfolgreiche Wohltätigkeits-Bälle, und 1870 wurde die erste Volksküche organisiert, welche die Ernährungsprobleme bedürftiger Einwohner in Pest beheben sollte.

Über Ziele und einige prominente Mitglieder des Feministischen Vereins
Um 1890 funktionierten in Ungarn schon etwa 800 wohltätige Frauenvereine, jedoch entwickelte sich neben diesen Vereinen die säkulare Frauenbewegung für die gesellschaftliche Gleichberechtigung. Die Frauenrechtlerinnen Ungarns kämpften seit dem Ende des 18. Jahrhunderts für die Selbstbestimmung der Frauen in der Familie und in der Gesellschaft, darunter für das Recht auf persönliches Vermögen, Mitbestimmung in der Kindererziehung und Zugang zu den Universitäten sowie Beteiligung an den Parlamentswahlen. Seit 1885 durf-

---

[9] Mehr über Bischitz bei Mária Lendvai, „A Pesti Izraelita Nőegylet megalakulása és szociális intézményrendszerének kiépülése (1866-1885)," in: *A zsidó nő* (Magyar Zsidó Múzeum és Levéltár: Budapest 2002), 55-65.

ten die ungarischen Frauen staatliche Ämter bekleiden und seit 1895 an den Landesuniversitäten studieren.

| Rózsa (Rosika) Bédy-Schwimmer | Vilma Glücklich | Eugénia Miskolczi-Meller |

Im folgenden sollen drei Frauen vorgestellt werden, deren Namen mit der organisierten feministischen Bewegung Ungarns verbunden sind. Alle drei kamen aus jüdischen Familien und wurden zu Leiterinnen der säkularen Frauenbewegung des 20. Jahrhunderts. Sie erlebten die Emanzipation als Jüdinnen und als Frauen. Der Ungarische Feministische Verein wurde 1904 von den Aktivistinnen des Landesvereins der weiblichen Angestellten (1896) gegründet. 200 Frauen und 50 Männer – Studenten und Arbeiterinnen, die sich damals in einem der Häuser am Franziskaner Platz versammelten – standen im Raum dicht aneinander, still wie in einer Kirche, und warteten auf die Eröffnung, wie die Zeitung *Pesti Napló* am 18. Dezember 1904 berichtete.[10]

Die Präsidentin des Vereins, Vilma Glücklich (1872–1927), war die erste ungarische Frau, die ihre akademische Ausbildung in Budapest erworben hatte. Seit 1896 studierte sie Physik und Mathematik und unterrichtete anschließend an der Universität zu Budapest. Seit 1902 war sie eine der Vorsteherinnen des Landesvereins der weiblichen Angestellten. 1915 leitete sie die ungarische Delegation auf dem Frauenweltkongress in Haag. Vor dem Horthy-Regime (1919-1944) ist Vilma Glücklich nach Österreich geflohen, wo sie 1927 verstarb.

Drei Jahre nach der Vereinsgründung (1907) erschien die erste Ausgabe der Vereinszeitung „Frau und die Gesellschaft". Sie gab bekannt, dass sich die

---

[10] Judit Acsády, „A hazai feminizmus fénykora," in: Ida Csapó / Mónika Török (Hg.), *Feminista Almanach* (Printer Art Kkt: Budapest 2005), 60-62.

ungarischen Frauen bereit wussten, die soziale Verantwortung mit den Männern zu teilen. Gewiss gab es auch Spannungen innerhalb des Vereins. Die „Radikalen"[11] forderten vom Staat die sofortige Besserung der Lebensumstände der Ärmsten und Arbeiterinnen. Der alte „elitäre" Feminismus, der nur Emanzipation für einige besonders gebildete bzw. begabte Frauen erringen wollte, unterschied sich grundsätzlich von der sozialdemokratischen Richtung, die nach einer tiefgreifenden gesellschaftlichen Wandlung strebte.

Diesem Verein gehörten von Anfang an auch Männer an – vor allem Pester Journalisten und Schriftsteller. So schrieb Zoltán Szász 1907 in „Frau und die Gesellschaft", dass die bürgerliche Gesellschaft den Begriff der Frauenwürde sexualisiert und die gesellschaftliche Existenz von Frauen auf ihre Sexualrollen reduziert habe. Die traditionellen Frauenrollen, so argumentierte er, stellten Frauen nur als Geschlechtswesen dar: als verliebte Frauen, Ehefrauen oder Mütter. Deshalb sei auch die größte „Frauensünde" die Prostitution in den unteren bzw. der Ehebruch in den oberen gesellschaftlichen Schichten.

Der Ungarische Feministische Verein forderte eine umfassende soziale Reform und lehnte die spontane Wohltätigkeit der Wohlhabenden als ungenügend ab. Solche Hilfeleistung schadete den notleidenden Frauen sogar, da sie die Armut als natürliches Begleitphänomen der gesellschaftlichen Entwicklung erscheinen ließ.[12]

1914 wurde der Name der feministischen Zeitung verändert. Als Hauptredakteurin der „Frau" arbeitete weiterhin Rosika (Rózsa) Bédy-Schwimmer (1877–1948), eine der Gründerinnen des Feministischen Vereins. Sie galt als ultramoderne Frau, die mit schockierenden Kleidern ohne Wespentaille herumlief und in der Öffentlichkeit ohne Begleitung ihres – eventuell nur auf dem Papier existierenden – Ehemannes erschien. Bédy-Schwimmer hatte Musik und Sprachen studiert und verfügte über Sprachkenntnisse in neun Sprachen. Ihrem diplomatischen Talent war es zu verdanken, dass zahlreiche ausländische Beziehungen entstanden und Besuche bzw. Vorträge wie der von

---

[11] Das Lexem „radikal" wurde von Feministinnen für die sozial-demokratische Gruppe des Vereins eingesetzt. Von den Kritikern des Vereins aber wurden alle Mitglieder der feministischen Organisation als „radikal" – das heißt für die Gesellschaft gefährlich – oder „materialistisch" bezeichnet. Siehe z. B: J. S., *Lássunk világosan* „Mit ígér és mit ad a radikális feminizmus," in: *Magyar Nő* (1918, I/1).

[12] Die sogenannten „christlichen Feministinnen", über die im nächsten Kapitel berichtet wird, forderten die Verordnung der Wohltätigkeits-Steuer für junge, alleinstehende Männer und reiche Familien.

Charlotte Perkins Gillman in Budapest zustande kamen, der das ungarische Publikum elektrisierte.[13] 1913 organisierte Bédy-Schwimmer zusammen mit Vilma Glücklich und Eugénia Miskolczi-Meller den VII. Kongress der IWSA (Woman Suffrage Alliance) in Budapest. 1914 arbeitete sie als Presseverantwortliche im Londoner Büro der IWSA. Sie vertrat 1918 die bürgerliche Regierung Ungarns als Botschafterin in der Schweiz und wurde zu einer der maßgeblichen Organisatorinnen der Friedensbewegung. 1937 wurde ihr der Weltfriedenspreis verliehen. (1947 wurde Bédy-Schwimmer sogar für den Friedensnobelpreis nominiert, den sie jedoch 1948 nicht bekommen hat).

Mit der Machtübernahme von Horthy musste sie Ungarn wegen des sich ausbreitenden Antisemitismus verlassen und in die USA emigrieren, die sie als Pazifistin aber nicht einbürgern wollten. Rosika Schwimmer (Rózsa Bédy-Schwimmer) starb 1948 in New-York.

Die dritte Stifterin des Feministischen Vereins – Eugénia Miskolczi-Meller (1872–?) – lebte in glücklicher Ehe, war Mutter von vier Kindern und finanziell sehr gut versorgt. Auch Miskolczi-Meller war eine leidenschaftliche Frauenrechtlerin und darüber hinaus Mitglied in der Sozialdemokratischen Partei. Sie war für ihre scharfsinnigen Artikel und öffentlichen Reden bekannt, wurde 1944 verhaftet und verschwand 1945 spurlos. 1946 wurde der Feministische Verein offiziell aufgelöst, weil seine Ziele in der Volksrepublik angeblich nicht mehr aktuell waren.

Das christlich-feministische Paradigma: „Ungarische Frau"

Auch manche katholische Wohltätigkeitsvereine änderten ihre Formen im Laufe der Jahre, da auch religiöse Frauen immer mehr sozial mitreden wollten. 1918 erschien die erste Nummer der „Ungarischen Frau", die sich als „Blatt des christlichen Feminismus" vorstellte.[14] Das neue Monatsblatt, hinter dem die Katholische Sozialmissions-Gesellschaft stand, betonte zwar seine kirchliche Verbundenheit, wollte jedoch für alle ungarischen Frauen sprechen, was der Feministische Verein sofort in Frage stellte.

Zwischen den beiden Organisationen gab es ständige gegenseitige Angriffe in der Presse. Bédy-Schwimmer polemisierte gegen die „Ungarische Frau"

---

[13] Der Titel des Vortrags lautete „Should women work?"
[14] *Magyar Nő*, Budapest, 1918. március. A keresztény feminizmus lapja. A Szociális Missziótársulat Országos Szervezetének Hivatalos Közlönye. I. évfolyam/1. szám (*Ungarische Frau*, Budapest, März 1918. Blatt des christlichen Feminismus. Offizielles Bulletin der Landesorganisation der Sozialmissions-Gesellschaft).

Women's traditions
Frauentraditionen
Tradiciones de mujeres

und behauptete, diese stünde hinter dem Verbot der „Frau" im Jahre 1918, da das Blatt die Feministinnen wegen „höllischer" Unsittlichkeit aus der Gesellschaft „herausgepredigt" habe.[15] Das Programm der Sozialmissions-Gesellschaft entstand aus der Auseinandersetzung und dem politischen Streit zwischen christlichen und säkularen Feministinnen. Der christliche Feminismus forderte zwar ebenfalls die Selbstbestimmung der Frauen in der Familie und Öffentlichkeit, betrachtete jedoch die Hausarbeit und Verpflegung der Familie – „die Wurzelarbeit" sozusagen – als vorrangige Frauenpflicht. Die christlichen FeministInnen vertraten nicht nur eine frauenrechtlerische, sondern auch eine national-chauvinistische Politik.[16] Sie wollten nicht nur die spezifisch weiblichen Eigenschaften von Frauen – wie Fürsorge, Mütterlichkeit und Altruismus – ins öffentliche Leben bringen, sondern strebten auch die totale „Christianisierung" des Landes an.

Die umstrittene Persönlichkeit des Bischofs Ottokár Prohászka hat das national-konservative Profil der „Ungarischen Frau" grundsätzlich bestimmt. Prohászka war allerdings auch bereit, die Bürgerrechte der Frau je nach deren Lebensweise massiv einzuschränken. So schlug Prohászka beispielsweise eine Ergänzung des Paragraphen 12/2 im Wahlgesetzentwurf vor, nach dem all jene Frauen, die wegen unwürdigen Verhaltens die Sorgerechte für ihre Kinder verloren hätten, vom Wahlrecht für mindestens 2 Jahre ausgeschlossen werden sollten.[17] Auch das Problem der unehelichen Kinder betraf nach Prohászkas Einstellung ausschließlich die Frauen. So machte er in einem Artikel in der „Ungarischen Frau" vom 27. April 1918 die Frauen dafür verantwortlich, dass die unehelichen Kinder vom Staat als nicht gesetzlich behandelt werden. Er plädierte dafür, die gesellschaftliche Abneigung nicht gegen die armen Kinder zu wenden, sondern die unordentlichen und gewissenlosen Mütter zu strafen.

---

[15] Das heißt: „verbannt". Die „Frau" des Feministischen Vereins wurde nach der Niederlage der kommunistischen bzw. bürgerlichen Regierung 1918 verboten, denn mehrere Mitglieder des Vereins waren eng mit der sozialdemokratischen Partei verbunden. Zu den größten Feinden der „Frau" gehörte Bischof Ottokár Prohászka als erbitterter Gegner der revolutionären Arbeiterbewegung und Anführer des modernen Antisemitismus. Vgl. z. B. Ferenc Szabó (SJ), *Prohászka önmagáról* (Szeged 1999).

[16] So forderten sie z. B. die Aufstellung des Kreuzes auf dem Parlamentsgebäude (1919 / 9-10), was die Vertreter der reformierten Kirche kategorisch ablehnten, weil das Parlament der Tempel aller Christen Ungarns sein solle. Dr. János Koncz, „Fel a keresztet a parlamentre," in: *Magyar Nő* (1919 / 11, november 16.)

[17] Ottokár Prohászka, „Eszmecsere a törvénytelen gyermekről," in: *Magyar Nő* (1918. I/1, április 27.)

Prohászka erklärte unmissverständlich, dass die Legitimität der Kinder ausschließlich durch die kirchliche Heirat zu erwerben sei.[18]

1918 war den Aktivitäten aller Pester Frauenrechtlerinnen der erste Erfolg vergönnt: Sie setzten das Wahlrecht für Frauen in Ungarn durch, durften aber erst ab 24 und nicht ab 21 Jahren wie Männer zur Wahl gehen. Schon 1920 wurde Schwester Margit Schlachta (1884 Kaschau – 1974 New York), eine der Aktivistinnen der katholischen Sozialmissions-Gesellschaft und Redakteurin der „Ungarischen Frau" Parlamentabgeordnete. Die christlichen Frauenrechtlerinnen wurden dadurch als erste gesellschaftlich legalisiert, was unter den damaligen gesellschaftlichen Verhältnissen (Dominanz der katholischen Kirche in allen Bereichen des gesellschaftlichen Lebens Ungarns) nicht verwunderlich war.

Schwester Margit Schlachta (Slachta)

Schwester Margit Schlachta blieb wegen ernsthafter Auseinandersetzungen mit der Leitung der Sozialmissions-Gesellschaft, die ihre politische Aktivität einschränken wollte, nicht lange in der Körperschaft der Gesellschaft. 1920 gründete sie eine neue Kongregation der Sozialschwestern, die wegen ihrer grauen Schleier auch „graue Schwestern" genannt wurden. Margit Schlachta und ihre

---

[18] Vgl. dagegen den Feministischen Verein, der eindeutig gegen Diskriminierung der unehelichen Kinder auftrat.

Schwestern versteckten Juden und halfen anderen Verfolgten während des faschistischen Terrors, was im damaligen Ungarn eher untypisch war. Für ihre Tapferkeit wurde Schwester Margit von Yad Vashem, der zentralen Gedenkstätte für die Opfer und Helden des Holocaust in Israel, post mortem als „Gerechte unter den Völkern" ausgezeichnet.

Rückblick auf die Geschichte: Tikkun olam[19]

Der 1866 gegründete jüdische Frauenverein leistete „Weltverbesserung" nicht nur im Wohltätigkeitsbereich. Vielen jüdischen Frauen verhalf dieser Verein zur aktiven Teilnahme am öffentlichen Leben und zugleich zur Verbesserung ihrer eigenen Lebensqualität.

Das öffentliche Auftreten der Frauen wurde in den meisten bürgerlichen jüdischen Familien akzeptiert, wenn es sich um religiöse Ziele oder das Wohlergehen der Gemeinde handelte. Die Modernität erreichte auch die jüdischen Familien und deren „Hauspriesterinnen", die nicht mehr in ihren Schranken bleiben wollten.[20] Bereits um die Jahrhundertwende erhielten jüdische Mädchen nicht selten die gleiche Erziehung wie die Knaben.[21] Diese „knabenhaften" jungen Frauen lieferten Nachschub für den harten Kern der kommunistischen bzw. sozialdemokratischen Bewegung Ungarns in der Zeit zwischen den beiden Weltkriegen. Im religiösen Umfeld konnten sie ihr ethisches Verlangen nach *tikkun olam* nicht mehr durchsetzen, weil sie sich von der traditionellen religiösen Lebensform eingeschränkt fühlten. So traten die emanzipierten Jüdinnen aus dem ethnisch-religiösen jüdischen Lebensraum heraus, um sich im bürgerlichen politischen Leben Ungarns zu sozialisieren.

---

[19] *Tikkun olam* (hebräisch) ist ein Ausdruck für „Verbesserung der Welt". Dieses humanistische Konzept stammt aus der frührabbinischen Periode des Judentums (R. Gamliel – Gittin, Mischnah 4:2), obwohl es in diesem Traktat ursprünglich um die Scheidung ging. Durch Mischnah 4:2 wurde die soziale Ordnung in der jüdischen Gemeinschaft verbessert. Im heutigen Judentum verfügt dieses Wort über eine zusätzliche Bedeutung der Förderung und Entwicklung der menschlichen Gesellschaft.

[20] „*Die Frau sei die Priesterin des Hauses*" – Zitat aus dem Jahresbuch 1938 des Ungarischen Israelitischen Frauenvereins. Mehr darüber bei Andrea Pető, „A fiúnak nevelt lányok és a tikkun olam szerepe a magyarországi zsidó nők politikai szerepvállalásban," in: *A zsidó nő* (Magyar Zsidó Múzeum és Levéltár: Budapest 2002), 77-87.

[21] Pető, „A fiúnak nevelt lányok …", 80. Pető weist dabei auf eine Arbeit von Marion A. Kaplan hin, welche die Frauenidentitätsprobleme in den jüdischen Familien Deutschlands thematisiert: *The Making of the Jewish Middle Class. Women, Family, and Identity in Imperial Germany* (Oxford University Press: New York u. a. 1991).

Die Ereignisse in Ungarn in den 30er- und 40er-Jahre des letzten Jahrhunderts zeigten jedoch, dass dieses Vertrauen verfrüht war. Weder der ungarische Staat noch die christlichen Frauenorganisationen wollten (oder konnten) sie beschützen. Als Schlachtas „graue Schwestern" die Juden vor den ungarischen und deutschen Faschisten versteckten, waren die gesellschaftlichen Verhältnisse im Lande durch Misstrauen und Feindlichkeit schon längst vergiftet. Auch zahlreiche Artikel in der „Ungarischen Frau" trugen zur Steigerung der allgemeinen antisemitischen Stimmung in Ungarn bei. So veröffentlichte die „Ungarische Frau", deren verantwortliche Redakteurin 1919 noch Schwester Margit Schlachta war, einen tabellenartigen Überblick über Angestelltenentlassungen, der den allgemein verbreiteten (übrigens durchaus falschen) Gedanken bekräftigte, dass die meisten Großunternehmer Ungarns Juden waren, die überwiegend den christlichen Angestellten kündigten.[22] Zur Zeit der wirtschaftlichen Rezession und politischen Unsicherheit wirkten solche Artikel hetzerisch.

Niemand könnte mit Sicherheit behaupten, dass die Frauen Ungarns allein durch vernünftige Zusammenarbeit eine gesunde Gesellschaftsbalance hätten herstellen können. Das Problem war, dass sie nicht einmal versuchten, einander zu verstehen. Die Idee eines interreligiösen bzw. sozialen Dialoges war im damaligen gesellschaftlichen Umfeld offensichtlich noch völlig fremd. Die geistigen Kapazitäten und reichen Erfahrungen der jüdischen Frauenbewegung wurden von der christlichen Frauenorganisation nie studiert, geschweige denn angenommen.

Dennoch: Trotz ihrer politischen Unterschiede trugen Frauen wie Johanna Bischitz, Rosika Schwimmer, Vilma Glücklich, Eugénia Miskolcsi-Meller und Sr. Margit Schlachta enorm dazu bei, dass sich das Selbstbestimmungsrecht und die gesellschaftliche Gleichberechtigung der ungarischen Frauen im zwanzigsten Jahrhundert deutlich verbesserten.

En este artículo se tratan los primeros movimientos feministas de Hungría. Los "caballeros" utilizaron las primeras asociaciones de mujeras católicas y judías para resolver los graves problemas de las metrópolis. Igualmente los altos jerarcas de la iglesia sacaron provecho de la asociación feminista cristiana. La asociación feminista fundada en 1904 se ocupó de muchos problemas sociales de Hungría, pero nunca llegó a tener influencia suficiente, porque una parte de los miembros de esta sociedad eran judías y tuvieron que huir ante el régimen fascista húngaro. El diálogo entre los grupos feministas, que tan importante hubiera sido, nunca se llegó a concretar.

---

[22] in: *Magyar Nő* (1919 / 12. szám (3), II (VII.) évfolyam, november 27.)

Women's traditions
Frauentraditionen
Tradiciones de mujeres

This article discusses the first feminist movements in Hungary. The men took advantage of the first associations of Catholic and Jewish women to solve grave problems in the metropolis. And the leading people in the church benefitted from the Christian feminist association. The feminist association established in 1904 devoted itself to many of the social problems in Hungary, but it did not have sufficient influence because a proportion of its members were Jewish and they had to flee from the Hungarian fascist regime. A dialogue between the feminist groups, which would have been most important, did not come about.

Larissza Hrotkó (*1945) ist Philologin, katholische Theologin und jüdische Kulturhistorikerin. Sie beschäftigt sich mit Kulturanthropologie der Juden Ungarns und widmet ihre Forschungen vor allem den unbekannten, „kleinen" Menschen der jüdischen Gemeinde in Budapest. Gerade erschien ihre Publikation „Dynamik, Geographie und Gesellschaftsspezifik der jüdischen Ansiedlung in Pest um die Mitte des 19. Jahrhunderts", in: *Acta Ethnographica Hungarica* 53 (2 / 2008), 207–300. Ihre jüngste Arbeit in ungarischer Sprache – „Zsidó nők régi arcképcsarnoka" (Alte Portraithalle der jüdischen Frauen) – wurde in der jüdischen Gesellschaftszeitschrift „*Remény*" (Hoffnung) zu Chanukka 2008 veröffentlicht.

Nuriye Duran Özsoy

Die Frauenbewegung in der Türkei

Die Entstehungs- und Erfolgsgeschichte der Frauenbewegung ist grundsätzlich vom jeweiligen Land und seiner Kultur abhängig. Die Emanzipationsbestrebungen in der Türkei bedürfen einer gründlichen Erforschung und genauen Analyse der Faktoren, die Ursache dieser Bewegung waren und sind. Dafür ist es hilfreich, diese in Phasen zu unterteilen. Als die erste Phase lässt sich die Osmanische Frauenbewegung ansehen, deren Anfänge auf das Ende der Tanzimat-Periode (Ende des 19. Jh.) zurückzuführen sind.[1] Im Anschluss daran etablierten sich Frauen, die die Kemalistischen Reformen miterlebten. Sie waren der Regierung gegenüber sehr loyal und galten als von ihr gelenkt und zur Schau gestellt. Bis in die 1970er Jahre hinein durchlebte die Frauenbewegung ihre ruhigste Phase. Danach gab es eine starke Orientierung an linken Ideologien. Nach dem Putsch vom 12. September 1980[2] entstand eine Frauenbewegung, die sich sowohl von der linken als auch von der islamischen Bewegung losriss und von diesen Ideologien Unabhängigkeit erlangte. Diese Phasen werden in der feministischen Literatur als die erste, zweite und dritte Welle der Frauenbewegung[3] bezeichnet, die sehr

---

[1] Vgl. Ömer Çaha, „Türk Kadın Hareketi: Kadınsı Bir Sivil Toplumun İmkanı" [Die Türkische Frauenbewegung: Die Möglichkeit einer femininen Zivilgesellschaft], in: *Kadın Çalışmaları Dergisi*, Nr. 3, 2006.

[2] Am 12. September 1980 übernahm die militärische Führung unter Generalstabschef Kenan Evren die Regierung. Es begann eine breit angelegte Jagd auf Linke. Diese Zeit, die manchen Informationen zufolge 4000 Menschen das Leben kostete, hinterließ in den Köpfen von Zeitzeugen ewige Spuren. Leider wurde mit öffentlichen militärischen Putschen, die etwa alle zehn Jahre 1960, 1971, 1980 – und später 1997 in modernisierter Form als postmoderner Putsch – stattfanden, die demokratische zivile Regierung aufgehoben. Diese militärischen Putsche wurden zum Thema von zahlreichen Filmen und Büchern. Schließlich wurden die kürzlich gescheiterten Bemühungen der Schließung der AKP, die mit 40% gewählt wurde, auch von rechten, einigen linken und liberalen Kreisen als die Fortsetzung dieser Putschversuche angesehen.

[3] Hinzuweisen ist in diesem Zusammenhang, dass die Bezeichnungen „Erste, Zweite und Dritte Welle" in Bezug auf die Frauenbewegung in der Türkei mit der Verwendung dieser

unterschiedliche Dynamiken, Paradigmen und Diskurse aufweisen. Diese sollen im Folgenden anhand der jüngsten feministischen Literatur in der Türkei erläutert werden.

Die „erste Welle" der Frauenbewegung
Die Existenz der Osmanischen Frauenbewegung kam erst infolge von Forschungen in den 1980er Jahren zutage. Es war die sogenannte „Erste Welle" der Frauenbewegung. Bis dahin betrachtete man die Rechte, die nach der Gründung der Republik den Frauen gewährt wurden, nicht als von Frauen eingeforderte Rechte, sondern als solche, die ihnen die Revolution einräumte. Es gab jedoch am Ende des Osmanischen Reiches – vor und nach der 2. Tanzimat-Periode – eine äußerst aktive Frauenbewegung und auch später eine weitere, die sich an der Gründung der Republik beteiligen wollte. Diese Osmanische Frauenbewegung blieb bis in die jüngere Zeit unentdeckt. Erst die Eröffnung der Frauenforschungszentren in den Universitäten nach westlichem Vorbild ermöglichte es, dass diese Bewegung nicht in völlige Vergessenheit geriet. Die nacheinander einsetzenden Forschungen zu Frauen an diesen Zentren einerseits und die Gründung einer Bibliothek der Frauenwerke und eines Informationszentrums im Jahre 1990 andererseits beschleunigten die Frauenforschung und wurden zum Wendepunkt der Frauenforschung in der Türkei.[4]

> In den letzten zwanzig Jahren bildete in der feministischen Geschichtsschreibung die Beleuchtung der verborgenen Frauengeschichte den ersten Schritt. Dies war, nach Skott „auch die Phase der Erschaffung eines neuen Wissens über die Frau und somit über die Gesellschaft".[5]

Es wird deutlich, dass der feministische Diskurs, der die Notwendigkeit einer neuen Geschichtsschreibung aus Sicht der Frau betont, nicht ignoriert werden sollte. Eine ganze Reihe von Arbeiten haben der Frauenforschung in der Türkei eine neue Dimension gegeben und den Weg für weitere Arbeiten über diesen Zeitraum geebnet: Zafer Topraks Arbeiten über osmanische

---

Bezeichnungen in der internationalen feministischen Literatur nicht übereinstimmt, sondern als eine letztendlich lokale Wortverwendung anzusehen ist.
[4] Vgl. Yeşim Arat, „Türkiye'de Kadın Çalışmaları: Kemalizm'den Feminizme" [Frauenarbeit in der Türkei: Vom Kemalismus zum Feminismus], in: *Kadın Çalışmaları Dergisi*, Nr. 3, 2006.
[5] Yaprak Zihnioğlu, *Kadınsız İnkılap* [Revolution ohne Frauen] (Metis Yayınları: Istanbul 2003), 16.

Frauenvereine (1988-89), Serpil Çakırs Schriften „Eine osmanische Frauenorganisation: Gesellschaft zur Verteidigung der Frauenrechte"[6] und „Osmanische Frauenbewegung"[7] (beide 1994), die Arbeiten von Şirin Tekeli (1986-90), Nüket Sirman (1993) und Yeşim Arat (1997) über die neuen feministischen Aktivitäten sowie Emel Aşas (1989) und Aynur Demirdireks (1993) Untersuchungen über osmanische Frauenvereine und Yaprak Zihnioğlus aktuelle Arbeit „Revolution ohne Frauen – Nezihe Muhiddin"[8] (2003).

Latife Hanım selbst, die Frau des Gründers der türkischen Republik Mustafa Kemal Atatürk, war eine äußerst starke Frau und stand in engem Kontakt mit den Feministinnen jener Zeit. İpek Çalışlars Werk „Latife Hanım"[9], das kürzlich veröffentlicht wurde und zu heftigen Diskussionen führte, zeigt sehr deutlich, wie die Geschichte bisher verzerrt dargestellt und die Rolle der Frauen während der Revolution ignoriert wurde. Nachdem ihr Mann, Mustafa Kemal, sich von ihr gemäß dem Familiengesetz des Osmanischen Reiches scheiden ließ, wurde Latife Hanım des Palastes verwiesen und zog sich in die Einsamkeit zurück. Die Geschichtsschreibung hat sie fast gänzlich ignoriert. Ihre Memoiren wurden der Gesellschaft für Sprache und Geschichte (Dil Tarih Kurumu) hinterlassen und sind der Öffentlichkeit und der Forschung bis zum heutigen Tage nicht zugänglich.

Die Erste Welle der Frauenbewegung selbst kann in drei Phasen unterteilt werden:

- von 1868, als der erste Brief einer Frau veröffentlicht wurde, bis zur 2. Tanzimat-Zeit (1908)
- der osmanische Feminismus der 2. Tanzimat-Periode (1908-1922)
- die Erste Welle des republikanistischen[10] Feminismus (1923-1935).[11]

Ab den 1870er Jahren schickten Frauen – zunächst ohne Namen, beziehungsweise unter Pseudonymen – Briefe an Zeitungen, später aber fingen

---

[6] Serpil Çakır, „Bir Osmanlı Kadın Örgütü, Osmanlı Müdafaa-i Hukuk-ı Nisvan Cemiyeti", in: *Tarih ve Toplum*, XI/66 (Haziran 1989), 18-19.
[7] Serpil Çakır, *Osmanlı Kadın Hareketi* (Metis Yayınları: Istanbul) 1994.
[8] Yaprak Zihnioğlu, *Kadınsız İnkılap – Nezihe Muhiddin, Kadınlar Halk Fırkası, Kadın Birliği* (Metis Yayınları: Istanbul 2003).
[9] İpek Çalışlar, *Latife Hanım* (Doğan Kitapçılık: Istanbul 2006).
[10] Anmerkung der Lektorin: Der Begriff „republikanistisch" wird hier für eine Haltung verwendet, die eine patriotische kemalistische Einstellung zur Republik stark herausstreicht und ideologisch überhöht.
[11] Yaprak Zihnioğlu, *Kadınsız İnkılap*, 21.

sie an, regelmäßig Artikel zu verfassen. Das Buch der ersten Romanautorin Fatma Aliye Hanım, Tochter des bekannten Historikers Cevdet Pascha, wurde in europäische Sprachen übersetzt. Zur selben Zeit wurde eine eigene Zeitung für Frauen mit dem Titel „Hanımlara Mahsus Gazete"[12] zu einem Presseorgan, über das die Frauen sprachen und diskutierten, und das die Tagesordnung der Presselandschaft mitbestimmte. Durch diese und ähnliche Zeitungen, Zeitschriften und Vereine begannen die Frauen für ihre Meinungs- und Bildungsfreiheit einzutreten, ebenso für das Recht auf Arbeit und das Recht, innerhalb der Familie eine geachtete Stellung einzunehmen. Sie setzten sich für die Abschaffung von Polygamie und das Scheidungsrecht ein, das bis dahin nur Männer für sich beanspruchen konnten. Şirin Tekeli beschreibt die Haltung der reformistischen Männer jener Zeit folgendermaßen:

> Obwohl sie die Reformen der Tanzimat vertraten, verhielten sie sich, was die Rechte der Frauen anbelangte, sehr konservativ. Sie versuchten, die althergebrachten osmanischen Werte über die Frauen aufrecht zu erhalten.[13]

Die Feministinnen jener Zeit kritisierten entschieden diese Haltung ihrer männlichen Genossen und setzten sich selber für ihre Interessen ein. Obwohl sie die Ansichten ihrer europäischen Genossinnen schätzten und als wichtig erachteten, rechtfertigten sie ihre Position mit dem Rückgriff auf die Religion und bedienten sich religiöser Argumente mit dem Verweis auf muslimische Frauen aus dem frühen Islam sowie muslimische Wissenschaftlerinnen aus der islamischen Geschichte.

Die Erste Welle republikanischer Feministinnen ging noch einen Schritt weiter. Sie forderten eine aktive Rolle in der Gründungsphase der Republik sowie das Wahlrecht. Sie waren der Ansicht, einer Revolution ohne Frauen fehle etwas. Zu diesem Zweck gründeten sie 1923 die *Frauenvolkspartei* (Kadınlar Halk Fırkası) und ein Jahr darauf die *Türkische Frauenunion* (Türk Kadınlar Birliği). Die von der Kemalistischen Ideologie beherrschte Einparteienregierung sah die Rolle der Frauen nicht als Mitbegründerinnen und aktive Elemente der Nation an, sondern lediglich als passiv, beobachtend und bestenfalls als unterstützend.

---

[12] Der Titel der Zeitung lässt sich mit „Zeitung für Frauen" übersetzen.
[13] Unveröffentlichter Beitrag von Şirin Tekeli im Rahmen des Internationalen Symposiums „Türkiye ve Avrupa Birliği'nde Kadınlar: Ortak Bir Anlayışa Doğru" [Frauen in der Türkei und der Europäischen Union: Hin zu einem gemeinsamen Standpunkt], 13.09.2004, in: http://bianet.org/bianet/bianet/43145-on-maddede-turkiyede-kadin-hareketi.

Infolge dieser Zurückdrängungspolitik wurden Frauen, die diesem Bild nicht entsprachen, isoliert, die Frauenvolkspartei verboten und die Aktivitäten ihrer Mitglieder unterbunden. Die neue Regierung setzte die Frauenrechte als starke demokratische Symbole gegen die Außenwelt ein, trug die Behauptung – „wir sind es, die den Frauen die Rechte gegeben haben" – wie ein Banner vor sich her und gewährte nur jenen Frauen ihre Unterstützung, die diesem Slogan folgten. Indem die führenden Frauenbilder der Vergangenheit aktiv in die Vergessenheit verbannt wurden, um sie so aus dem kollektiven Gedächtnis der Kulturgeschichte zu löschen, wurde ein neuer Frauentyp geschaffen.[14]

Diesen neuen Frauentyp, den die kemalistische Ideologie in der Türkei kreierte, können wir „Republikanistische Frau"[15] nennen. Sie wird dadurch charakterisiert, dass sie eine geschlechtsspezifische Betrachtung von gesellschaftspolitischen Angelegenheiten nicht für richtig hält. Forscherinnen und Schriftstellerinnen wie Elif Şafak und Ferhunde Özbay kritisieren, dass diese republikanistisch orientierten Akademikerinnen in der Türkei der Meinung sind, sie würden aufgrund ihres Geschlechts kaum benachteiligt:

> Wenn wir das, was uns widerfährt, nicht als Frau, sondern aus männlicher Ideologie heraus betrachten, ist die Diskriminierung nicht so ersichtlich. Die Diskriminierung setzt sich aus kleinen Erfahrungen in unserem täglichen Leben zusammen. In der Türkei wurden in den 1930er Jahren Akademikerinnen voller Überzeugung aktiv: Sie glaubten von Herzen daran, eine neue Gesellschaft zu schaffen, waren fleißig und dabei auch der Regierung gegenüber treu, die ihnen diese Gelegenheit ermöglichte (...) Dieses Gefühl der Treue wurde von Generation zu Generation übertragen, durch die Behauptung, die Republik sei bedroht, gefestigt und mit der Theorie des „inneren Feindes" gesteigert. Schließlich entstand sowohl in den Gesellschafts- als auch Naturwissenschaften ein neuer Typus: „Treue und missionarische Akademikerinnen". Weder demokratisch, noch objektiv, rational oder wissenschaftlich (...)[16]

Die wichtigste Vertreterin des republikanistischen Frauentyps und somit der Kemalistischen Ideologie ist Afet İnan mit ihren Schriften.[17] Die wichtigste

---

[14] Vgl. Yaprak Zihnioğlu, *Kadınsız İnkılap*, 17-18.
[15] Vgl. Anm. 10.
[16] Elif Şafak, „Bilim Kadınları" [Gelehrtinnen], in: *Zaman Gazetesi*, 23.05.2006: http://www.zaman.com.tr/yazar.do?yazino=287473
[17] Vgl. Yeşim Arat, „Türkiye'de Kadın Çalışmaları: Kemalizm'den Feminizme" [Frauenarbeit in der Türkei: Vom Kemalismus zum Feminismus], in: *Kadın Çalışmaları Dergisi*, Nr. 3, 2006.

Women's traditions
Frauentraditionen
Tradiciones de mujeres

Arbeit İnans ist *Atatürk und die Erlangung der Frauenrechte in der Türkei und die Rechte und Pflichten der türkischen Frau im Verlauf der Geschichte.*[18]

Die „zweite Welle" der Frauenbewegung

Die zweite Welle der Frauenbewegung hat sich nach 1973 zur linken Bewegung bekannt. Die Vertreterinnen dieser Welle deuteten die Unterdrückung der Frau als Folge der kapitalistischen Ordnung und Ausbeutung und konnten dabei den Einfluss des patriarchalischen Systems nicht erkennen, dessen Wurzeln noch viel weiter zurückliegen, als die des Kapitalismus. Sie glaubten fest daran, dass ihre Befreiung durch den sozialistischen Kampf verwirklicht werden würde, in dem „Frau und Mann Seite an Seite" stünden.[19] Die marxistischen Feministinnen, die noch immer dieses Argument anführen, beschuldigen die sozialistischen Feministinnen, die eine Frauenbewegung außerhalb der linken Männerbewegung schufen, dadurch die Bewegung gespalten zu haben.[20]

Die „dritte Welle" der Frauenbewegung

Die dritte Welle der feministischen Bewegung fiel infolge des Militärputsches von 1980 in eine Phase der Selbsthinterfragung. Dieser neue Zustand brachte eine aktive Frauenbewegung hervor und ermöglichte die Einbeziehung von Frauen, die anderen Ideologien als der Linken angehörten. Nacheinander wurden Vereine und Arbeitsgruppen gebildet, die sich mit verschiedenen gesellschaftspolitischen Problemen auseinander setzten. Entscheidend waren dafür der Einfluss des Demokratisierungsprozesses und die Stärkung der Zivilgesellschaft in der Amtsperiode des Ministerpräsidenten Turgut Özal. Die Ratifizierung des UN-Übereinkommens zur Beseitigung jeder Form von Diskriminierung der Frau (CEDAW) von Seiten der Türkei im Jahre 1985 und die Beschlüsse der 3. Weltfrauenkonferenz in Nairobi waren ebenfalls bedeutsam.

---

[18] *Atatürk ve Türk Kadın Haklarının Kazanılması. Tarih Boyuncu Türk Kadınının Hak ve Görevleri*, 1964 (4. Auflage: İstanbul 1982).

[19] Führende Frauen der *linken* Bewegung wie Stella Ovadia, Handan Koç, Firdevs Gümüşoğlu und Yüksel Selek haben dies in verschiedenen Zeitungsinterviews nach den 80er Jahren deutlich zur Sprache gebracht. Vgl. Nurten Kaya, „80 ve 90'larda Türkiye'de Feminist Hareketler" [Feministische Bewegungen in der Türkei in den 80er und 90er Jahren], in: *Kadın Çalışmaları Dergisi*, Nr. 3, 2006.

[20] Ebd. 19.

In dieser Phase der Neustrukturierung bemühten sich Frauenorganisationen, lockerere demokratische und unbürokratische Strukturen aufzubauen, in denen gleichberechtigte Beziehungen angestrebt wurden. Auch wenn ihre Erfolge diesbezüglich kritikwürdig sind, muss eingeräumt werden, dass die von ihnen geschaffenen Strukturen im Vergleich zu denen anderer Nichtregierungsorganisationen weniger bürokratisch sind.

Dennoch fällt es den heutigen Frauenrechtlerinnen in der Türkei aufgrund ihrer ausgeprägten nationalistischen und laizistischen Einstellung sehr schwer, kurdische – sowie religiöse – Feministinnen einzubeziehen. Sie sind der Auffassung, dass die Religion hauptsächlich dazu beiträgt, die Frau als Mensch zweiter Klasse einzustufen. Sie beziehen äußerst ungern religiöse Frauen in ihre gemeinsamen Aktivitäten mit ein und nehmen sich widerwillig ihrer Probleme an. Dass sich diese feministischen Organisationen – abgesehen von einem kleinen Teil, der sich gegen das aktuelle und heiß diskutierte Kopftuchverbot an Universitäten positionierte – regierungsloyal zeigen, bringt ihre Haltung klar auf einen Nenner. Laut der bekannten linken Feministin Ayşe Durakbaşa ist „die Gemeinsamkeit der türkischen Feministinnen womöglich ihre Unwissenheit und ihr Desinteresse am Islam".[21]

Muslimische Frauenforschung: historische Perspektiven
Dies ist eine zutreffende Feststellung. Entgegen aller Behauptungen der laizistischen Feministinnen in Europa und der Türkei bietet der Koran aber, auch wenn in ihm ein dominant patriarchalisches Bild deutlich wird, muslimischen Frauen eine Grundlage, um innerhalb der Religion eine feministische Haltung zu entwickeln, da er der Frau die gleichen Verantwortungen und Werte wie dem Manne zugesteht. Diese Auffassung blieb auch in der Praxis der frühislamischen Gesellschaft bestehen, obwohl die *sahâba*[22] sich von Zeit zu Zeit dieser emanzipatorischen Entwicklung widersetzten. Ein Beweis für diese Auffassung ist, dass Aisha, die Frau des Propheten, eine der wichtigsten Personen

---

[21] Ayşe Durakbaşa, „Türkiye'de Kimlik Siyaseti Üzerine" [Über die Identitätspolitik in der Türkei], in: Aynur İlyasoğlu, *Örtülü Kimlik* [Verschleierte Identität] (Metis Yayınları: Istanbul 1994), 8.
[22] *Sahâba*: Gefährten des Propheten Muhammad, die zu seiner Zeit lebten und gläubig waren. Muslime messen ihnen besondere Bedeutung bei, da sie die Ersten waren, die sich der islamischen Religion annahmen und sie den folgenden Generationen überlieferten.

Women's traditions
Frauentraditionen
Tradiciones de mujeres

innerhalb der Hadithwissenschaften[23] ist. Sie gehört bis heute zu den wichtigsten Hadithüberliefernden. In ihren Hadithüberlieferungen[24] und Koraninterpretationen ist eine deutliche Frauenperspektive zu erkennen. Bemerkenswert ist auch, dass später, als im Mittelalter in Europa bestimmte Frauen als „Hexen" bezeichnet und verbrannt wurden, so viele muslimische Überlieferinnen und berühmte Frauen im Bereich der Kunst und Wissenschaft hervortraten, dass sie zum Thema einzelner Bücher wurden. Einige erstaunliche statistische Informationen können das belegen.[25]

Der große Hadithgelehrte Al-Mundhirî (656/1258) erwähnt in seinem Werk *Al-Takmila* („Die Vollendung") über 200 Hadithwissenschaftlerinnen (*muhadditha*)[26], wobei dieses Werk lediglich einen Zeitraum von hundert Jahren abdeckt. Allen voran erwähnt besonders der berühmte Al-Dhahabî (748/1347) in seinen Werken die meisten gelehrte Frauen. In seinem Buch *Mu'dscham schuyûkh al-Dhahabî* (Konkordanz der Lehrenden von al-Dhahabî) erzählt er über seine Lehrer. Er berichtet, dass unter ihnen 104 Lehrerinnen waren, und führt detailliert aus, wo und in welcher Form er von ihnen unterrichtet wurde. Nach Al-Dhahabî erwähnt Al-Sakhavî in seinem Werk *Al-Daw' al-lâmi'*

---

[23] Hadithwissenschaft: Eine der fundamentalen Wissenschaften der islamischen Theologie, die sich mit Aussagen und Verhaltensweisen des Propheten beschäftigt und sie in Textform (*Hadith*, pl. *Hadithe*) tradiert. Hadithe wurden von Generation zu Generation übertragen, sehr früh verschriftlicht und entwickelten sich dabei zu einem Wissenschaftszweig.

[24] Eines der wichtigsten Beispiele hierfür ist die Kritik von Aisha an dem bekannten „Unglücks"-Hadith in islamischen Quellen. Sie widersetzte sich dem Hadith „Das Unglück liegt in drei Dingen: Dem Haus, der Frau und dem Pferd" von Abu Khurayra (ein Prophetengefährte, der die meisten Hadithe überlieferte) und sagte, er habe es falsch gehört, der Gesandte Gottes habe vor diesem Satz „Gott verdammt die Juden, denn sie sagen:..." und kritisierte so den berühmten Überlieferer Abu Khurayra. In der Hadithwissenschaft ist Aisha eine der ersten, die im Sinne der Textkritik die Technik des Koran- und Hadtihvergleichs anwendet. Vgl. Bedruddin Ez-Zerkeşi, *Hz. Aişe'nin Sahabeye Yönelttiği Eleştiriler* [Die Kritik Aishas an den Sahaba] (Kitabiyat: Ankara 2000), 42. Außerdem vgl. Hidayet Şefkatli Tuksal, *Ataerkil Söylemin İslam Geleneğindeki İzdüşümleri* [Spuren des frauenfeindlichen Diskurses in der islamischen Tradition] (Kitabiyat: Ankara 2003), 218.

[25] An dieser Stelle möchte ich Herrn Kazım Sever danken, der mir Ergebnisse seiner Promotionsarbeit zugänglich machte, die bald unter dem Titel *Gelehrte Frauen in der Geschichte des Islam* auf Deutsch und Türkisch erscheinen wird. Für nähere Informationen wende man sich an diese Arbeit.

[26] *Muhaddith/muhaddita*: Bezeichnung sowohl für diejenigen, die die Hadithe von Generation zu Generation überliefern, als auch für die, die sich mit diesem Überlieferungsgut, vor allem mit seiner Authentizität befassen. Diese Arbeit bezeichnet eine wissenschaftliche und ehrwürdige Tätigkeit, die einer besonderen Befähigung bedurfte.

(„Leuchtendes Licht") 1075 gelehrte Frauen. Eine jüngere Arbeit hierzu ist das im Jahre 1878 veröffentlichte zweibändige Werk von Hacı Mehmet Zihni Efendi, *Meşâhir-i Nisâ'* („Berühmte Frauen"). Er stellt dort etwa tausend Frauen vor, die sich mit verschiedenen Bereichen der Hadithwissenschaften, der Dichtung, der Medizin bis hin zur Magie beschäftigten. Ein weiteres wichtiges Werk in diesem Bereich ist das gleichnamige fünfbändige, im Jahre 1909 verfasste Werk von Umar Rıdâ Kahhâla. Er führt ungefähr 2800 Frauen an, die auf verschiedenen Gebieten Berühmtheit erlangten. In diesem Zusammenhang gibt es noch zahlreiche weitere Werke. Schon die Existenz dieser Frauen, die in diesen und anderen Werken Erwähnung finden, steht im absoluten Widerspruch zu der Behauptung, die Frau stünde in der ganzen Geschichte des Islam an zweiter Stelle.

Suchprozesse muslimischer Frauen nach 1980

Die offenere Atmosphäre, die in der Zeit Özals[27] nach 1980 im Zuge der Demokratisierung und Liberalisierung vorherrschte, in der Kopftuchträgerinnen begannen, an Universitäten und im Arbeitsleben eine Rolle zu spielen, führte dazu, dass auch in diesem Milieu eine Frauenbewegung einsetzte. Diese Frauen lehnten meistens die Bezeichnung „Feministin" ab. Dennoch hinterfragten sie die aktuelle Situation der Frau[28] und suchten nach Lösungsvorschlägen. Aufgrund der westlichen Herkunft des Begriffes „Feminismus", des kritischen Umganges der Feministinnen mit der Religion und der Aussagen radikaler Feministinnen, die mit der Religion nicht zu vereinbaren sind, schreckt sie der Ausdruck „Feministin" ab.[29] Wenn man aber ihre Kritik, die sie nicht nur an religiöse Männer, sondern auch an herrschende Islamauffassungen richten, und den Wandel, den sie durchleben, analysiert, erkennt man, dass ihre Aktivitäten im Grunde auf die Verteidigung von Frauenrechten zielen.

Die Ende 1995 in Ankara gegründete *Başkent Kadın Platformu* (Hauptstadt Frauenplattform) zeigt sich im Zusammenhang mit diesem Thema mutiger und

---

[27] Turgut Özal, der nach dem Militärputsch von 1980 gewählt wurde, verfolgte eine Politik, die den Übergang zur zivilen Regierung beschleunigen sollte.
[28] Vgl. Cihan Aktaş, *Bacı'dan Bayan'a* [Von Schwester zu Dame] (Pınar Yayınları: Istanbul 2001); Fatma Karabıyık Barbarosoğlu, „Babalar Günü Münasebetiyle Piknik Babası" [Der Picknick-Papa anlässlich des Vatertags], in: *Yeni Şafak Gazetesi*, 17.06.2008: http://yenisafak.com.tr/Yazarlar/?i=11447&y=FatmaKBarbarosoglu
[29] Zu diesem Thema vgl. Ülkü Özel Akagündüz, „İslami Feminizm: Adı var Kendi yok" [Islamischer Feminismus: Ein Begriff ohne Inhalt], in: *Derkenar Edebiyat Dergisi*, 17.12.2006: http://derkenar.wordpress.com/2006/12/17/islami-feminizm-adi-var-kendi-yok/

Women's traditions
Frauentraditionen
Tradiciones de mujeres

erfüllte später eine wichtige Funktion dabei, die Stimme der religiösen Frauen innerhalb der Frauenbewegung zu vertreten. Hatice Güler, die zu den Gründungsmitgliedern des Vereins zählt und eine Zeit lang den Vorsitz innehatte, äußert sich im Mitteilungsblatt des Vereins, das zum zehnjährigen Bestehen herausgegeben wurde, folgendermaßen zu dessen Gründung:

> ... Ich erinnere mich an den Beginn unserer Gemeinschaft; wir waren hauptsächlich Frauen in ihren Dreißigern, die ihre Ausbildung abgeschlossen hatten, verheiratet waren und Kinder hatten; und ein Teil von uns war im Arbeitsleben. Einige Frauen unter uns hatten eine akademische Laufbahn begonnen. Wir tauschten Dinge aus, die wir gelesen hatten, und diskutierten Themen, die auf der Welt und im Land aktuell waren. Einerseits versuchten wir die Rolle der Ehefrau und Mutter, die wir im Laufe des Lebens übernommen hatten, zu erfüllen und andererseits hinterfragten wir die traditionelle Bedeutung, die diesen Rollen auferlegt wurde. Dazu kamen noch Schwierigkeiten, die das Arbeitsleben mit sich brachte (...). Seit der Entstehung dieser Plattform stießen viele Theologinnen hinzu, die mittlerweile Mitglieder sind. – Diese kamen u.a. zu folgenden Forschungsergebnissen: Der Einfluss der patriarchalischen Auslegung der religiösen Traditionen auf die Vorstellung von der Rolle der Frau und der Beziehung zwischen Männern und Frauen innerhalb der türkischen Gesellschaft ist nicht gering. Im Hinterfragen solcher Stereotypen, die zunächst in Form einer Art Unterhaltung geschah, bei der Probleme besprochen wurden, entstand die erste Idee und emotionale Vorbereitungsphase, die später zu einer Plattform weiterentwickelt werden sollte.
>
> Der „Aufruf zur Organisation" von der 1994 in Istanbul gegründeten Gökkuşağı Kadın Platformu (Regenbogen Frauenplattform) erweiterte unseren Horizont und brachte die Idee einer Organisation wie die einer „Plattform" hervor. Wir bedanken uns hiermit erneut bei Dr. Gülsen Ataseven und ihrem Team, die uns ermutigte und uns diese Organisationsform empfahl, welche die Möglichkeit bot, Frauen aus verschiedenen Bereichen in flexiblen Rahmen zusammen kommen zu lassen. Man kann natürlich nicht behaupten, dass am Anfang alles einfach war ... Einigen gefiel es nicht, dass Frauen einer Organisation beitraten, die unabhängig von ihnen war. Diese Frauen konnten ja, wenn sie unbedingt wollten, bei Stiftungen und Vereinen oder bei den Frauensektionen der Parteien arbeiten; was waren schon Frauenrechte; man könnte sich an Organisationen beteiligen, die im Bereich der Menschenrechte gegründet worden waren. Eigentlich wäre es besser, wenn sie zu Hause blieben, denn schließlich hätten sie ohnehin alle Rechte bekommen (...). Sie sollten bloß nicht zu Feministinnen werden?![30]

---

[30] Hatice Güler, „Uzun Yılların Kısa Hikayesi" [Die kurze Geschichte der langen Jahre], in: *Dünden Bugüne Başkent Kadın Platformu* (Oktober 1995, Mai 2007), Ankara 2007, 6. Der ganze Artikel ist im Internet abrufbar: http://www.baskentkadin.org/bizkimiz/onuzunyilinhikayesi.htm

Mit der Gründung der Regenbogen Frauenplattform und der Hauptstadt Frauenplattform haben praktizierende muslimische Frauen in der Türkei Traueninitiativen gegründet, die von Männern, von religiösen Verbänden und Vereinen, von Parteien jeglicher Couleur unabhängig waren und sich somit ihrer Kontrolle entzogen. Dies verdient insofern große Beachtung, weil es in der Türkei ein Novum darstellt. Diese unabhängige Organisation von Frauen wurde insbesondere von vielen Männern und auch von einigen Frauen mit großer Skepsis und Misstrauen beobachtet und mit dem Etikett des Feminismus versehen, was in diesen religiösen Kreisen einem Schimpfwort gleich kommt. Dennoch hat insbesondere die Hauptstadt Frauenplattform bis in das türkische Parlament und im Ausland mit ihren Forderungen und Aktivitäten ihrer Stimme Gehör verschafft und große Erfolge erzielt.[31]

Die Promotionsarbeit über frauenfeindliche Hadithe von Hidayet Şefkatli Tuksal, Gründungsmitglied und zeitweilige Vorsitzende der Hauptstadt Frauenplattform, mit dem Titel „Spuren des frauenfeindlichen Diskurses in der Islamischen Tradition"[32] zeigte weitergehende Auswirkungen als eine gewöhnliche wissenschaftliche Arbeit auf diesem Gebiet. Es gelang ihr innerhalb der religiösen Kreise, eine sichtbare Veränderung im Hinblick auf deren patriarchalische Auslegungen des Koran und der Hadithe zu erlangen. Diese Doktorarbeit entstand in der Zeit, in der das Kopftuchverbot an Universitäten gelockert wurde.[33] Ähnliche Arbeiten wurden leider dadurch unterbunden, dass sehr viele kopftuchtragende Mädchen und Frauen von den Universitäten ferngehalten wurden.[34]

---

[31] Ermutigt durch die Gründung dieser unabhängigen Organisationen haben sich in der gesamten Republik mit der Unterstützung der Hauptstadt Frauenplattform unabhängige Fraueninitiativen nach dem gleichen Muster gegründet. Diese Frauenforen sind eng miteinander vernetzt und führen gemeinsame Aktivitäten durch. Sie treffen sich einmal im Jahr und diskutieren aktuelle politische, soziale, religiöse und wirtschaftliche Themen aus der Perspektive religiöser Frauen. Darüber hinaus hat die Hauptstadt Frauenplattform eine Brückenfunktion zwischen säkularen Feministinnen und religiösen Aktivistinnen übernommen.

[32] Hidayet Şefkatli Tuksal, *Kadın Karşıtı Söylemin İslam Geleneğindeki İzdüşümleri* (Kitabiyat: Ankara 2003).

[33] Das Kopftuchverbot, das an Universitäten angewandt wird, hat im Grunde keine gesetzliche Grundlage. Es existiert lediglich für Personen im öffentlichen Dienst eine Regelung zur Kleiderordnung. Je nach Haltung der Regierung wird die Umsetzung des Gesetzes willkürlich gelockert oder verschärft.

[34] Für weitere Informationen, wie und in welchem Ausmaß die Gesetze die Frauen in der Türkei beeinflusst haben, siehe die Untersuchung der Hazar Gruppe für ANAR: www.hazargrubu.org/basortusudosyasi.htm

Dass mit dem Ausschluss der Kopftuchträgerinnen aus öffentlichen Räumen in der Türkei ein wichtiges Potential an emanzipatorisch eingestellten Frauen ausgegrenzt wird, zeigen die Untersuchungen der Soziologin Nilüfer Göle zum Thema Kopftuch. In ihnen wird deutlich, dass kopftuchtragende Frauen nicht notwendig politisch-islamistisch orientiert sind. Vielmehr kehrt in ihnen die muslimische Frau auf die historische Bühne zurück. Bisher Unterdrücktes sucht sich neue Wege der Darstellung. Es weist Ähnlichkeiten mit feministischen, Umwelt- und ethnischen Bewegungen auf und widersetzt sich der globalen und monistischen Konzeptualisierung der Modernität.[35]

> Das Kopftuch islamischer Mädchen unterscheidet sich grundlegend von dem traditionellen Tuch ihrer Mütter. Während das traditionelle Tuch die ungebildete, passive und dem Haus verbundene Frau symbolisiert, steht das neue Tuch oder Turban, wie es in der Öffentlichkeit genannt wird, für das junge, städtische und gebildete Mädchen. Während das erste viel mehr vormodern als antimodern war, symbolisiert das zweite aktive und sichtbare Akteurinnen einer Bewegung, die sich als Alternative zur westlichen Moderne sieht. Die Präsenz kopftuchtragender Mädchen führt zur Hinterfragung sowohl des traditionellen islamischen Verständnisses, das die Frau im privaten Bereich definiert, als auch des homogenen laizistischen öffentlichen Raumes, der durch die kemalistische Elite entstanden ist.[36]

Die wichtigste Eigenschaft dieser neuen islamischen Akteurinnen ist laut Göle die Tatsache, dass sie einer Mittelschicht angehören, die gebildet, berufstätig und städtisch ist. Daher würde ihre Beschreibung als klassische passive muslimische Frau die Wirklichkeit verfehlen. Diese Frauen hinterfragen sowohl ihre biologische und gesellschaftliche Identität als auch ihre festen gesellschaftlichen Normen und wollen ihre Identität neu definieren. Deshalb kann die Präsenz der islamischen Frau in der heutigen muslimischen türkischen Gesellschaft nicht nur durch Glauben und Kopftuch erklärt werden, sondern ist ein Phänomen, das in ein kulturelles Begriffssystem eingebettet werden muss. Denn die Frauen begnügen sich nicht damit, ihren Kopf zu bedecken, sondern schaffen einen neuen Lebensstil, veranschaulichen unterschiedliche gesellschaftliche Alltagspraktiken und versuchen in der modernen Stadt ein konsequentes Glaubens- und Lebenssystem zu entwickeln. Wenn man diese

---

[35] Vgl. Nilüfer Göle, *İslamın Yeni Kamusal Yüzleri – Bir Atölye Çalışması* [Die neuen öffentlichen Gesichter des Islam – Eine Workshop-Untersuchung] (Metis Yayınları: Istanbul 1999), 29.

[36] Ebd. 42f.

selbstbewusste Repräsentanz muslimischer Frauen in den öffentlichen Räumen als eine neue Bewegung begreift, muss auch erkannt werden, dass dabei eine neue Form muslimischer Identität entwickelt wird.

Dennoch darf auch dies nicht darüber hinweg täuschen, dass die islamische Frauenbewegung eine ausgegrenzte und marginalisierte Bewegung darstellt. Laut Nilüfer Göle lässt sich diese Bewegung weniger als „klassische künstliche Krise" oder als „Ausdruck gemeinsamer Interessen" charakterisieren als durch das Paradigma neuer sozialer Bewegungen.[37] Soziologische Phänomene durch bestimmte Paradigmen zu erklären, birgt meines Erachtens die Gefahr vereinfachter Deutung. Dadurch wird wenig zu ihrem Verständnis beigetragen. Komplizierte Phänomene werden auf diese Weise in einfache Schemata gepresst, wodurch die Bildung von Stereotypen gefördert und die Stigmatisierung und Ausgrenzung bestimmter Gruppen erleichtert wird. Solcherart diskriminierende Einstellungen zum Thema Kopftuch sind heutzutage nicht nur in der Türkei zu beobachten, sondern überall, wo es ein Streitthema darstellt. Auf diese Weise wird das Problem nicht gelöst, sondern gänzlich in eine Sackgasse getrieben.

Im Unterschied dazu eröffnet Defne Suman eine neue Sichtweise des öffentlichen Raumes. Ihr zufolge

> weist der öffentliche Raum der Republikzeit Ähnlichkeit mit dem öffentlichen Raum der liberalen Bourgeoisie von Habermas auf. Vor allem sind beide auf weltliche und globale Begriffe gegründet. Der Eintritt in den öffentlichen Raum ist sowohl im Habermas'schen Modell als auch in der Türkei nur durch das Ablegen der persönlichen Eigenschaften und einem Verhalten gemäß globaler Normen möglich. Eine weitere Gemeinsamkeit besteht darin, dass beide Pluralität ablehnen und glauben machen, in der Gesellschaft könne Fortschritt nur durch einen öffentlichen Raum erreicht werden. Dagegen wird Demokratie, wie Nancy Fraser zeigt, nicht durch Ignorieren von Vielfältigkeit, sondern durch ihre Hervorhebung erlangt.[38]

Es bleibt festzuhalten, dass der Staat und die Mehrheit der Feministinnen sich in einer Definition des öffentlichen Raumes treffen, in der die Grenzen der

---

[37] Ebd. 44f.
[38] Vgl. Defne Suman, *Feminizm, İslam ve Kamusal Alan* [Feminismus, Islam und öffentlicher Raum], in: Nilüfer Göle, *İslamın Yeni Kamusal Yüzleri – Bir Atölye Çalışması* [Die neuen öffentlichen Gesichter des Islam – Eine Workshop-Untersuchung] (Metis Yayınları: Istanbul 1999), 72f.

Women's traditions
Frauentraditionen
Tradiciones de mujeres

Freiheiten – seien es geschlechtliche, ethnische, kulturelle oder religiöse – auf Ablehnung der Differenzen basieren.[39]

Die Entwicklung einer gesunden Persönlichkeitsstruktur braucht die Möglichkeit, eine eigene, von anderen unterschiedene Identität zu entwickeln, die in Harmonie mit anderen Identitäten leben kann. Die Unterdrückung oder Ablehnung von Identitätsmerkmalen führt hingegen dazu, dass im Blick auf unterdrückte Merkmale eine radikale Position eingenommen wird und dadurch eine Entfernung von der Normalität geschieht. Die aktuellen Diskussionen um das Kopftuch haben ein hohes Reizpotential aufgebaut und dazu geführt, dass die Menschen sich genötigt sahen, Partei für das Kopftuch zu ergreifen. Auf jeden Fall blockiert eine Beibehaltung seines Verbotes die Entwicklung von Frauen. Sie werden auf diese Weise aus dem öffentlichen Leben ferngehalten und dazu gezwungen, ins Haus zurückzukehren, um dort wie eine Gefangene zu verharren. In der Türkei wurden Frauen schon immer sowohl als Mittel der Modernisierung als auch der Hinwendung zur Religiosität benutzt; der Kampf wurde seit jeher und noch immer über ihre Köpfe hinweg geführt. Ayşe Durakbaşa beschreibt diesen Kampf um Modernität und Traditionalismus, der auf dem Rücken der Frau ausgetragen wird, wie folgt:

> In den politischen Programmen der Linken und der Rechten wurde dieses Thema als „Frauenproblem" behandelt und es wurde zum Grundsatz, den Status der Frau im Rahmen des Fortschritts und der Entwicklung zu erhöhen. Laut dieser modernisierungsfreudigen Denkweise, deren Begriffe und Rahmen hauptsächlich von Männern bestimmt wurden, wurden Frauen als ein „Problem" angesehen, das korrigiert werden musste. Die Rückständigkeit der Gesellschaft wurde auf die Unwissenheit der Frau zurückgeführt. Demgegenüber will die feministische Geschichtsschreibung die Frauen nicht als Objekte, sondern als Subjekte der Geschichte hervorheben und empfiehlt, sie nicht als unschuldige Opfer, sondern als

---

[39] An dieser Stelle soll eine neuere frauenpolitische Entwicklung erwähnt werden. Am 13. März 2008 haben sich rund 1500 Akademikerinnen und Schriftstellerinnen unterschiedlicher Couleur zusammengefunden und sich mit einer Resolution unter der Überschrift „wenn eine von uns nicht frei ist, sind wir alle gefangen" Gehör verschafft und gegen das Kopftuchverbot an den Universitäten ihren Unmut zum Ausdruck gebracht. Das Interessante an dieser Entwicklung ist, dass unter den Unterzeichnerinnen Kurdinnen, Alevitinnen, orthodoxe Muslimas, Laizistinnen und sich offen bekennende lesbische Frauen befanden. Dies ist ein absolutes Novum für die Türkei. Ca. 150 Aktivistinnen unter ihnen haben sich dann zu einer E-Gruppe formiert, die sich täglich schreibt. Dort diskutieren sie mit großer Offenheit kontrovers über ihre Ansichten und sind bemüht, einander besser zu verstehen. Diese Gruppe kann für die Zukunft der feministischen Debatte ein positives Beispiel und ein Wegweiser sein.

Macherinnen von Geschichte zu definieren. Aus diesem Blickpunkt betrachtet stellen wir fest, dass die Modernisierungsgeschichte in der Türkei im Hinblick auf die Frauen noch nicht geschrieben wurde. Historische Untersuchungen enthalten beispielsweise nichts darüber, wie die kemalistischen Reformen von Frauen verschiedener Generationen erlebt wurden, wie sie sich auf die Wahl und Lebensweise der Frauen auswirkten und zu welchen Widersprüchen diese Reformen bei den Frauen führten. Wie gut, dass diese Frage von RomanautorInnen gestellt wurde. Die Romanfigur *Aysel* von Adalet Ağaoğlu hat sich wie eine historische Figur in unser Gedächtnis eingeprägt.[40]

In einer beeindruckenden Passage aus einem Artikel von Adalet Ağaoğlu in der Zeitung Cumhuriyet, der kurz nach dem Tode von Mevhibe İnönü, der Frau des zweiten türkischen Staatspräsidenten İsmet İnönü[41], veröffentlicht wurde, heißt es:

…ich denke oft an sie, an die Frauen, die bewegte Zeiten durchlebten, aber nie darüber sprachen. Warum sind „diese Frauen" diejenigen, für deren Gefühle man sich am wenigsten interessiert? Warum hat man sich nicht intensiv mit ihnen beschäftigt und über sie geschrieben? Und wenn, warum nur aus Sicht ihrer Aufgaben in der Gesellschaft?

Wie konnten diese Frauen zu einem Zeitpunkt, der tatsächlich für die Geschichte wichtig war, die Last eines ganz neuen Lebens dermaßen unvorbereitet und mit ihren schwachen Schultern tragen? Vieles war für die Frauen ein Problem, was für die Männer weniger schlimm war, wenn überhaupt nicht direkt ihre „Ehre" schädigte. Sie waren Frauen, die nicht aus dem Gleichgewicht gerieten und denen es gelang, den bösen Blicken auszuweichen. Frauen, die noch gestern Arabisch schrieben und heute das Lateinalphabet beherrschen müssen, von denen erwartet wird, dass sie sich unter Kontrolle haben, wenn sie mit „fremden Männern" tanzen und selbst dann angezogen aussehen, wenn sie den Schleier ablegen.

Das Beispiel von Mevhibe İnönü erinnert uns an zahlreiche Frauen, die mit uns verwandt sind. Unsere Mütter, Tanten und sogar unsere Großmütter aus vorheriger Generation … Modernistische Männer wollten immer bestimmen, wann und wie eine Frau modern und traditionell sein sollte, und haben dies meistens auch getan.[42]

---

[40] Ayşe Durakbaşa: „Türkiye'de Kimlik Siyaseti Üzerine" [Über die Identitätspolitik in der Türkei], in: Aynur İlyasoğlu, *Örtülü Kimlik* [Verschleierte Identität] (Metis Yayınları: Istanbul 1994), 8-9.
[41] İnönü war ein Waffen- und Revolutionsfreund des Staatsgründers Atatürk.
[42] Adalet Ağaoğlu, *Karşılaşmalar* [Begegnungen] (Yapı Kredi: İstanbul 1993), 148.

Women's traditions
Frauentraditionen
Tradiciones de mujeres

Auch heute wird leider der Identitätskonflikt der modernistischen und religiösen Männer zu Lasten der Frauen ausgetragen. Trotz allem ist die Frauenbewegung in der Türkei – im Gegensatz zu der Weltfrauenbewegung, die aus verschiedenen Gründen an Geschwindigkeit verloren hat – eine starke Bewegung. Auch wenn sie sich schwer tut, kurdische und religiöse Frauen mit ihren jeweiligen Identitäten zu akzeptieren, und auch wenn sie bei manch wichtigen Themen aufgrund ihrer noch nicht gefestigten gesellschaftlichen Identitätsstrukturen keinen Konsens erreichen konnte, hat sie doch recht akzeptable Erfolge zu verzeichnen. Dem Konto dieser Frauen sind die Verbesserungen im Zivilrecht vom Jahre 2001 gutzuschreiben. Die Organisationen, die es sich zur Aufgabe gemacht haben, die Umsetzung dieser Gesetzesänderungen zu beobachten, sind fest entschlossen, der Alptraum jener Männer zu sein, die wollen, dass diese Gesetze lediglich auf dem Papier gelten.

Der Beitrag bietet einen Überblick über die erste, zweite und dritte Welle der Frauenbewegung in der Türkei und betrachtet jeweilige religiöse Implikationen dieser Phasen. Er beginnt bei der Osmanischen Frauenbewegung, deren Anfänge auf das Ende der Tanzimat-Periode (Ende des 19. Jh.) zurückzuführen sind, führt über die Entwicklung von Frauenrechten während der Kemalistischen Reformen über die Unruhen nach den 70er Jahren und dem Putsch vom 12. September 1980 bis in die Gegenwart. In ihr diagnostiziert die Autorin eine starke und engagierte türkische Frauenbewegung, die in vieler Hinsicht hoffnungsvolle Aufbrüche verspricht. Insbesondere die Debatte um das Kopftuch zeigt, dass dabei ein neues, stark von Frauen bestimmtes islamisches Selbstbewusstsein entsteht, das eine eigenständige Position für sich in Anspruch nimmt.

This contribution provides a review of the first, second and third stages of the women's movement in Turkey and examines the religious implications specific to each phase. It starts with the Ottoman women's movement, the beginnings of which can be traced back to the end of the Tanzimat period (end of the 19th century), and continues with the development of women's rights during the Kemalist reforms, the disturbances after the 1970s and the putsch of September 12th 1980 though to the present. In this development, the author recognises a strong, committed Turkish women's movement promising hopeful new beginnings in many respects. Especially the debate about headscarves demonstrates that a new Islamic self-confidence is coming into being that is strongly influenced by women and claims to exist in its own right.

En este artículo se resumen las tres olas del movimiento de mujeres en Turquía y se analizan las implicaciones religiosas de las mismas. La primera fase la constituye el movimiento de mujeres osmanas, que surgió al final del período del Tanzimat (a finales del siglo XIX); luego se analiza la situación de los derechos de la mujer en el período de las reformas kemalistas, pasando luego por los desórdenes después de los años 70 y el golpe del 12 de septiembre de 1980, hasta llegar al presente. La autora diagnostica un fuerte movimiento de mujeres turcas muy comprometido, y muy prometedor desde varios puntos de vista. En especial el debate sobre el velo demuestra que está surgiendo una nueva autoconsciencia islámica acuñada por las mujeres y que reclama ser reconocida como algo autónomo.

Nuriye Duran Özsoy (*1964), 1982-1987 Studium an der Theologischen Fakultät der Universität Ankara. Ab 1987 Religions- und Arabischlehrerin in verschiedenen Schulen. Seit 1996 Mitbegründerin und Mitglied der Hauptstadt-Frauenplattform (2003-2005 Vorsitzende). Seit 2007 Mitglied der Gesellschaft zur Förderung der Islamstudien (GEFIS). 2009 Mitbegründerin und Mitglied des Kompetenzzentrums Muslima Rhein Main (KoZeMa). Forschungsschwerpunkte: Frauenbewegung in der Türkei, Frauenfrage im Islam, Orientalistische Koranforschung. Laufende Magisterarbeit über *Kritische Analyse der orientalistischen Arbeiten über die Inhalte des Koran am Beispiel der Zeitschrift „Der Islam"*. Verheiratet, 2 Kinder.

Naime Çakir

Muslimische Frauen in Deutschland: zwischen Viktimisierung, Kriminalisierung, Rechtfertigung und Selbstbehauptung

Das Bild der bekennenden Muslima in Deutschland ist im Wesentlichen durch zwei Vorstellungen geprägt: einerseits als vorgestelltes Opfer ihrer männlichen Verwandten, das unterdrückt und entmündigt wird, zum anderen von der der „obskuren Fundamentalistin".[1] Je mehr moderne Musliminnen für sich in Anspruch nahmen, selbst Verantwortung zu übernehmen und somit beispielsweise auch öffentliche Ämter für sich beanspruchten, umso mehr verlor sich das verführerisch-romantizistische Faszinosum, das im 18. Jahrhundert über die Orientalin transportiert wurde. Dagegen wuchs das bedrohlich-fremdscheinende an. So kommt es, dass sich praktizierende muslimische Frauen besonders in jüngerer Zeit zunehmend einem Islamismusverdacht ausgesetzt sehen.

Die Gründe einer allenthalben feststellbaren Re-Islamisierung von Frauen werden aus der vorurteilsbeladenen Beurteilungsperspektive meist entweder auf eine „Verarmung und Perspektivlosigkeit breiter Bevölkerungsschichten" oder – im schlimmsten Fall – auf „hinterhältige Manipulationsstrategien machtgieriger Mullahs" zurückgeführt.[2] Die Möglichkeit, dass die Zuwendung zu ihren religiösen Wurzeln in einem zunehmend emanzipatorischen Interesse muslimischer Frauen selbst begründet sein könnte, wird dagegen kaum in Erwägung gezogen. Für praktizierende muslimische Frauen bedeutet dies, dass sie eine doppelte Rollenzuschreibung erfahren: Sie werden einerseits mit dem latenten islamistischen Fundamentalismusverdacht kriminalisiert und andererseits mit der zugeschriebenen Opferrolle viktimisiert.

---

[1] Irmgard Pinn, „Von der exotischen Haremsschönheit zur obskuren Fundamentalistin", in: Houdda Youssef, (Hg.), *Abschied vom Harem. Selbstbilder – Fremdbilder muslimischer Frauen* (Orlanda Frauenverlag: Berlin 2004), 137-153, hier 137.
[2] Pinn, „Von der exotischen Haremsschönheit zur obskuren Fundamentalistin", 138.

Women's traditions
Frauentraditionen
Tradiciones de mujeres

Dies gilt insbesondere für Frauen, die ein Kopftuch tragen, wie beispielsweise dem folgenden Zitat des hessischen Verfassungsschutzberichtes des Jahres 2004 unter dem Titel *„Das Kopftuch: Die ‚Fahne' für Islamisten"* zu entnehmen ist:

> Für alle Islamisten ist das Kopftuch (sofern sie nicht sogar noch weitergehende Verhüllungen der Frau vorschreiben) ein demonstrativer und zentraler Ausdruck ihrer politischen Überzeugung. In welchem Ausmaß das Kopftuch ein Symbol für den Islamismus ist, zeigte die Islamistin Merve Kavakci, eine ehemalige türkische Parlamentsabgeordnete, als sie das Kopftuch als ‚ihre Fahne' im Kampf bezeichnete. Das Kopftuch ist so für Islamisten ein offensiv eingesetztes Agitationsinstrument zur Verbreitung ihrer Ideologie (...). Vor allem aber ist das Kopftuch eine Manifestation der von Islamisten angestrebten verfassungsfeindlichen und patriarchalischen Ordnung. Das Kopftuch darf nicht isoliert gesehen werden. Es ist nur ein – allerdings wichtiges und zudem augenfälliges – Teilelement einer islamistischen Parallelgesellschaft, in der wesentliche, verfassungsrechtlich verankerte Menschenrechte Frauen vorenthalten bzw. für diese eingeschränkt werden. Der Islamismus,[3] der Frauen rechtlich und faktisch massiv unterprivilegiert oder unterdrückt, steht im diametralen Gegensatz zu den westlichen Verfassungsordnungen mit Gleichberechtigung und freier Persönlichkeitsentfaltung von Frauen und Männern.[4]

Beide Sichtweisen werden weder der Heterogenität noch der Lebensrealität muslimischer Frauen gerecht. Vielmehr zeigen sie, dass auch in den angeblich offenen Gesellschaften Frauenrollen nicht nur nach patriarchalem Grundmuster besetzt werden, sondern auch nach dem Grad der Anerkennung einer ethnischen oder religiösen Minderheit.

---

[3] Es gibt mehrere auf den islamischen Radikalismus bezogene Begriffe. Diese können an dieser Stelle nicht ausreichend definiert werden. Der Begriff des Islamismus meint hier das „ideologische Moment der radikal islamischen Vorstellungen..." (Peter Heine, „Islamismus – ein ideologiegeschichtlicher Überblick", in: Bundesministerium des Innern (Hg.), Islamismus (GGP Media GmbH: Pößneck 2006, 5-20, hier 5). Das Bundesamt für Verfassungsschutz definiert Islamismus wie folgt: „Islamismus ist eine – in sich heterogene – politische, zumeist sozialrevolutionäre Bewegung, die von einer Minderheit der Muslime getragen wird. Ihre Anhänger, die Islamisten, fordern unter Berufung auf den Urislam des 7. Jahrhunderts die ‚Wiederherstellung' einer ‚islamischen Ordnung' als der nach ihrem Verständnis einzig legitimen Staats- und Gesellschaftsform, die alle anders geprägten Ordnungssysteme ersetzen soll." (Bundesamt für Verfassungsschutz, *Islamismus und islamistischer Terrorismus*, in: http://www.verfassungsschutz.de/de/arbeitsfelder/af_islamismus/ – Zugriff am 27. 12. 08).

[4] Hessisches Ministerium des Innern und für Sport (Hg.), *Verfassungsschutz in Hessen*, Bericht 2004, 25.

Die Neo-Muslima

Nökel und Klinkhammer haben um die Jahrtausendwende in Deutschland den Begriff der „Neo-Muslima" und der „exklusivistisch islamischen Lebensführung" in die wissenschaftliche Debatte eingebracht. Sie haben damit dem Stereotyp der unterdrückten muslimischen Frau ein anderes Bild gegenüber gestellt, das sich allerdings bis heute im öffentlichen Diskurs nicht wesentlich durchsetzen konnte.[5] In der Biographie dieser Frauen nimmt eine qualifizierte Berufsausbildung, ihre Familie und das Befolgen der islamischen Gebote die zentrale Rolle ein. Oft wird eine „ideale islamische Lebensweise" konstruiert, die sie mit islamischen Glaubensgrundsätzen begründen. Ihr Anliegen ist es, die im Qur'an enthaltenen Regeln und Gebote, die als unveränderliches Wort Gottes begriffen werden, durch den hermeneutischen Zugang neu zu interpretieren.

Der Qur'an als verschriftlichter Wille Gottes steht hier im Zentrum eines neuen islamischen Selbstverständnisses, das nach Erneuerung durch den Rückbezug auf die Wurzeln des Islam strebt. Gegenüber einem traditionellen Umgang mit islamischen Regeln zeichnet sich ein solches Verständnis durch eine Intellektualisierung und Kodifizierung islamischer Lebensführung aus, die für jeden nachvollziehbar, gültig und verbindlich ist. Im Zuge des im Verlauf der 90er Jahre einsetzenden Islamisierungsprozesses innerhalb der zweiten Generation schien sich dieser Prozess zunehmend für Migrantinnen als produktiv wirkende Anschubkraft zur Selbstbehauptung in der gegebenen sozialen Ordnung zu erweisen.[6]

Ins höhere öffentliche Bildungswesen integriert, definieren Bikulturalität und Bildungskarrieren deren spezifische, von der ersten Generation unterscheidbare soziale Position. In Kombination von Religiosität und moderner Lebensauffassung scheinen diese Frauen einen eigenen authentischen islamischen Weg jenseits traditioneller familiärer Orientierungen und elterlicher Kontrollansprüche gefunden zu haben. In ihm suchen sie nach Möglichkeiten, der

---

[5] Vgl. Sigrid Nökel, „Migration, Islamisierung und Identitätspolitiken: Zur Bedeutung der Religiosität junger Frauen in Deutschland", in: Ingrid Lukatis / Regina Sommer / Christof Wolf (Hg.), *Religion und Geschlechterverhältnis* (leske + budrich: Opladen 2000), 261-270; Gritt Klinkhammer, *Moderne Formen islamischer Lebensführung: Eine qualitativ-empirische Untersuchung zur Religiosität sunnitisch geprägter Türkinnen der zweiten Generation in Deutschland* (diagonal: Marburg 2000), 286 f.

[6] Vgl. Nökel, „Migration, Islamisierung und Identitätspolitiken", 261 ff. Nökel wählt hier den Begriff „neo-islamisch", um ihn, orientiert an einem modernen interpretationsfähigen und interpretationswürdigen Islam, von orthodoxen und staatspolitischen Varianten des Islam abzugrenzen (vgl. ebd. 264).

Women's traditions
Frauentraditionen
Tradiciones de mujeres

marginalisierenden Fremdzuordnung, die sie beständig als Opfer einer zurückgebliebenen patriarchalischen Ordnung identifiziert, zu entgehen. Als sichtbares äußeres Zeichen im Sinne einer „Ästhetisierung" bzw. „Aristokratisierung des Selbst" fungiert nach Nökel neben dem bewusst gewählten Kleidungsmodus (zum Beispiel des Kopftuches) der Neo-Muslimas, der unter anderem die Funktion der Abgrenzung vom Gastarbeiter-Milieu des „Aldi-Türken" hat, ein spezifisches, zum Teil am Oberschicht-Habitus orientiertes neo-islamisches Verhalten, das Nökel als Ausdruck von Klassenaffirmation sieht:

> Zentral ist eine reflektierte Selbstdisziplinierung als Mittel zur Konstruktion eines Respekt einfordernden, Autonomie beanspruchenden Selbst, das sich ins Spiel der Definitionen und Rangzuordnungen einklinkt.[7]

Mit der Konstruktion eines modernen islamischen Selbst konturieren sich zudem neue innerfamiliäre Konfliktmuster. Beispielsweise indem schriftkundige Töchter, die meist den unreflektiert-mechanistischen islamischen Habitus der Eltern als unislamisch ablehnen, mit dem Verweis auf den authentischen Islam die elterlichen Kontrollansprüche elegant abwehren oder sich bemühen, das Verhältnis der Geschlechter und die Rolle der Frau in der Konfrontation mit modernen Vorstellungen von Weiblichkeit neu zu ordnen.

> Ein zentraler Aspekt ist die Absage an das Hausfrauenmodell und die damit einhergehende Geschlechterasymmetrie. In diesem Zusammenhang wird festgestellt, dass die Heirat eine Frau nicht zwangsläufig zur Hausfrau und damit zum Gegenstand patriarchalischer Attitüden mache. Der Mann habe die Pflicht, seiner Ehefrau den Lebensstandard zu bieten, den sie vor der Ehe gewohnt war. Das bedeutet im Hinblick auf die aktuelle Lebenssituation der jungen Frauen ein unbestreitbares Recht auf die Fortführung von Ausbildung oder Berufstätigkeit.[8]

Es zeigt sich hier insgesamt eine Verschiebung der Machtbalance, mit der sich die Neo-Muslima durch ihre offensiv dokumentierte islamische Kompetenz den elterlichen und männlichen Autoritätsansprüchen entzieht. Das äußert sich unter anderem auch darin, dass die traditionelle Praxis einer Ehevermittlung auf diesem Weg umgangen und die Partnerwahl selbst in die Hand genommen

---

[7] Nökel, „Migration, Islamisierung und Identitätspolitiken", 266.
[8] Nökel, „Migration, Islamisierung und Identitätspolitiken", 268.

wird, weil die Eltern immer erfolgreicher von der eigenen religiösen Inkompetenz bei der Suche nach dem guten Muslim überzeugt werden können, weshalb sie die Suche nach dem geeigneten Partner immer öfter ihren Töchtern selbst überlassen.[9]

All dies kann belegen, dass Islamisierungsprozesse nicht zwangsläufig in Unterdrückung und Desintegration enden müssen. Dessen ungeachtet findet der von Nökel und Klinkhammer beschriebene Typus muslimischer Frauen im öffentlichen Diskurs wenig Resonanz. Vielmehr scheinen diese Frauen durch die medial vermittelten Bilder eine Umdeutung in Richtung zu einem radikalen Islamismus zu erfahren, dem durch das dokumentierte Kopftuch im Sinne eines politischen Islam ein unerschütterlicher Fanatismus zur Seite gestellt wird. Neben einer demokratiefeindlichen Haltung stehen sie im Verdacht, eine islamistische Unterwanderung der Gesellschaft zu betreiben, mit der am Ende die islamische Revolution nach dem Modell des Iran angestrebt werden könnte.

Die beschriebene Typisierung der islamischen Lebensführung in den aufgezeigten Ausprägungen macht deutlich, dass islamische Religiosität wesentlich komplexer strukturiert ist, als es das vermeintlich eindeutige Zeichen des Tragens eines Kopftuches zeigt. Folglich ist vor dem Hintergrund wissenschaftlicher Forschung und gesellschaftspolitischer Entscheidungen eine differenzierte Betrachtung islamischer Religiosität erforderlich. Durch das vorschnelle Anlegen von eurozentrischen Erklärungsfolien, die einen produktiven Zusammenhang von gesellschaftlicher Modernisierung und Religionsentwicklung vorab ausschließen, werden zwangsläufig inhaltliche und strukturelle Aspekte dieses Zusammenhangs bei der Beschreibung der gegenwärtigen so genannten „Reislamisierung" in europäischen Ländern übersehen. Nach Meinung von Klinkhammer reicht deshalb eine kritische Abgrenzung oder Distanzierung von westlicher Moderne im Kontext der Selbstbeschreibung von Muslimen und Musliminnen nicht aus, um eine grundsätzliche nichtmoderne Gegenbewegung in deren Lebensführung zu diagnostizieren.[10] Stattdessen verweist der Typus der exklusivistischen islamischen Lebensführung der so genannten „Neo-Muslima" auf ein Ringen um gesellschaftliche Anerkennung der differenzierten symbolischen Repräsentation der eigenen Gruppe. Gerade diesen Frauen, die als ein Paradebeispiel für Integration gelten würden, wenn

---

[9] Vgl. Nökel, „Migration, Islamisierung und Identitätspolitiken", 269.
[10] Vgl. Klinkhammer, *Moderne Formen islamischer Lebensführung*, 288 ff.

sie kein Kopftuch trügen, wird die Anerkennung ihrer Anpassungs- und Integrationsleistung verweigert. Ihr Beharren auf einer islamischen Identität, die sich vom konservierend-traditionalistischem Islam einerseits und von den zugeschriebenen Rollen andererseits abhebt, scheint sie nach allen Seiten als bedrohlich auszuweisen.

Islamische Feministinnen und Aktivistinnen in Deutschland

Im Zuge der genannten Reislamisierungstendenzen, die überwiegend im Sinne eines weltweiten Gender-Diskurses, teilweise als „Gender Jihad"[11], von urbanen, sozial gut integrierten akademischen Schichten getragen werden, findet eine zunehmende Auseinandersetzung mit emanzipatorischen Positionen statt. In Deutschland wird diese Auseinandersetzung im Wesentlichen von islamischen Feministinnen[12] bzw. muslimischen Aktivistinnen getragen, die grob in drei Gruppen unterteilt werden können, die dies auf völlig unterschiedliche Art und Weise tun.[13]

Das Zentrum für islamische Frauenforschung und Frauenförderung (ZIF)[14] bemüht sich neben der stetigen Beratungsarbeit um einen hermeneutischen und geschlechtergerechten Zugang zum Qur'an. Das ZIF ist die Gruppe mit einem theologisch-feministischen Ansatz. Es ist ihnen wichtig, mit einem Qur'anischen Ansatz nicht die bestehende Rollenklischees, die dem Patriarchat nur in die Hände spielen würden, zu bestätigen, sondern ein eigenständiges Reflektieren muslimischer Frauen über Geschlechterdifferenz und Rollenzuweisung zu erreichen.

---

[11] Wobei hier „Jihad" nicht als Krieg, sondern als „große Anstrengung" verstanden wird.

[12] Hier ist zu unterscheiden zwischen einem „muslimischen Feminismus", dessen Begründungen gegen Geschlechterungerechtigkeit nicht primär islamisch begründet sein müssen, und einem „islamischen Feminismus", der sich in seinen Begründungen explizit auf den Qur'an bezieht (vgl. Indre Monjezi-Brown, „Islamischer Feminismus – Leitbilder, Selbstverständnis und Akteure", in: Heinrich-Böll-Stiftung [Hg.], *DOSSIER Muslimische Vielfalt in Deutschland*, http://www.migration-boell.de/web/integration/47_1139.asp [o.J.], 1 – Zugriff am 17. 08. 2008). Es existieren unterschiedliche, auf Länder bezogene Formen von Feminismus, die jeweils ihre individuellen Schwerpunkte setzen wie: Kampf um Zulassung von Richterinnen (Ägypten); rechtliche Gleichstellung mit Männern (Iran); gesellschaftliche Anerkennung von unehelichen Kindern und deren Müttern (Marokko); gegen Diskriminierungen am Arbeitsplatz (Deutschland, Frankreich).

[13] Die Aktivitäten muslimischer Frauen sind breit gefächert. Sie ausführlich zu untersuchen kann diese Arbeit nicht leisten, da es bisher keine wissenschaftlichen Untersuchungen in Deutschland in diesem Bereich gibt.

[14] http://www.zif-koeln.de

HUDA ist eine Vernetzungsplattform für muslimische Frauen.[15] In ihren Veröffentlichungen bemühen sich die Frauen, ein breites Spektrum muslimischer Meinungen zu Wort kommen zu lassen. Das ist eine wichtige Möglichkeit, auch Frauen in konservativen Kreisen mit liberalen, theologisch-fundierten Ansichten zu konfrontieren, aber auch orthodoxe Perspektiven den liberalen Kreisen näher zu bringen und somit immer wieder ein Stück Realität in die Szene zu bringen.

Das BFmF[16] setzt bei der gesellschaftlichen Problematik an. Durch ein reichhaltiges Angebot an sozialen Kursen und Beratungsmöglichkeiten bietet dieses Frauenzentrum vor allem muslimischen Frauen die Möglichkeit, durch Schul- und andere Bildungsabschlüsse in der hiesigen Gesellschaft Fuß zu fassen.

Darüber hinaus gibt es religiös orientierte Frauen, die sich als Privatpersonen oder Verbandsvertreterinnen mit anderen Frauen zusammenschließen und sich ebenfalls für die Gleichberechtigung von Frauen und Männern einsetzen.

Bei allen – zumindest seitens des *„islamischen Feminismus"*, der sich hier vom *„muslimischen Feminismus"* unterscheidet – scheint es wichtig, darauf zu achten, dass bei den Argumentationen gegen Geschlechterungerechtigkeiten die Qur'anischen Wurzeln nicht aus dem Blick geraten.[17] Das heißt konkret: Die Vertreterinnen dieser islamischen Position befürworten in einem islamischen Rahmen verankerte Frauenrechte, jedoch jeweils in völlig unterschiedlicher Form. Indem einige also eine weiblich-emanzipatorische Position in der frühen islamischen Geschichte betonen, verteidigen sie nicht nur ihre Religion gegen diffamierende Angriffe von „Außen", sondern wenden sich gleichzeitig nach „Innen", indem sie sich im gleichen Zuge gegen eine traditionell patriarchalisch-männliche Deutungshoheit des Qur'an richten und sich somit auch innerhalb des Islam als „innerislamische Kritikerinnen" angreifbar machen. So verweisen insbesondere weibliche Islam-Gelehrte vermehrt auf die Frauenfeindlichkeit bestimmter Text-Auslegungen und fordern neben einer Neuinterpretation dieser Texte insbesondere die Aufdeckung von

---

[15] HUDA – Netzwerk für muslimische Frauen e.V.: http://www.huda.de/index2.php (Zugriff am 27. 12. 08).
[16] Begegnungs- und Fortbildungszentrum muslimischer Frauen e.V.: http://www.bfmf-koeln.de/bfmf/bfmf/index.php (Zugriff am 27. 12. 08).
[17] Zur Unterscheidung zwischen einem *„muslimischen Feminismus"* und einem *„islamischen Feminismus"* s. Anm. 12 (vgl. Monjezi-Brown, „Islamischer Feminismus").

patriarchalen Machtstrukturen im innerislamischen Diskurs. Es geht dabei nach Monjezi-Brown um folgendes:

> Patriarchale, religiös legitimierte Denkstrukturen, Verhaltens- und Kontrollmechanismen mancher muslimischer Männer werden mittels religiöser Argumentation die Grundlagen entzogen.[18]

Emanzipatorisch-feministisch interessierte Musliminnen wenden sich mit ihrer internen Kritik natürlich auch gegen solche Positionen, mit denen im Rahmen einer „islamistischen Utopie", bzw. einer „Philosophie der Rückkehr" suggeriert wird, „Männer und Frauen – jeweils im Rahmen ihrer natürlichen Möglichkeiten – würden ohnehin gleichberechtigt sein, sobald das islamische System errichtet ist".[19] Bis dahin solle sich die Muslima bescheiden und sich ihren vorgeschriebenen frauenspezifischen und religiösen Pflichten widmen. Aus dieser Perspektive wird tendenziell versucht, die Frauenfrage lediglich als ein Problem westlicher Gesellschaften zu werten und patriarchale Strukturen im eigenen System zu verschleiern. Kritischen Muslimas kann nicht verborgen bleiben, dass sich hinter der biologistisch begründeten zugewiesenen Rolle der gefügsamen Frau, die wegen ihrer „zarten" und „passiv-introvertierten Natur" den (Pseudo-)Schutz des Häuslichen mit den damit verbundenen, quasi heilig gesprochenen Aufgaben der Mutterpflichten vorzuziehen habe, primär patriarchale Interessen verbergen. Insofern wehren sie sich vehement gegen einen solchermaßen offen propagierten Biologismus, mit dem selbst islamische Autoritäten darauf hinweisen, „dass die Frau schon von Natur aus anders sei als der Mann" und auf diese Weise versuchen, „ihren auf das Innere des Hauses beschränkten Wirkungskreis zu legitimieren".[20] So gibt es immer mehr Frauen, die sich weigern, den polarisierende Archetypen – „starker Mann" versus „schwache Kindfrau" – Folge zu leisten und ein eingeschränktes Leben in der Rolle der Ehefrau und Mutter zu führen, während der religiös inspirierten Legende nach der von Natur aus mehr „extrovertiert-aktive Mann" ohne

---

[18] Monjezi-Brown, „Islamischer Feminismus", 1.
[19] Nilüfer Göle, *Republik und Schleier: Die muslimische Frau in der modernen Türkei* (Babel: Berlin 1995), 156.
[20] Göle, *Republik und Schleier*, 153. Göle zeigt hier an einem Beispiel, wie eine öffentlich geführte Debatte zu dieser Thematik in der Türkei so weit eskalierte, dass die Einstellung der Debatte eingeklagt wurde mit der Begründung, eine „illegale Feministenseite" geschaffen zu haben (vgl. ebd. 155).

jegliche Einschränkungen ein spät-pubertierendes Leben unter Seinesgleichen führen darf und auf diese Weise von den Annehmlichkeiten der Moderne profitiert.

Auch die potenzielle islamische Überhöhung des Genderaspektes wird kritisch in den Blick genommen. Sie wird in jenen religiös inspirierten islamisch-emanzipatorischen Positionierungen gesehen, die behaupten, Frauen wären schon zu Lebzeiten des Propheten alle Rechte zugestanden worden, die sich „westliche Frauen" erst mühsam erkämpfen mussten.[21] Es geht hierbei vielmehr darum wahrzunehmen, dass der Koran, historisch gesehen, zwar die Rechte der Frau in seiner Zeit gestärkt hat, ohne dabei – eben aus heutiger Perspektive – patriarchale Züge ganz überwinden zu können. Es gilt also zu sehen, dass der Koran kein feministisches Handbuch ist, sondern es ist hier die Frage zu stellen, welche Antworten aus dem Koran mittels Textverständnis und Exegese auf dem Hintergrund heutiger Problemlagen herauszulesen sind.

Fazit

Die neuen Musliminnen repräsentieren nicht länger die unterdrückte, von patriarchalen Strukturen dominierte Frau. Die Rückbesinnung auf den Islam scheint ihnen vielmehr die Kraft zu geben, sich von diesen Strukturen zu befreien und mit den Herausforderungen der Moderne fertig zu werden, ohne auf diesem Wege mit der eigenen Religion und Kultur brechen zu müssen.[22]

Mit ihrem selbstbewussten Auftreten in der Öffentlichkeit hat die Wahrnehmung von Musliminnen einen Bedeutungswandel erfahren. Hierfür ist die hitzig geführte „Kopftuch-Debatte" – nicht nur in Deutschland – ein gutes Beispiel. Mit dem Anspruch, das Kopftuch auch in öffentlichen Institutionen tragen zu wollen, erfuhr dieses bis dahin relativ bedeutungslose Tuch einen signifikanten Bedeutungszuwachs. Erst mit diesem formulierten Anspruch wurde das Tuch gewissermaßen markantes Zeichen des Feindlichen, das mit dem Makel der potenziellen territorialen Grenzüberschreitung des Eigenen behaftet ist. So konnte das Kopftuch im Zuge verschwörungstheoretischer Konstruktionen als „Fahne für Islamisten" (s.o.) hochstilisiert und deren Trägerinnen unter potenziellen Generalverdacht gestellt werden.[23]

---

[21] Diese Lesart des Qur'an übersieht allzu leicht, dass der Qur'an dem Glaubensanspruch nach kein feministisches Handbuch, sondern eine göttliche Offenbarung ist, die eine neue Gemeinschaft hervorbringen solle, vgl. Göle, *Republik und Schleier*.
[22] Vgl. Göle, *Republik und Schleier*, 156.
[23] Vgl. den hessischen Verfassungsbericht aus dem Jahre 2004 (vgl. Anm. 4).

Women's traditions
Frauentraditionen
Tradiciones de mujeres

Indem emanzipatorisch-feministisch orientierte Musliminnen als selbstbewusste Persönlichkeiten ihren Platz im öffentlichen Raum beanspruchen, finden sie sich in einem kaum auflösbaren Dilemma wieder: Sie drohen in den ihnen zugewiesenen Rollen gefangen zu bleiben. Je nach Perspektive und festgezurrten Interessenssphären legen diese sie als armes, von patriarchalen Mächten drangsaliertes Opfer fest, als gefährliche, das Eigene bedrohende islamistische Fundamentalistin oder als glaubensschwache Muslima, die, von westlich-emanzipatorischen Ideologien infiziert, vom korrekten Weg ihrer eigentlichen religiös vorgezeichneten Bestimmungen und den daraus resultierenden Aufgaben einer Frau abgekommen ist. Für einige etablierte säkulare Feministinnen bleiben sie mysteriös und unglaubwürdig, so lange sie einem Glauben anhängen, der aus deren vermeintlich aufgeklärten Perspektive per se frauenfeindlich ist. Es scheint, dass diesen Frauen trotz aller redlichen Bemühungen von keiner Seite Glauben geschenkt wird. Das mag möglicherweise auch ihre Stärke ausmachen. Denn gerade diese von vielen Seiten kaum nachvollziehbare Rückbesinnung auf den Islam innerhalb einer von einem ethisch-moralischen Vakuum gekennzeichneten säkularen Spät- oder Postmoderne[24] scheint diesen Frauen die Kraft zu geben, sich auf dem Hintergrund ihrer Glaubensgewissheit für demokratisch-humanistische Selbstverständlichkeiten von Gleichberechtigung und Chancengleichheit einzusetzen, für die es im Grunde keiner religiösen Begründung bedarf.

Es bleibt also festzuhalten, dass die genannten typisierenden Konstruktionen dem differenzierten Bild der Muslima in keiner Weise gerecht werden. Tatsächlich ist bei jungen Frauen und Mädchen in der zweiten und dritten Generation eine Hinwendung zur islamischen Religion zu beobachten, in der der islamischen Religion eine große Bedeutung als Identitätsmerkmal zukommt. Jenseits jeglicher Zuschreibungen beansprucht diese zunächst lediglich „Andersheit". Somit liegt auch die muslimische Frau ganz im Individualisierungstrend, wie dies in postmodernen Gesellschaften üblich, bzw. im Grunde erwünscht ist. Doch hier wirkt die Betonung der „Andersheit" als ein Protest im positiven Sinne gegen die Fremdzuschreibung, die sie als unmündige unterdrückte Wesen einerseits und als islamistische Fundamentalistinnen andererseits festschreibt.

Die starke Hinwendung muslimischer Frauen zur islamischen Religion wird dadurch allerdings nicht ausreichend erklärt. Spicer, ein Vertreter des symbolischen Ansatzes in der Ethnisierungs-Diskussion, vermutet, dass denjenigen

---

[24] Vgl. Zygmunt Bauman, *Postmoderne Ethik* (hamburg edition: Hamburg 1995).

Kulturelementen im Identitätssystem eine überhöhte symbolische Bedeutung zugeschrieben werden, die Gegensätzlichkeit zu anderen Kultureinheiten am besten ausdrücken. Gerade der Assimilationsdruck der Majorität führe dazu, dass Symbole und ihre Bedeutungen ins Identitätssystem eingebracht werden.[25] Nach dieser These ist anzunehmen, dass diejenigen religiösen Rituale und Symbole an Bedeutung gewinnen, die von der Majorität als „unerwünscht" deklariert werden. Das legt die Prognose nahe, dass beispielsweise das Kopftuch als religiöses Identitätsmerkmal an Bedeutung zunehmen wird, je mehr der Druck auf muslimische Frauen wächst, ihr Kopftuch abzulegen.

Die Handlungsweise einer wachsenden Zahl muslimischer Frauen, die aus eigenem Entschluss ihr Leben an religiösen Vorschriften orientieren, kann nicht monokausal als Folge einer Unterdrückung ihrer männlichen Verwandten interpretiert werden. Muslimische Frauen sind als mündige Personen ebenso wie andere Frauen in der Lage, eigene Lebensentwürfe in der postmodernen „Multioptionsgesellschaft"[26] zu wählen. Dabei sind sie in ihren Identitätsentwürfen – wie andere auch – durch die jeweiligen Sozialisationsbedingungen und den damit verbundenen Einflussfaktoren ihrer Umwelt geprägt.[27]

This description of the situation in which Muslim women with emancipatory feminist views live in the public context which they claim for themselves reveals their almost insoluble dilemma. In the course of their efforts at emancipation, specific roles are assigned to them from different sides. On the one hand, that of victims oppressed by patriarchal forces, or of activists inspired by fundamentalist Islamic

---

[25] Vgl. Spicer, zit. nach: Marco Heinz, *Ethnizität und ethnische Identität* (Holos-Verlag: Bonn 1993), 139.

[26] Vgl. Peter Gross, *Die Multioptionsgesellschaft* (suhrkamp: Frankfurt/Main 1994).

[27] Vgl. Heiner Keupp u.a., *Identitätskonstruktionen: Das Patchwork der Identitäten in der Spätmoderne* (rowohlt: Reinbek bei Hamburg ²2002).
Zum gesamten Artikel vgl. außerdem die folgenden Titel: Iris Bednarz-Braun / Ulrike Heß-Meining, *Migration, Ethnie und Geschlecht: Theorieansätze – Forschungsstand – Forschungsperspektiven* (VS Verlag: Wiesbaden 2004); Naime Çakir, „Die Position des Anderen", in: Beatrix Caner, (Hg.), *Doppelte Heimat: Türkische Migranten berichten* (Heinrich&Hahn: Frankfurt/Main 2008), 265-285; Nilüfer Göle, / Ludwig Ammann (Hg.), *Islam in Sicht: Der Auftritt von Muslimen im öffentlichen Raum* (transcript: Bielefeld 2004); Claudia Rademacher / Peter Wiechens (Hg.), *Geschlecht – Ethnizität – Klasse: Zur sozialen Konstruktion von Hierarchie und Differenz* (leske + budrich: Opladen 2001); Bernhard Waldenfels, *Grenzen der Normalisierung: Studien zur Phänomenologie des Fremden* (suhrkamp: Frankfurt/Main 1998); Ders., *Topographie des Fremden: Studien zur Phänomenologie des Fremden* (suhrkamp: Frankfurt/Main 1999); Zentrum für islamische Frauenforschung und Frauenförderung (ZIF) (Hg.), *Ein einziges Wort und seine große Wirkung* (Staffeldruck: Köln 2005).

interests. On the other hand, the orthodox religious approach tends to suspect that these self-confident women are Muslima who have departed from the true faith and been seduced by western ideologies hostile to religion.

Al describir la situación de las mujeres musulmanas orientadas a la emancipación y al feminismo en el espacio público que ellas reclaman para sí, se muestra cuál es el dilema casi sin solución en el que viven. En su lucha por la emancipación, se les adjudican determinados roles, que son por un lado la víctima oprimida por poderes patriarcales o la activista guiada por intereses fundamentalistas-islamistas, y por el otro lado, se presume por parte de la perspectiva ortodoxa que son mujeres musulmanas que han renunciado a la verdadera fe, habiendo sido tentadas por ideologías occidentales antirreligiosas.

Naime Çakir (*1969), geboren im Nord-Osten der Türkei, kam im Alter von 7 Jahren nach Deutschland. Abgeschlossenes Studium der Sozialpädagogik (Migrationssozialarbeit) an der Fachhochschule Darmstadt. Derzeit Studium der Religionswissenschaften mit Schwerpunkt Islam an der Johann-Wolfgang-Goethe-Universität in Frankfurt. Freischaffende Referentin zu Islam und Integration. Ehrenamtliche Tätigkeiten: Muslimische Vorstandsvorsitzende des islamisch-christlichen Arbeitskreises in Hessen (ICA), Mitglied der Sara und Hagar Fraueninitiative Rhein/Main, Vorstandsmitglied des hessischen Islamforums und Vorstandsmitglied des Interkulturellen Rates in Deutschland.

Pilar de Miguel, Lucía Ramon Carbonell,
Rosa Cursach Salas

Logros y retos de la teología feminista en España[1]

> *"Todas las instituciones de nuestra cultura nos dicen a través de las palabras, de las acciones y, peor aún, de los silencios, que nosotras somos insignificantes. Pero nuestra herencia es nuestro poder"*
> Judy Chicago[2]

1. La realidad española: breve cronología ubicadora

Compartimos con la filósofa española Celia Amorós su afirmación de que *"nada es mejor que una buena cronología"*. De otro modo, corremos el riesgo de que nuestras descendientes crean que siempre ha sido así y olviden la pasión y la vida luchadora de tantas, antes y ahora; como si la conquista de derechos sociales, políticos, culturales, económicos y religiosos fueran asuntos que han ido cayendo del cielo cual maná, u otorgados por quienes los poseían por "derecho divino", gracias a su benevolencia o magnanimidad, dejándolas así a la intemperie creyendo ingenuamente que mañana será mejor y que llegan las cosas sólo porque el tiempo pasa.

Si algo nos muestra la historia es que se puede ir a peor si no se anda con ojo, y aún así. Algo vamos aprendiendo de ello, por eso sabemos que es bueno visibilizar nuestros logros para interrumpir la dinámica de esta opresión, que la solidaridad asertiva nos es imprescindible para avanzar mejor y constatamos con gusto que nos hemos vuelto interesantes para nosotras mismas.

En España, el feminismo tiene una singularidad: no podemos encontrar figuras en el pensamiento feminista español antes de la década de los setenta del

---

[1] El siguiente artículo ha sido elaborado a partir de las reflexiones ya realizadas en diferentes ámbitos por parte de Pilar de Miguel.
[2] Explicando *The Dinner Party (La Cena)*, su obra artística sobre la invisibilidad de las mujeres.

siglo XX. Las anteriores, o son débiles, o han de ser más bien reinterpretadas en clave feminista, debido a que aquí hemos sufrido lo que la prestigiosa filósofa española Amelia Valcárcel llama *"ablación de la memoria histórica"*. Esta se refiere a todo lo que truncó la guerra civil y el período posterior: la memoria de lo que había sido y de lo que hubiera sido posible.

Cuando pretendemos hacer historia del feminismo español y leemos a las personas que han escrito desde finales del siglo XIX hasta los años treinta, o sabemos de sus biografías, en realidad estamos recuperando, con la ayuda de un puente larguísimo, una memoria que no nos pertenece del todo.

> "Una memoria de la que pretendemos apropiarnos, pero que no es memoria que se haya hecho en nosotras carne propia. Nuestras vidas se vivieron como si todas esas personas no hubieran existido jamás. Supimos de ellas cuando ya éramos personas adultas, con nuestras claves estabilizadas por otras vías. Recuperar esa memoria, a esas personas, es una labor muy importante. Pero tal recuperación no podrá evitar nunca nuestra primitiva orfandad."[3]

Pablo VI incorporó a la tercera sesión del concilio Vaticano II, aceptando así la interpelación del cardenal Suenens, a 23 mujeres (10 religiosas y 13 seglares), la mayoría de éstas elegidas entre las dirigentes de las organizaciones internacionales católicas. Esta situación insólita hasta el momento está cargada de anécdotas indescriptibles que ha transmitido con humor Pilar Belosillo[4], una española entre las 13 seglares elegidas.

2. Tejiendo redes

Lo que es destacable es que en esta circunstancia se gesta una primera red de mujeres, diríamos hoy, que posteriormente y gracias a las relaciones establecidas, dentro del espíritu conciliar, y convocando a otras incluso de otras tradiciones cristianas, constituyen un núcleo de diálogo ecuménico. Cuenta Pilar

---

[3] Amelia Valcárcel, *Rebeldes. Hacia la paridad* (Plaza y Janés: Barcelona 2000), 21-23.
[4] Sobre todo esto y las complejas relaciones del feminismo y la teología feminista, puede verse Maria Salas (recientemente fallecida y cuya vida celebramos agradecidas), *De la promoción de la mujer a la teología feminista* (Sal Terrae: Santander 1993); y el trabajo de Pilar de Miguel, *Los movimientos de mujeres y la teología feminista. Una visión panorámica desde nuestro contexto* (DDB: Bilbao 2002); trad. Portuguesa: "A teologia e as mulheres. Uma visão a partir do contexto español", en: *Communio*, Revista Internacional Católica (ed. Portuguesa) Lisboa, UCP, año XXII (3/2005), 319-328; trad. Inglesa: "The womeńs movements and feminist theology: Reviewing the context in Spain (*Journal of the ESWTR* 13; Peeters: Leuven 2005), 41-64.

Belosillo[5] que descubrió a mujeres protestantes de mucha categoría, muy preparadas en teología y Biblia.

Tras mucho trabajo y mucha historia se constituye *El Foro Ecuménico de mujeres cristianas* en 1982 en Gwatt (Suiza). En 1986 se funda también en Suiza (Magliaso), the *European Society of Women in Theological Research* (ESWTR); desde 2009 se llama tambien la *"Sociedad Europea de Mujeres Investigatoras en Teología"*

Gracias a la presencia de mujeres españolas significativas en estas organizaciones, junto a inquietudes que se despertaban en muchas, van naciendo también en España en los 80 algunos grupos. Es interesante destacar como nuestra socialización europea es un hecho desde el comienzo.

En 1986 se crea en España, por iniciativa de Pilar Belosillo, el *Foro de Estudios sobre la Mujer (FEM)*. Es miembro del *Foro Ecuménico de Mujeres Cristianas de Europa*. El mismo año nace también el primer grupo de *Mujeres y Teología*, como primer grupo de estudiantes y licenciadas en teología de España. Y se funda también el *Col·lectiu de Dones en L´Esglesia* de Cataluña.

La Asociación de Teólogas Españolas (ATE)[6] nace en 1992 porque cada vez hay más mujeres que elaboran una teología feminista desde una perspectiva académica y casi todas se unen con el fin de hacer ciencia teológica propia e impulsar también el pensamiento multidisciplinar. La ATE ha sido y es canal de debate y encuentro entre teólogas y entre investigadoras feministas de distintas disciplinas y religiones. Canalizados a través de las Jornadas que la asociación organiza anualmente hemos debatido sobre "Espiritualidad y Empoderamiento" 2005, "Historia, Memoria y Género" 2006, "Mujeres, Salud y Salvación" 2007 y "Mujer, Palabra y Comunidad Eclesial" 2008, sólo para citar los debates más recientes.

Y todo ello teniendo en cuenta que nuestra universidad no tiene la opción de la Teología como carrera civil, asunto que en otros países ha facilitado mucho el acceso a los estudios de cualquiera que así lo deseara. Nuestras facultades de teología son eclesiásticas y en general fueron pensadas para instruir a los futuros presbíteros y religiosos, obviamente todos varones.

La mayoría de las teólogas españolas tienen otros estudios universitarios previos, con lo cual acceden con mayor bagaje cultural y experiencia vital

---

[5] Maria Salas / Teresa Rodriguez de Lecea, *Pilar Belosillo. Nueva imagen de mujer en la Iglesia* (Acción católica: Madrid 2004).
[6] La web de la Asociación de Teologas Españolas es www.asociaciondeteologas.org.

y eclesial a la reflexión teológica (esto, por cierto, no favorece como cabría pensarse a las estudiantes), ampliando así horizontes hermenéuticos, incluyendo contenidos y renovando metodologías en muchos casos. La Teología española hecha por mujeres es sobre todo vocacional, de otro modo, no se entenderían los precios personales que se pagan para acceder y especialmente, para permanecer en ella.

El desarrollo de la teología feminista española está ligada, como toda la europea, a la recepción de la teología feminista americana. Aunque, como ya hemos visto, caía en terreno preparado. Autoras como Mary Daly, Rosemary Radford Ruether, Letty Russell, Elisabeth Schüssler Fiorenza y otras muchas forman parte también de nuestra tradición. Asimismo, fueron importantes otros nombres de tradición alemana como Dorothee Sölle o Elisabeth Moltmann-Wendel, Ida Raming o la holandesa Catharina Halkes. Con el paso del tiempo, comenzaron a formar parte de nuestra tradición también autoras como las brasileñas Ivone Gebara, Ana María Tepedinho, María Clara Bingemer, la mexicana M. Pilar Aquino o la uruguaya M. Teresa Porcile con las que se ha ido compartiendo también el quehacer teológico y otros proyectos.

La obra colectiva *Diez mujeres escriben teología*, dirigida por Mercedes Navarro en 1993, es de algún modo la presentación primera y amplia de la teología feminista o la teología hecha por mujeres en España. La directora dice en su presentación:

> "Nuestro libro tiene mucho de teología feminista, más o menos explícita. Los artículos de las diferentes autoras tienen estas características: a) una postura crítica de los temas y disciplinas ante el pasado en lo que a la mujer se refiere, b) una toma de postura desde la mujer y a favor de ella en el presente, que quiere hacer justicia a un olvido histórico y que pertenece al pecado de la Iglesia patriarcal, c) una decidida y valiente apertura creativa al futuro, en el que las mujeres nos sentimos sujetos responsables de la marcha de la Iglesia y de la reflexión de la fe que es la teología y d) el uso de la interdisciplinariedad y la apertura ecuménica en la elaboración de dicha teología."[7]

En los 90 surge también la iniciativa *Sínodo Europeo de Mujeres*, un movimiento renovador que pretende dar cabida a un mayor abanico de mujeres, teniendo en cuenta las nuevas realidades de las pertenencias eclesiales: hay muchas mujeres de inspiración cristiana que no se sienten representadas por

---

[7] Mercedes Navarro (ed.), *Diez mujeres escriben teología* (EVD: Estella 1993).

las iglesias, ni por sus instituciones, aunque sean femeninas. Creen que se empeñan más en defender sus respectivas instituciones y programas que en comprometerse con los asuntos feministas específicos. Es ya fruto también de la reflexión teológica expresamente feminista y no sólo de la hecha por mujeres. La ATE entra en relación con este movimiento en 1994 y participó activamente en la realización *del Primer Sínodo Europeo de mujeres*, que tuvo lugar en Gmunden (Austria) en 1996, bajo el lema: *Las mujeres por el cambio en el siglo XXI*.[8]

El Segundo Sínodo Europeo tuvo ya lugar en Barcelona en agosto del 2003, con el título *Compartir Culturas*.[9] Si en el Primero se habían hecho especialmente presentes la realidad y las mujeres del Este de Europa, en este tienen lugar varias circunstancias interesantes, según nuestra opinión. En primer lugar, se hace presente la teología feminista española en Europa de un modo más visible. Cabe destacar la magnífica ponencia de Mercedes Navarro: "Mujeres y religiones: visibilidad y convivencia en el sur de Europa" y a partir de ahí la invitación expresa a participar en el Congreso de Budapest de la EWSTR del 2005 (primera vez que se oye una ponencia en español). En segundo lugar, se consigue una interrelación y cooperación significativa entre los grupos de España. De hecho, la realización del Sínodo en Barcelona es posible gracias a la colaboración de algunos de estos grupos (*Creyentes y feministas* de Mallorca, *Arnasatu* de Bilbao, la colaboración de la *ATE, Mujeres y teología* de Sevilla, Galicia, etc.) y la asociación catalana *Col·lectiu de Dones en L'Església*.[10] En tercer lugar, la presencia numerosa de mujeres italianas y algunas destacadas teólogas como Marinnella Perroni (Presidenta del Coordinamento di Teologhe Italiane-CTI) o Adriana Valerio, presidenta a la sazón de la EWSTR, fue definitiva para la colaboración futura que de ahí resurgirá entre España e Italia.[11]

Las teólogas italianas organizan un gran Congreso en Roma el año siguiente: *Teólogas, en qué Europa*, a donde acude ya un nutrido grupo de españolas y se van conformando redes y proyectos conjuntos como publicaciones, etc. Cabe

---

[8] Pilar de Miguel (ed.), *Europa con ojos de mujer. Primer Sínodo europeo de mujeres* (EVD: Estella 1996).
[9] Pilar de Miguel / María Josefa Amell (eds), *Atreverse con la diversidad. Segundo Sínodo europeo de mujeres* (EVD: Estella 2004).
[10] Pilar de Miguel / Sefa Amella, *Atrevir-se a la diversitat* (Editorial Mediterrània: Barcelona 2004).
[11] Hubiéramos deseado igualmente ese contacto más asiduo apenas esbozado con alguna portuguesa, pero aún no se ha dado, así como con alguna francesa que aún queda pendiente.

destacar el proyecto de publicación para los próximos siete años *La Biblia y las Mujeres*. Pretende ser un recorrido exhaustivo, de carácter enciclopédico, por toda la historia de la Biblia y de su exégesis en relación con las mujeres y los temas importantes en la perspectiva de género. Será un proyecto en cuatro idiomas (alemán, español, inglés e italiano) dirigido por Irmtraud Fischer, Mercedes Navarro, Jorunn Okland, Adriana Valerio y contará con muchas y variadas colaboradoras. El primer volumen sobre la *Torá* está previsto para octubre del año 2008.

Hay que destacar también el hecho de contar ya no sólo con publicaciones en Teología feminista sino con colecciones dedicadas a esta, así debemos destacar, la colección *En clave de mujer*, dirigida por Isabel Gómez Acebo, que desde 1999, impulsa la teología y el pensamiento en perspectiva de género, a fecha de hoy la colección cuenta con abundantes títulos sobre espiritualidad, historia, temas bíblicos y teológicos.

Más recientemente han visto la luz dos nuevas colecciones de textos de Teología Feminista. Por una parte la colección Aletheia perteneciente a la ATE y dirigida por Carmen Bernabé, ha publicado ya algunos títulos. Pretende ser una vía para que las teólogas españolas, bien de forma colectiva o individualmente puedan dar salida a sus textos e investigaciones, aunque tiene asimismo previsto traducir al castellano obras relevantes de Teología Feminista. La otra colección va ligada a EFETA,[12] *Escuela Feminista de Teología de Andalucía*, que en colaboración con la editorial Arcibel, publica textos relacionados con la Escuela de Teología Feminista, ya sean los temarios de las clases que se dictan en los cursos presenciales o investigaciones de las profesoras.

3. ¿Mayoría de edad con diez años?

Teníamos aún las teólogas feministas españolas dos retos pendientes enunciados que parecen haberse comenzado a poner en práctica con el cumplimiento de la decena de años de la mayoría de nuestras organizaciones. Por un lado, nuestro contacto y conocimiento más sistemático y "en-redado" con los países de la América de habla hispana y por otro, la relación que queríamos mejorar o en su caso entablar con la Universidad civil española y sus pensadoras feministas.

Hemos tenido contacto o proyectado conjuntamente algunos encuentros con el *CESEP, Centro Ecuménico de Servicios de Evangelización y Educación*

---

[12] Para más información sobre EFETA www.efeta.org.

Popular, de Brasil, *Anudando* de Ecuador (Marcia Moya), *Teologanda* (Argentina) y algunos otros en cuya estela de ida y vuelta quisiéramos continuar. Hemos sido amablemente invitadas desde Nápoles por Elisabeth Schüssler Fiorenza a presentar el proyecto EFETA en San Diego (USA) en noviembre del 2007; así como al Congreso que organizó *Teologanda* y *Agenda* (Alemania) para la Semana de Pascua del 2008 en Buenos Aires. Y también algunas teólogas españolas fueron invitadas al Primer Summer Forum organizado por WATER (Women's Alliance for Theology, Ethics and Ritual) y el FSR (Feminist Studies in Religion) que tuvo lugar el pasado mes de Junio del 2008 en Washington, donde 35 investigadoras feministas de la Teología y la Religión procedentes de diferentes partes del mundo, reflexionaron y debatieron sobre el pasado, el presente y el futuro de las investigaciones feministas en religión, de modo que las redes se van ensanchando.

Expresaba Ivone Gebara,[13] con motivo de la celebración del décimo aniversario de *Conspirando* que si una organización, sobre todo si es de mujeres, resistía 10 años, podía ya considerarse que había hecho historia dentro de la gran Historia; la mayoría de nuestras organizaciones ya han cumplido los 10 años algunas hasta ya han celebrado la mayoría de edad, y en estos años han nacido algunas más dando respuesta a nuevas necesidades. El trabajo prestado a la sociedad es significativo. En la introducción de *Diez palabras clave en teología feminista*, texto que conmemoró el décimo aniversario de la ATE, se explica el contexto nuevo en que se encuentra nuestro quehacer:

> "Ha de moverse en un contexto social, cultural y religioso de creciente indiferencia hacia la religiosidad institucional, pero en búsqueda de sentido y espiritualidad, al que debe escuchar; un contexto además cambiante y abocado a un multiculturalismo y una multirreligiosidad a la que tendrá que preparase ecuménica y creativamente; una teología patrikyriarcal con la que coexistir como 'residente extranjera'."[14]

Entre los desafíos que se nos presentaban; y se nos siguen presentando, a las teólogas españolas, está el reto de dialogar con un pensamiento feminista

---

[13] Ivone Gebara, "Presentación", en: Mary Judith Ress, *Lluvia para florecer. Entrevistas sobre el ecofeminismo en América Latina* (Colectivo Con-spirando: Santiago, Chile 2002), 9-17.

[14] Pilar de Miguel / Mercedes Navarro (eds), *10 palabras clave en teología feminista* (EVD: Estella 2004) 11-12. Hemos asistido recientemente (2007) al décimo aniversario de *Arnasatu* (Bilbao) y al de *Creients i feministes* de Mallorca.

maduro y prestigioso como Celia Amorós, Amelia Valcárcel, Mª Jesús Izquierdo, Teresa del Valle, Mª José Urruzola (recientemente fallecida), Mª Angeles Durán, Victoria Camps, Victoria Sau y otras. Por aquí hay un camino fecundo. Y también en el surgimiento de pensadoras cristianas de otras disciplinas afines, sociología de la religión, psicología, historia, antropología. Esto comienza, no sin dificultades, a ser posible porque nos hemos ido encontrando en la vida, en la academia y en la práctica militante por conseguir la ciudadanía plena en un contexto sur europeo y trabajando por superar la exclusión y la explotación que resulta del sistema patriarcal.[15] De ahí puede salir el pensamiento teológico feminista original y auténticamente nuestro, que responda a nuestra idiosincrasia. Participamos de los asuntos universales comunes evidentemente, pero también debemos reflejar lo original y diferente de nuestras realidades. Algo de esto también comienza a vislumbrarse en los últimos volúmenes (Amparo Pedregal, Angela Muñoz, etc....) de la colección mencionada *En clave de mujer*.[16]

Es cierto que se está empezando a acusar el agotamiento de tanto voluntariado y la escasez de recursos para la investigación. Éste es, ahora mismo, uno de los grandes desafíos de futuro, así como un "contragolpe"[17] institucional más agudo y pertinaz con varios frentes y metodología diferente.

Sin hablar con seriedad de apoyos económicos, de solidaridad efectiva de los grupos, comunidades e instituciones, el futuro es un interrogante muy abierto. Es carísimo y esforzadísimo mantenerse en la producción y quehacer teológicos en las condiciones actuales. Quizás es el momento de un discernimiento para comunidades, organizaciones, grupos, personas, etc. sobre asuntos que merezcan ser subvencionados en beneficio de un cambio de paradigma que ayude a un mundo donde los recursos estén mejor distribuidos. De todas formas podemos afirmar con Mª Pilar Aquino que nuestra existencia *"es una muestra de la actividad del Espíritu de Dios transformando las realidades y las conciencias desde dentro de un mundo de pecado"*[18].

---

[15] La relación o pertenencia a AUDEM (Asociación Universitaria de Estudios de Mujeres)s también un signo de este proceso.
[16] Un ejemplo reciente entre otros, puede ser Pilar de Miguel (ed.), *En qué creen las mujeres. Creyendo y creando* (DDB: Bilbao 2007).
[17] Ver Mary Hunt, "Remodelar el contragolpe", en: *Concilium* 263 (1996), 67-76, aquí 71ss.
[18] Mª Pilar Aquino, "El movimiento de mujeres: fuente de esperanza", en: *Concilium* 283 (1999), 787-794.

3.1. *EFETA: un ensayo de mayoría de edad, auto-reconocimiento y autoridad*

El feminismo siempre es tardío. Todavía no es lengua materna, ni cultura básica escolar, ni pensamiento universitario formativo, como se ha ido viendo. Cada una debe hacer su experiencia personal a contracorriente y tras haber vivido un trecho largo de vida y experiencias patriarcales marcadoras.

Cada segundo, los medios de comunicación, la mayoría de las escuelas y de las iglesias, y desde luego las familias, difunden los valores, las interpretaciones y el sentido de la vida patriarcal. Cada hecho refuerza lo aprendido. Millones de mujeres son actualizadas de manera permanente en creencias y visiones misóginas y machistas.

> "Si no fuera por los placeres de la mismidad, la sororidad y la solidaridad, y por el goce de intervenir en la propia vida y en el mundo positivamente – que se generan en la experiencia feminista- nadie persistiría".[19]

Entre el 30 de Marzo y el 1 de Abril del 2006 en el Congreso de Roma organizado por el CTI (Coordinamento Teologhe Italiane) se visibilizaron muchas mujeres plurales. Los escenarios de la vida pública y civil ya establecía vínculos significativos que eran por una parte desafío, mirando con coraje al futuro, y por otra resultado, recogiendo decenas de años de intentos, ilusiones, trabajo y producción teológica. El congreso se inauguró en la Sala del Consejo de la ciudad de Roma, con la presencia de autoridades eclesiásticas y de la vida política civil de la ciudad y de Italia. En ese ámbito, precisamente, se dio a conocer públicamente la Escuela Feminista de Teología de Andalucía (EFETA), en el primer esbozo de sus Jornadas, equivalentes a las clases presenciales de la programación de sus cursos.

Los días 10 y 11 de junio del 2006 tuvo lugar su inauguración solemne en la ciudad de Sevilla, en la sede de la Universidad Internacional de Andalucía (UNIA), escenario académico civil, primera universidad en conceder créditos académicos a la Escuela. No es casualidad que, junto con las personalidades políticas, el discurso de apertura fuera pronunciado por la mujer (Mercedes Arriaga) que le ha abierto las puertas universitarias. No parece casualidad tampoco que entre las 130 personas matriculadas en estas clases presenciales se encontrara un número significativo de agnósticas y ateas, interesadas y buscadoras de un pensamiento que, por teológico y riguroso, les

---

[19] Marcela Lagarde, "Aculturación Feminista", en: www.ciudadanas.org (1/12/2008).

From the Countries
Aus den Ländern
Desde los distintos Países

brindaba horizontes de sentido y bases para una espiritualidad de raíces claramente cristianas. La diversidad de actitud religiosa se sumaba a la diversidad de género, de generaciones (en profesoras y alumnado) y pertenencias (desde religiosas, hasta políticas, académicas, mujeres de movimientos, feministas militantes...). EFETA es sobretodo una Escuela on-line de Teología Feminista a la que en los pocos años que lleva funcionando le llegan demandas de formación desde 17 países de América Latina, Portugal y España. El título del primer seminario era claro "Introducción a la Teología Feminista", las conferencias eran introducciones a los diferentes ámbitos en los que trabaja la Teología Feminista: Metodología de Investigación, Exégesis y Hermenéutica, la Cuestión de Dios, Cristología, Antropología, Ética, etc. Se han realizado dos seminarios más "De lo Sagrado y de lo profano: mujeres/entre/sin fronteras" (2007) y "Mujeres ¿Menos religión y más espiritualidad?" (2008).

A la par, y sin ponerse explícitamente de acuerdo, el grupo de mujeres catalanas *Col·lectiu de Dones en l'Esglessia*, lograba el reconocimiento de un curso sobre mujeres y Biblia en la facultad de filosofía de la Universidad Central de Barcelona, que consta de 2 semestres con créditos académicos reconocidos, y en la Universidad de Sevilla se acepta un curso de doctorado en la facultad de filología sobre las Sagradas Escrituras y las mujeres con varios créditos reconocidos. En estos momentos ya se está realizando el tercer curso y estos se han hecho extensivos a la Universitat de Girona y la Universitat Pompeu Fabra.

Desde diversos lugares también era convergente la percepción de que se ha dado un salto cualitativo en el discurso religioso teológico de las mujeres. Muchas, llegamos incluso a formular que algo ha madurado y, al hacernos conscientes, hemos llegado a tiempo. Dice Mercedes Navarro:

> "No tenemos, todavía, la suficiente perspectiva temporal, pero no nos abandona la certeza de haber cruzado un umbral, haber roto barreras de separación no sólo ya entre confesiones y religiones, sino entre actitudes ante la vida y su sentido que permiten convergencias que en un país como éste no han sido posibles hasta ahora, y mucho menos en y desde las mujeres."[20]

Los datos que conectan estos acontecimientos entre sí, por citar sólo los más inmediatos en el tiempo, no son improvisaciones. Van precedidos de anhelos y logros como hemos ido desgranando en estas páginas.

---

[20] De la presentación de Efeta en Nápoles.

El Comité científico valora en los siguientes términos el acontecimiento:

"A primera vista podríamos pensar que esos intentos han propiciado el éxito final, la creación de EFETA. Es una lectura posible y algunos datos parecen confirmar su pertinencia. Sin embargo la percepción que tenemos es que los resultados no obedecen a la ecuación causa-efecto, sino que se ha producido un salto de nivel el cual, más que buscar su sentido lineal, necesitamos leer en otros registros que exceden lo meramente local y relativo a ciertas personas e instituciones. Mucho más no sabemos decir, necesitamos más tiempo para hacer una valoración más precisa, incluso en la perspectiva de la fe cristiana."[21]

3.2. *El desafío del Diálogo interreligioso*
Entre los retos que se le presentan a la teología feminista española en el nuevo siglo, está el asumir y trabajar desde un contexto multicultural y multirreligioso. Es algo en lo que desde diferentes ámbitos e instituciones se ha ido trabajando, aunque reconocemos el camino que nos queda todavía por recorrer.

No debemos olvidar que el Sur de Europa tradicionalmente, como hemos dicho, ha sido de mayoría católica y además en España hasta la Constitución del 78 no se puede hablar de abertura a la pluralidad religiosa; en este sentido debemos reconocer que son muchos más los pasos que nos quedan por dar que los realizados.

Un momento importante fue el Forum del Parlamento de las Religiones de Barcelona 2004, en el que hubo un espacio importante para el encuentro y el diálogo interreligioso.

En algunas ocasiones, en los grupos que hemos ido mencionando se ha invitado a personas de otras tradiciones religiosas para acoger sus reflexiones y para abrir las diferentes tradiciones al diálogo; no obstante queda un largo camino.

Cabe destacar desde una perspectiva no confesional la Asociación UNESCO para el Diálogo Interreligioso, que aglutina y moviliza personas de diferentes tradiciones religiosas con el objetivo de promover el conocimiento mutuo entre éstas, el diálogo y la cooperación.

Recientemente, entre los pasos que se van dando debemos destacar la experiencia del grupo Sophia, que nace a partir de la Cátedra de las Tres Religiones de la Universidad de Valencia. El grupo está integrado por mujeres de diferentes tradiciones religiosas de la Ciudad de Valencia; se trata de una de

---

[21] *Ib.*

las pocas iniciativas que no parten de una tradición religiosa particular. La asociación Sophia que vio la luz en Mayo del 2007 está formada por mujeres judías, católicas, musulmanas, bramakhumaris, budistas, etc., y pretende ser un foro abierto a todos y todas las *"que deseen participar en el desarrollo de una conciencia de paz y amor que el mundo de hoy tanto necesita"*.

Como hemos dicho, este camino es aún incipiente. Las teólogas y las estudiosas de la religión españolas tenemos varios retos y campos abiertos ante nosotras, hay un camino recorrido y un gran trecho todavía por hacer.

Die Autorinnen zeigen, wie sich im katholisch dominierten Spanien nach dem Ende der Diktatur Schritt für Schritt ein Netzwerk feministisch denkender Frauen entwickelt, die nach Anschlüssen an die feministische Theologie in Europa, USA und Lateinamerika suchen, bzw. erste Verknüpfungen zu diesen aufgenommen haben. Im Kern sind ihre Reflektionen ökumenisch ausgerichtet, beziehen die nicht-religiösen Frauen nach Möglichkeit ein und tragen das Potential der Öffnung für interreligiöse Verständigung in sich. Für diese Entwicklung bringt der Beitrag zahlreiche Beispiele, sowie Themen, Namen von Gruppen, Bewegungen und Einrichtungen.

The authors show how, in Catholic dominated Spain after the end of the dictatorship, a network of feminist inspired women has developed step by step who have been seeking contacts with feminist theology in Europe, the USA and Latin America or have already established initial links in this field. The core of their reflections has an ecumenical emphasis; wherever possible, they include non-religious women and they reflect a potential openness for interreligious understanding. This contribution offers many examples of these developments together with subjects and names of groups, movements and institutions.

Pilar de Miguel (*1957), Coordinadora del Departamento de Ciencias de la Religión de la Escuela Universitaria de Magisterio Begoñako Andra Mari (Universidad del País Vasco). Es miembro de diversas asociaciones españolas, europeas e internacionales, es profesora presencial de EFETA. Entre sus publicaciones destacan Pilar de Miguel (ed.), *Europa con ojos de mujer. Primer Sínodo europeo de mujeres* (EVD: Estella 1996); Pilar de Miguel y Mercedes Navarro (eds), *10 palabras clave en teología feminista* (EVD: Estella 2004); Pilar de Miguel y Maria Josefa Amell (eds), *Atreverse con la diversidad. Segundo Sínodo europeo de mujeres* (EVD: Estella 2004). Ha dirigido varios de los títulos de la Colección *En Clave de Mujer* Ed. Desclée de Brower.

Lucía Ramón Carbonell (*1970), ha sido la Directora del Congreso Internacional de Mística de Ávila en 2008, Licenciada en Teología (Facultad de Teología San Vicente Ferrer de Valencia) y Licenciada en Filosofía (Universidad Autónoma de

Barcelona). Profesora de la Cátedra de las Tres Religiones de la Universidad de Valencia. Secretaria de la ESWTR. Ha sido vocal hasta hace poco de la Junta de la Asociación de Teólogas Españolas, es miembro del comité científico y profesora de EFETA. Tiene varios artículos en diferentes publicaciones.

Rosa Cursach Salas (*1967), estudió teología en el Centro de Estudios Teológicos de Mallorca (CETEM) y Filosofía en la Universitat de les Illes Balears (UIB). Es vocal de la Junta de la Asociación de Teólogas Españolas y presidenta de la Asociación "Creients i Feministas" de Mallorca. Profesora presencial de EFETA y de los cursos organizados por el Col·lectiu de Dones en l'Església de Catalunya en la Universitat de Barcelona. Es miembro del grupo de Investigación de Política, Trabajo y Sostenibilidad de la UIB. Tiene varios artículos en diferentes publicaciones. Ha sido miembro del Comité Científico y del Comité Ejecutivo del IV Congreso Iberoamericano de Estudios de Género que tuvo lugar en Julio-Agosto del 2008 en la Universidad Nacional de Rosario (Argentina).

I. EUROPEAN ELECTRONIC JOURNAL FOR FEMINIST EXEGESIS: LECTIO DIFFICILIOR CELEBRATES ITS 10TH ANNIVERSARY

Ulrike Sals

Reading the Difficult Way – for Ten Years

There is an anniversary to announce: *lectio difficilior* (www.lectio.unibe.ch) has existed for ten years now! The first issue of this European Electronic Journal for Feminist Exegesis was published in the year 2000 and since then we have had more than 72 articles in three languages (English, German and French) on far-reaching feminist exegetical topics in feminist exegesis, hermeneutics and related disciplines (classical philology, archaeology, Egyptology, studies of the Ancient Near Middle East, ancient history, Judaic studies, history of art, social sciences, psychology, etc). We still are the only European Electronic Journal for Feminist Bible Studies.

It turned out that there are some focal points in our publications. So many articles on deutero-canonical texts were published,

- Luzia Sutter Rehmann, "Sexuelle Differenzen. Geschichten des Missbrauchs in den Apokryphen Apostelakten – Grundzüge einer Hermeneutik des Konflikts", in: *lectio difficilior* 2 (2000);
- Janet S. Everhart, "Naked Bodies: Transgendering the Gospel of Thomas," in: *lectio difficilior* 1 (2005);
- Cornelia B. Horn, "The *Pseudo-Clementine Homilies* and the Challenges of the Conversion of Families", in: *lectio difficilior* 2 (2007);
- Christina Leisering, "Susanna im Garten: Eine feministisch-intertextuelle Lektüre der Susannaerzählung", in: *lectio difficilior* 1 (2008);
- Elisabeth Esch-Wermeling, "Paulus lehrt – Thekla lauscht? Annäherungen an textstrategische Phänomene in den Theklaakten", in: *lectio difficilior* 2 (2008);

Book market
Büchermarkt
Feria de Libros

and as well on feminist social and religious history,

- Irène Schwyn, "Kinderbetreuung im 9.-7. Jahrhundert. Eine Untersuchung anhand der Darstellungen auf neuassyrischen Reliefs", in: *lectio difficilior* 1 (2000);
- Silvia Schroer, "Häusliche und außerhäusliche religiöse Kompetenzen israelitischer Frauen – am Beispiel von Totenklage und Totenbefragung", in: *lectio difficilior* 1 (2002);
- Silvia Schroer, "Feministische Anthropologie des Ersten Testaments. Beobachtungen, Fragen, Plädoyers", in: *lectio difficilior* 1 (2003);
- Silvia Schroer, "Liebe und Tod im Ersten (Alten) Testament", in: *lectio difficilior* 2 (2004);
- Luzia Sutter Rehmann, "Der Glanz der Schekhinah und Elisabeths Verhüllung (Lukas 1,24)", in: *lectio difficilior* 1 (2005);
- Erhard S. Gerstenberger, "Women in Old Testament Legal Procedures", in: *lectio difficilior* 1 (2005);
- Angela Standhartinger, "Frauen in Mahlgemeinschaften. Diskurs und Wirklichkeit einer antiken, frühjüdischen und frühchristlichen Praxis", in: *lectio difficilior* 2 (2005);
- Silvia Schroer, "Gender and Iconography from the Viewpoint of a Feminist Biblical Scholar", in: *lectio difficilior* 2 (2008);

on feminist Judaic studies,

- Irene Pabst, "The interpretation of the Sarah-Hagar-stories in rabbinic and patristic literature. Sarah and Hagar as female representations of identity and difference", in: *lectio difficilior* 1 (2003);
- Susanne Plietzsch, "Zwischen Widerstand und Selbstaufopferung. Die rabbinische Rezeption der Gestalt der Hanna (Babylonischer Talmud, Berachot 31a-32b)", in: *lectio difficilior* 2 (2006);
- Tal Ilan, "Gender and Lamentations: 4Q179 and the Canonization of the Book of Lamentations", in: *lectio difficilior* 2 (2008);
- Christiane Steuer, "Der Fetus ist ein Glied seiner Mutter (ubar yerekh imo): Eine rabbinische Interpretation von Exodus 21:22-24", in: *lectio difficilior* 2 (2008);

and on masculinity and men's studies,

- Ernst Axel Knauf, "Bull-jumping David Crosses Gender-lines (Once Again). Three additional remarks to Philippe Guillaume", in: *lectio difficilior* 2 (2004);
- Moisés Mayordomo Marin, "Construction of Masculinity in Antiquity and Early Christianity", in: *lectio difficilior* 2 (2006);
- Peter-Ben Smit, "Manliness and the Cross – A Note on the Reception of Aspects of Early Christian Masculinity in Athanasius' *Life of Anthony*", in: *lectio difficilior* 1 (2007);

- Cynthia R. Chapman, "Sculpted Warriors: Sexuality and the Sacred in the Depiction of Warfare in the Assyrian Palace Reliefs and in Ezekiel 23:14-17", in: *lectio difficilior* 1 (2007);
- Thomas Staubli, "Geschlechtertrennung und Männersphären im Alten Israel", in: *lectio difficilior* 1 (2008);

or postcolonial biblical studies,

- Elzbieta Adamiak, "Gestohlene Bibel. Feministische Exegese im Kontext Mittel-Ost-Europa", in: *lectio difficilior* 1 (2001);
- Hanna Stenström, "Is a liberating feminist exegesis possible without liberation theology?", in: *lectio difficilior* 1 (2002);
- Seong Hee Kim, "Rupturing the Empire: Reading the Poor Widow as a Postcolonial Female Subject (Mark 12:41-44)", in: *lectio difficilior* 1 (2006);
- Surekha Nelavala, "Jesus Asks the Samaritan Woman for a Drink: A Dalit Feminist Reading of John 4", in: *lectio difficilior* 1 (2007).

Apart from these groups of subjects, readers could also find special, unexpected, even surprising themes. Examples of what I mean by "far-reaching articles" are: The reception of the Book of Job by Simone Weil;[1] text-critical questions of the translation and pronunciation of YHWH;[2] the holy family in Jesus-films;[3] clothing in the Book of Esther;[4] archaeological gender research;[5] questions of canon;[6] feminist approaches to the Image Ban;[7] reflections on

---

[1] Elisabeth Pernkopf, "Ich will dich fragen... Simone Weil im Gespräch mit Hiob", in: *lectio difficilior* 2 (2006).

[2] Kristin De Troyer, "The Names of God. Their Pronunciation and Their Translation. A Digital Tour of Some of the Main Witnesses", in: *lectio difficilior* 2 (2005).

[3] Adele Reinhartz, "Die 'Glückliche Heilige Familie' in den Jesus-Filmen", in: *lectio difficilior* 2 (2002).

[4] Jopie Siebert-Hommes, "'On the third day Esther put on her queen's robes' (Esther 5:1). The Symbolic Function of Clothing in the Book of Esther", in: *lectio difficilior* 1 (2002).

[5] Julia Müller-Clemm, "Archäologische Genderforschung: (K)ein Thema für die Palästina-Archäologie? Ein Forschungsüberblick mit Beispielen zur 'Archäologie des Todes'", in: *lectio difficilior* 2 (2001).

[6] Mieke Bal, "Religious Canon and Literary Identity. Plenary lecture Nijmegen, Conference 'Literary Canon and Religious Identity'", in: *lectio difficilior* 2 (2000); Ilse Müllner, "Dialogische Autorität. Feministisch-theologische Überlegungen zur kanonischen Schriftauslegung", in: *lectio difficilior* 2 (2005).

[7] Kune Biezeveld, "Der Splitter und das Bild. Das Bilderverbot aus neuer Perspektive", in: *lectio difficilior* 2 (2003).

the categories of 'pure' and 'impure';[8] female mediation;[9] women as possible authors of biblical texts;[10] and many others.

This electronic journal enables many people all over the world to read about feminist scholarship. "All over the world" means exactly that: *lectio difficilior* has more than 550 readers per month in more than 40 countries, mainly in Western Europe and the U.S., but also in countries like Poland, Iran, Lebanon, Haiti, or Nigeria.

Comparable to this is the range of emails written to the administration (lectio@theol.unibe.ch). Several demands for help in research on certain topics, thanks for decisive ideas for sermons, education, bible reading groups or women's meetings. An example of positive response is Ovidiu Creanga's email from King's College in London in August 2008: "I'm writing to congratulate the editors of this great electronic journal for their assiduous work in promoting quality scholarship on the Hebrew Bible via the Internet. Personally, I have found many of the articles published by you very stimulating and, in fact, I wish to use them in my own scholarship." In the main we have very few negative reactions to articles or to the journal as a whole.

Other reactions: There has developed close contact and even cooperation with other internet journals, especially with "Open Theology" (www.opentheology.org/), an open and inclusive journal concerning any particular academic programme, country or religion. Again and again we have emails about one and the same article, for example, our 'best-seller': Esther A. de Boer, "Mary Magdalene and the Disciple Jesus Loved", in: *lectio difficilior* 1 (2000). There must be about four per half year. They range from generally positive (or a few negative) reactions to letters with detailed exegetical discussions. And then there are the small things: one day we received an email from Betty Fox whose father was Joseph Rumshinsky. His yet un-played opera was discussed by Helen Leneman ("Ruth and Boaz Love Duets as Examples of Musical

---

[8] Veronika Bachmann, "Die biblische Vorstellungswelt und deren geschlechterpolitische Dimension – Methodologische Überlegungen am Beispiel der ersttestamentlichen Kategorien 'rein' und 'unrein'", in: *lectio difficilior* 2 (2003).

[9] Mercedes L. García Bachmann, "'And YHWH saw and was displeased': Mediation as human responsibility (Isaiah 59)" in: *lectio difficilior* 1 (2005).

[10] Ernst Axel Knauf, "Vom Prophetinnenwort zum Prophetenbuch. Jesaja 8,3f im Kontext von Jesaja 6,1-8,16", in: *lectio difficilior* 2 (2000); Mayer I. Gruber, "Women's Voices in the Book of Micah", in: *lectio difficilior* 1 (2007).

Midrash", in: *lectio difficilior* 1 (2006)). She was delighted by that and emailed Helen via *lectio difficilior*. I do not know what came out of this contact.

In fact working for this journal does not only involve administration and editing. The redactional work in *lectio difficilior* is a way to move feminist scholarship on from theoretical reflection to practice: What exactly is feminist exegesis? Does the combination of a female author and a women's topic suffice? And the question that has existed since the beginning of feminist scholarship: Can male scholars do feminist research?

The commendable work in the production of such a journal is done by many women. The beginning of *lectio difficilior* was in 1998: At a meeting of contributors to the *Kompendium Feministische Bibelauslegung*, edited by Luise Schottroff and Marie-Theres Wacker, that took place in Münster (Germany) in December 1998, the suggestion was made to start with a journal. Its aim was especially to give young scholars the possibility to publish their research. From the very beginning an electronic version was preferred, because it is less expensive and it corresponds to the current needs of internationally oriented scholars better than a printed version. And as pointed out above: it enables so many women and men not living near to a University to read feminist research. So Silvia Schroer founded *lectio difficilior* together with Caroline Vander Stichele (Amsterdam, 2000-2005) and an interdisciplinary and cross-confessional editorial board consisting of Eleni Kasselouri (Thessaloniki, 2000-2006), Judith Frishman (Utrecht, 2000-2007), Christl Maier (Berlin, Yale, Marburg, 2000-now), Shelly Mathews (Greenville/USA, 2008-now), Susanne Scholz (Dallas/USA, 2004-now) and Hanna Stenström (Uppsala, 2000-now). Caroline Vander Stichele retired in 2005 from being a main editor and Tal Ilan from Berlin took over her task in 2006. The administrative work was done by Irène Schwyn (2000-2003), Alison Sauer (2003-2004) and Ulrike Sals (2004-now). Although it is much work for us all and financing the lectio difficilior is difficult, for every issue it all seems worthwhile! We are listed in several databases, cited in several scholarly works and have become well known meanwhile so that the *lectio difficilior* team can look back on a story of success and forward to exciting and intriguing articles in the future. Ad multos annos!

Lectio difficilior (LDiff) es una revista electrónica de exégesis feminista muy conocida, que se fundó hace diez años. En el artículo se presentan los temas principales, los contactos con las lectoras y los lectores, su intercambio de cartas electrónicas con la administración y se da un resumen de la historia de la revista.

Book market
Büchermarkt
Feria de Libros

Lectio difficilior (LDiff) ist eine weithin bekannte elektronische Zeitschrift für feministische Exegese, die vor zehn Jahren gegründet wurde. Dieser Artikel gibt einen Überblick über die thematischen Schwerpunkte, gibt Einblicke in die Kontakte mit den Leserinnen und Lesern und deren Email-Korrespondenzen mit der Administration und fasst die Geschichte der Zeitschrift kurz zusammen.

Ulrike Sals (*1971) works as Assistant at the Chair of Old Testament and Biblical World (Prof. Dr. Silvia Schroer), Faculty of Theology at the University of Berne, and she has done the administrative work for *lectio difficilior* since 2004.

II. Selected Bibliography:
Feminist Approaches to Interreligious Dialogue

Bechmann, Ulrike / Sevda Demir / Gisela Egler, **Frauenkulturen. Christliche und muslimische Frauen in Begegnung und Gespräch**, Düsseldorf: Klens Verlag 2001

Boys, Mary C. / Sara S. Lee, **Christians and Jews in Dialogue: Learning in the Presence of the Other**, Woodstock, NY: Skylight Paths 2006

von Braun, Christina / Bettina Mathes, **Verschleierte Wirklichkeit. Die Frau, der Islam und der Westen**, Berlin: Aufbau-Verlag 2007

Chung, Meehyun (ed.), **Breaking Silence. Theology from Asian Women**, Delhi: ISPCK / EATWOT 2006

Chung, Sook Ja / Marlene Perera (eds), **Sustaining Spirituality with Living Faith in Asia, in the Context of Globalization**, Colombo, Srilanka: CRS Press 2002

Cornille, Catherine, **The Im-Possibility of Interreligious Dialogue**, New York: Crossroad 2008

Donaldson, Laura E. / Kwok Pui-lan (eds), **Postcolonialism, Feminism, and Religious Discourse**, New York / London: Routledge 2002

Eck, Diana, **Encountering God: From Bozeman to Benares**, Boston: Beacon Press 2003

Egnell, Helene, "Dialogue for Life: Feminist Approaches to Interfaith Dialogue", in: Viggio Mortensen (ed.), **Theology and the Religions: A Dialogue**, Grand Rapids, MI: Eerdmans 2003

Egnell, Helene, **Other Voices. A Study of Christian Feminist Approaches to Religious Plurality East and West**, Studia Missionalia Svencana 100, Uppsala: Swedish Institute of Mission Research 2006

Esser, Annette, **Interkontexte feministischer Spiritualität. Eine enzyklopädische Studie zum Begriff religiöser Erfahrung von Frauen in ökumenischer Perspektive**, Theologische Frauenforschung in Europa 23, Berlin u. a.: Lit Verlag 2007

Hill Fletcher, Jeannine, "Shifting Identity: The Contribution of Feminist Thought to Theologies of Religious Pluralism", in: *Journal of Feminist Studies in Religion* 19,2 (2003), 5-24

Hill Fletcher, Jeannine, **Monopoly of Salvation: A Feminist Approach to Religious Pluralism**, New York: Continuum 2005

Lobo Gajiwala, Astrid, "Weaving the Human Web: Inter-faith Families as Basic Human Communities", in: *Word & Worship* 34, 3&4 (2001), 119-127

Gross, Rita M., "Feminist Theology as Theology of Religions", in: *Feminist Theology* 26 (January 2001)

Gross, Rita M. / Rosemary Radford Ruether, **Religious Feminism and the Future of the Planet: A Buddhist-Christian Dialogue**, New York: Continuum, 2001

Haker, Hille / Susan Ross / Marie-Theres Wacker (eds), **Andere Stimmen – Frauen in den Weltreligionen:** *Concilium* 42 (August 2006)

Heintz, Bettina, "Die Macht des Globalen. Frauenrechte im Kontext der Weltgesellschaft", in: Irene Dingel (ed.), **Feministische Theologie und Gender-Forschung. Bilanz – Perspektiven – Akzente**, Leipzig: Evangelische Verlagsanstalt 2003, 197-227

Impulse für eine geschlechtergerechte Sozialpolitik auf der Basis jüdischer, christlicher und muslimischer Traditionen, Frankfurt / Main: *epd Dokumentation* 6, 2006

Jonker, Gerdien, "Vor den Toren: Bildung, Macht und Glauben aus der Sicht religiöser muslimischer Frauen", in: Mechthild Rumpf / Ute Gerhard / Mechtild M. Jansen (ed.). **Facetten islamischer Welten. Geschlechterordnungen, Frauen- und Menschenrechte in der Diskussion**, Bielefeld: transcript 2003, 219-241

Kaddor, Lamya / Rabeya Müller, **Der Koran für Kinder und Erwachsene**, München: C.H. Beck 2008

King, Ursula / Tina Beattie (eds), **Gender, Religion & Diversity: Cross-Cultural Perspectives**, New York: Continuum 2004

Kratz Mays, Rebecca (ed.), **Interfaith Dialogue at the Grass Roots**. With a Preface by Leonard Swidler, Philadelphia: Temple University Press 2009

Mehlhorn, Annette, "Geschlechtsspezifische Dimensionen im interreligiösen Lernen – Erkundungen in Zwischenräumen", in: Peter Schreiner / Ursula Sieg / Volker

Elsenbast (eds), **Handbuch interreligiöses Lernen**, Gütersloh: Gütersloher Verlagshaus 2005, 315-329

Mehlhorn, Annette, "Difference as a Bridge to Religious Encounter. Facing Interfaith Dialogue through Gender Studies", in: Sabine Bieberstein / Kornélia Buday / Ursula Rapp (eds), **Building Bridges in a Multifaceted Europe: Religious Origins, Traditions, Contexts, and Identities**, Journal of the ESWTR 14, Leuven: Peeters 2006, 143-156

Mehlhorn, Annette (Red.), "Feministische Theologie und Praxis in der christlichen und interreligiösen Ökumene", in: Gisela Matthiae / Renate Jost / Claudia Janssen / Annette Mehlhorn / Antje Röckemann (eds), **Feministische Theologie. Initiativen, Kirchen, Universitäten – eine Erfolgsgeschichte**, Gütersloh: Gütersloher Verlagshaus 2008, 296-377

Meyer, Lidwina, "Feministische Theologien und interreligiöses Lernen", in: Peter Schreiner / Ursula Sieg / Volker Elsenbast (eds), **Handbuch interreligiöses Lernen**, Gütersloh: Gütersloher Verlagshaus 2005, 192-205

Mubarak, Fatheena, **Women's Interfaith Initiatives in the UK – A Survey**, London: Interfaith Net Work, 2006, http://www.interfaith.org.uk/publications/womenssurvey06.pdf

Mwaura, Ndirangu / L. D. Chirairo (eds), **Theology in the Context of Globalization. African Women's Response**, Nairobi, Kenya: City Square 2005

O'Neill, Maura, **Mending A Torn World: Women in Interreligious Dialogue**, Maryknoll, NY: Orbis Books 2007

Pui-lan, Kwok, **Postcolonial Imagination & Feminist Theology**, Louisville, KY: Westminster John Knox Press 2005

Richardson Jensen, Jane / Patricia Harris-Watkins (eds), **She Who Prays: A Woman's Interfaith Prayer Book**, Harrisburg, PA: Morehouse Publishing 2005

Riesebrodt, Martin, **Die Rückkehr der Religionen: Fundamentalismus und der "Kampf der Kulturen"**, München: C. H. Beck 2000

Ruether, Rosemary Radford, **Integrating Ecofeminism, Globalization and World Religions**, Oxford: Rowman & Litterfield Publishers 2005

Röckemann, Antje, "Wie hältst du's mit—? Die Sarah-Hagar-Religionen in 20 Jahrgängen Schlangenbrut", in: *Schlangenbrut* 85 (2004), 38-40

Book market
Büchermarkt
Feria de Libros

Rohr, Elisabeth / Ulrike Wagner-Rau / Mechtild Jansen (eds), **Die halbierte Emanzipation? Fundamentalismus und Geschlecht**, Königstein: Ulrike Helmer Verlag 2007

Slee, Nicola, **Faith and Feminism**, London: Darton, Longman and Todd 2003

Stauch, Karimah Katja, **Die Entwicklung einer islamischen Kultur in Deutschland. Eine empirische Untersuchung anhand von Frauenfragen**, Berliner Beiträge zur Ethnologie 8, Berlin: Weißensee-Verlag 2004

Strahm, Doris / Manuela Kalsky (eds), **Damit es anders wird zwischen uns. Interreligiöser Dialog aus der Sicht von Frauen**, Ostfildern: Matthias-Grünewald-Verlag 2006

Traitler, Reinhild (ed.), **In the Mirror of Your Eyes. Report of the European Project for Interreligious Learning**, Zürich / Beirut: EPIL 2004

Wyse, Marion, **Variations on the Messianic Theme: A Case Study of Interfaith Dialogue**, Brighton, MA: Academic Studies Press 2009.

Zentrum für Islamische Frauenforschung und Frauenförderung (ed.), **Ein einziges Wort und seine große Wirkung. Eine hermeneutische Betrachtungsweise zu Qur'an Sura 4, Vers 34, mit Blick auf das Geschlechterverhältnis im Islam**, Köln: Selbstverlag 2005.

III. BIBLIOGRAPHIE – BIBLIOGRAPHY – BIBLIOGRAFÍA*

III.1 Exegese (Erstes Testament, Neues Testament, Jüdische und frühchristliche Schriften) und Hermeneutik / Biblical Studies (Old Testament, New Testament, Literature of Early Judaism and Early Christianity) and Hermeneutics / Exégesis (Antiguo Testamento, Nuevo Testamento, escritos judíos y del cristianismo primitivo) y Hermenéutica

Mary-Anna Bader, **Tracing The Evidence. Dinah in Post-Hebrew Bible Literature**, Studies in Biblical Literature 102, Frankfurt a. M. / New York / Oxford / Wien: Peter Lang 2008, 223 p., ISBN 978-0-8204-8853-0, € 58,40 (D) / € 60,10 (A) / SFR 85,00

Dörte Bester, **Körperbilder in den Psalmen. Studien zu Psalm 22 und verwandten Texten**, Forschungen zum Alten Testament 2. Reihe, Bd. 24, Tübingen: Mohr Siebeck 2007, 304 p., ISBN 978-3-16-149361-4, € 49,00 (D)

Fiona Black, **The Artifice. Grotesque Bodies**, The Library of Hebrew Bible / Old Testament Studies 392, London: T&T Clark 2009, 272 p., HB 978 0 8264 6985 4, $ 125,00

Sarah Jane Boss (ed.), **Mary. The Complete Resource Book**, London: T&T Clark 2009, 580 p., PB 978 0 8264 2758 8, £ 21,41

Frank Crüsemann / Kristian Hungar / Claudia Janssen / Rainer Kessler / Luise Schottroff (Hg.), **Sozialgeschichtliches Wörterbuch zur Bibel**, Gütersloh: Gütersloher Verlagshaus 2009, 800 p., ISBN 978-3-579-08021-5, € 68,00

Patricia Dutcher-Wals (ed.), **The Family in Life and in Death. The Family in Ancient Israel. Sociological and Archaeological Perspectives**, The Library of Hebrew Bible / Old Testament Studies 504, London: T&T Clark 2009, 104 p., HB 978 0 567 02757, $ 135,00

*Sigrid Eder, **Wie Frauen und Männer Macht ausüben. Eine feministisch-narratologische Analyse von Ri 4**, Herders Biblische Studien 54, Freiburg u.a. 2008, 384 p., ISBN 978-3-451-29784-7, € 60,00 / SFR 99,90

---

* Zu Büchern mit * siehe unter "Rezensionen" – Books marked * are reviewed below – Los libros marcados con un asterisco * remiten al apartado de "Recensiones".

Karin Emmerich, **Machtverhältnisse in einer Dreiecksbeziehung. Die Erzählung von Abigajil, Nabal und David in 1 Sam 25**, Arbeiten zu Text und Sprache im Alten Testament 84, St. Ottilien: EOS Verlag 2007, 345 p., ISBN 978-3-8306-7294-4, € 36,00 (D) / € 37,10 (A)

Allie M. Ernst, **Martha from the Margins. The Authority of Martha in Early Christian Tradition**, Vigiliae Christianae Supplements 98, Leiden: Brill 2009, 370 p., ISBN 978 90 04 174900, € 121,00

Elisabeth Esch-Wermeling, **Thekla – Paulusschülerin wider Willen? Strategien der Leserlenkung in den Theklaakten**, NTA N.F. 53, Münster: Aschendorff 2008, 376 p., ISBN 978-3-402-11436-0, € 56,00 (D) / € 57,60 (A) / SFR 95,00

Irmtraud Fischer / Mercedes Navarro Puerto (Hg.), **Tora. Die Bibel und die Frauen. Eine exegetisch kulturgeschichtliche Enzyklopädie Band 1,1**, Stuttgart: Kohlhammer 2009, ca. 480 p., ISBN 978-3-17-020975-6, ca. € 36,00 (D) / SFR 57,90

Judith Hartenstein, **Charakterisierung im Dialog. Maria Magdalena, Petrus, Thomas und die Mutter Jesu im Johannesevangelium im Kontext anderer frühchristlicher Darstellungen**, Novum Testamentum et Orbis Antiquus / Studien zur Umwelt des Neuen Testaments 64, Göttingen: Vandenhoeck & Ruprecht 2007, 347 p., ISBN 978 3 525 53987 3, € 60,90 (D)

Judith Hartenstein / Silke Petersen / Angela Standhartinger (Hg.), **"Eine gewöhnliche und harmlose Speise"? Von den Entwicklungen frühchristlicher Abendmahlstraditionen**, Gütersloh: Gütersloher Verlagshaus 2008, 368 p., ISBN 978-3-579-08027-7, € 39,95 (D) / € 41,10 (A) / SFR 68,50

*Anni Hentschel, **Diakonia im Neuen Testament. Studien zur Semantik unter besonderer Berücksichtigung der Rolle von Frauen**, Wissenschaftliche Untersuchungen zum Neuen Testament 2. Reihe, Bd. 226, Tübingen: Mohr Siebeck 2007, 498 p., ISBN 978-3-16-149086-6, € 79,00

Karin Hügel, **Homoerotik und Hebräische Bibel**, 2009, ISBN 978-3-8366-7213-9; http://www.diplom.de/katalog/arbeit/12237, OLP: € 68,00

Othmar Keel, **Gott weiblich. Eine verborgene Seite des biblischen Gottes**, Gütersloh: Gütersloher Verlagshaus 2008, 144 p., ISBN 978-3-579-08044-4, € 25,00 (D) / € 25,70 (A) / SFR 43,90

Amy-Jill Levine / Maria Mayo Robins (eds), **A Feminist Companion to Patristic Literature**, Feminist Companion to the New Testament and Early Christian Writings 12, London: T&T Clark 2008, 256 p., PB 978 0 567 04555 3, $44,95

Amy-Jill Levine / Maria Mayo Robins (eds), **Feminist Companion to Early Christian Apocalyptic Literature**, Feminist Companion to the New Testament and Early Christian Writings, London: T&T Clark 2009, 304 p., PB 978 0 8264 6651 8, $ 49,95

Christl M. Maier, **Daughter Zion, Mother Zion. Gender, Space, and the Sacred in Ancient Israel**, Minneapolis: Fortress Press 2008, 285 p., ISBN 978 0 8006 6241 7, $ 21,00

Eleonore Reuter (Hg.), **Frauen- und Männer-Strategien**, FrauenBibelArbeit 22, Stuttgart: Katholisches Bibelwerk 2009, 88 p., ISBN 978-3-460-25302-5, € 10,90 (D) / € 11,30 (A)

Caroline Vander Stichele / Tod Penner (eds), **Contextualizing Gender in Early Christian Discourse**, London: T&T Clark 2009, 256p, PB 978 0 567 03036, $ 22,95.

III.2 Kirchen- und Religionsgeschichte / Church history and history of religions/ Historia de la Iglesia y de las Religiones

Christa Bertelsmeier-Kierst (Hg.), **Elisabeth von Thüringen und die neue Frömmigkeit in Europa**, Kulturgeschichtliche Beiträge zum Mittelalter und zur Frühen Neuzeit 1, Frankfurt a. M. / New York / Oxford / Wien: Peter Lang 2008, 349 p., ISBN 978-3-631-56992-4, € 56,00 (D) / € 57,50 (A) / SFR 82,00

Anne Conrad, **Rationalismus und Schwärmerei. Studien zur Religiosität und Sinndeutung in der Spätaufklärung**, Hamburg: Dobu Verlag 2008, 214 p., ISBN 3-934632-25-4, 28,80 €

Jacques Dalarum, **"Dieu changea de sexe, pour ainsi dire". La religion faite femme (XIe-XVe siècle)**, Vita regularis 37, Münster: LIT 2008, 464 p., ISBN 978-3-8258-1319-2, € 39,90 (D)

*Christiana de Groot / Marion Ann Taylor (eds), **Recovering Nineteenth-Century Women Interpreters of the Bible**, Society of Biblical Literature Symposium Series 38, Leiden: Brill u.a. 2007, 244 p., ISBN 978-90-04-15109-3, € 93,00 / US$ 139,00

Ulrike Gleixner / Erika Hebeisen (Hg.), **Gendering Tradition. Erinnerungskultur und Geschlecht im Pietismus**, Korb: Didymos-Verlag 2007, 292 p., ISBN 978-3-939020-41-7, € 29,00 / SFR 49,00

Book market
Büchermarkt
Feria de Libros

Christine Kleinjung, **Frauenklöster als Kommunikationszentren und soziale Räume. Das Beispiel Worms vom 13. bis zum Beginn des 15. Jahrhunderts**, Korb: Didymos-Verlag 2008, 368 p., ISBN 978-3-939020-21-9, € 59,00 / SFR 99,00

Franka Maubach, **Die Stellung halten. Kriegserfahrungen und Lebensgeschichten von Wehrmachthelferinnen**, Göttingen: Vandenhoeck und Ruprecht 2009, 349 p., ISBN 978 3 525 36167 2, € 46,90

Monika Mommertz / Claudia Oppitz-Belakhal (Hg.), **Das Geschlecht des Glaubens. Religiöse Kulturen Europas zwischen Mittelalter und Moderne**, Frankfurt u. a.: Campus 2008, 304 p., ISBN 9783593384504, € 34,90 (D) / SFR 59,00

Annerose Sieck, **Fromme Frauen im Mittelalter. Weisheiten und Visionen von Mystikerinnen und Heiligen**, Wien: Tosa-Verlag, 2008, 128 p., ISBN 978-3-85003-258-2, € 9,95 / SFR 12,90

Thérèse Taylor, **Bernadete of Lourdes, Her life, death and visions: new anniversary edition**, London: T&T Clark 2008, 304 p., PB 978 0 8264 2085 5, $ 19,95

Jane Tylus, **Reclaiming Catherine of Siena. Literacy, Literature, and the Signs of Others**, Chicago: University of Chicago Press 2009, 344 p., ISBN 9780226821283, $ 45,00

Haruko Nawata Ward, **Women Religious Leaders in Japan's Christian Century, 1549–1650**, Women and Gender in the Early Modern World, Aldershot, London: Ashgate 2009, c.a. 400 p., ISBN 978-0-7546-6478-9, £ 65,00.

III.3 Systematische Theologie, Ökumene und Interreligiöser Dialog / Systematic Theology and Interreligious Dialogue / Teología sistemática, Ecumenismo y Diálogo interreligioso

Marcella Althaus-Reid, **Liberation Theology and Sexuality**, London: SCM Press 2009, ISBN 978-0-334-04185-6, £ 24,99

Marcella Althaus-Reid / Lisa Isherwood (eds), **Controversies in Body Theology**, London: SCM Press 2007, 188 p., ISBN 978-0-334-04112-2, £ 18,99

Bethania Assy, **Hannah Arendt – An Ethics of Personal Responsibility**, Hanna Arendt Studien 3, Frankfurt a. Main u. a.: Peter Lang 2008, 191 p., ISBN 978-3-631-54990-2, € 38,10 (D) / 39,20 (A) / SFR 56,00

Bibliographie
Bibliography
Bibliographía

Wendy Beckett, **Encounters with God. In Quest of the Ancient Icons of Mary**, New York Maryknoll: Orbis Books 2009, 144 p., ISBN 978-1-57075-832-4, $ 22,00

*Christina von Braun / Bettina Mathes, **Verschleierte Wirklichkeit. Die Frau, der Islam und der Westen**, Berlin: Aufbau Verlag 2007, 476 p., ISBN 978-3-351-02643-1, € 24,95 / SFR 47,60

Kathy Coffey, **Mary**, New York Maryknoll: Orbis Books 2009, 128 p., ISBN 978-1-57075-724-2, $ 10,00

Marlene Crüsemann / Carsten Jochum-Bortfeld (Hg.), **Christus und seine Geschwister. Christologie im Umfeld der Bibel in gerechter Sprache**, Gütersloh: Gütersloher Verlagshaus 2009, 288 p., ISBN 978 3 579 05442 1, € 39,95 (D) / € 41,10 (A) / SFR 68,90

Alice Dermience, **La "question feminine" et l'église catholique. Approches biblique, historique et théologique**, Dieux, Hommes et Religions 11, Frankfurt a. M. / New York / Oxford / Wien: Peter Lang 2008, 207 p., ISBN 978 905 20 13787, € 27,70 (D) / € 28,50 (A) / SFR 41,00

Debórah Dwork, **The Terezín Album of Mariánka Zadikow**, Chicago: University of Chicago Press 2008, 280 p., ISBN 9780226511863, $ 35,00

Christiane Eckstein, **Geschlechtergerechte Familienpolitik. Wahlfreiheit als Leitbild für die Arbeitsteilung in der Familie**, Forum Systematik. Beiträge zur Dogmatik, Ethik und ökumenischen Theologie 37, Stuttgart: Kohlhammer 2009, 240 p., ISBN 978-3-17-021037-0, € 36,00 (D) / SFR 57,90

Christian Feichtinger, **Weiblichkeitskonzeptionen in den Shiva-Puranas**, Pontes 36, Münster: LIT 2007, 96 p., ISBN 978-3-8258-0464-0, € 19,90 (D)

Bärbel Fünfsinn / Kerstin Möller (Hg.), **Sister, carry on! Ökumenische Feministische Theologie**, Nordelbisches Missionszentrum 2009, € 3,00

Antonia Grunenberg / Waltraud Meints / Oliver Bruns / Christine Harckensee (Hg.), **Perspektiven politischen Denkens. Zum 100. Geburtstag von Hannah Arendt**, Hannah Arendt-Studien 4, Frankfurt a. Main: Peter Lang 2008, 220 p., ISBN 978-3-631-56659-6, € 34,00 (D) / € 35,00 (A) / SFR 50,00

Andrea Günter, **Vätern einen Platz geben. Aufgabe für Frauen und Männer**, Rüsselsheim: Christel Göttert Verlag 2007, ISBN 978-3-939623-01-4, 104 p., € 5,00

Andrea Günter, **Geist schwebt über Wasser. Postmoderne und Schöpfungstheologie**, Wien: Passagen-Verlag 2008, 112 p., ISBN 9783851658132, €14,90 / SFR 25,20

Book market
Büchermarkt
Feria de Libros

Andrea Günter, **Mutter – Sprache – Autorität. Sprechen lernen und Weltkompetenz**, Rüsselsheim: Christel Göttert Verlag 2009, 100 p., ISBN 978 3 939623 14 4, € 5,00

Meret Gutman-Grün, **Zion als Frau. Das Frauenbild Zions in der Poesie von al-Andalus auf dem Hintergrund des klassischen Piyyuts**, Judaica et Christiana 23, Frankfurt a. M. / New York / Oxford / Wien: Peter Lang 2008, 527 p., ISBN 978-3-03911-446-7, € 62,30 (D) / € 63,00 (A) / SFR 89,00

Eva Maria Hinterhuber, **Abrahamischer Trialog und Zivilgesellschaften: Eine Untersuchung zum sozialintegrativen Potential des Dialogs zwischen Juden, Christen und Muslimen**, Lucius & Lucius: Stuttgart 2009, 262 p., ISBN 978-3-8282-0467-6, € 46,00

Paula Hyman / Dalia Ofer (eds), **Jewish Women: A Comprehensive Historical Encyclopedia**, http://jwa.org/encyclopedia, 2009

Lisa Isherwood / Kathleen McPhillips (eds), **Post-Christian Feminisms. A Critical Approach**, Aldershot: Ashgate 2008, 254 p., ISBN 978-0-7546-5380-6, £ 55,00, eBook 978-0-7546-8739-9 www.ashgate.com/ebooks

Lisa Isherwood, **That Fat Jesus. Feminist Explorations in Boundaries and Transgressions**, London: Darton, Longman and Todd 2008, 168 p., ISBN 9780232526389, £ 12,95

Hilke Jabbarian, **Der Schleier in der Religions- und Kulturgeschichte. Eine Untersuchung von seinem Ursprung bis zu den Anfängen der Islamischen Republik Iran**, Interreligiöse Perspektiven 4, Münster: LIT 2009, 136 p., ISBN 978-3-8258-1938-5, € 19,90

Ian Jones / Janet Wootton / Kirsty Thorpe (eds), **Women and Ordination in the Christian Churches. International Perspectives**, London: T&T Clark 2008, 256 p., HB 978 0 567 03154 9, $ 140,00

Gesine von Kloeden-Freudenberg / Heike Koch / Brunhild von Local / Sonia Parera-Hummel / Liz Vuadi Vibila (eds), **It Takes Two. The Ordination of Women in the Member Churches of the United Evangelical Mission**, Wuppertal: Verlag der Vereinten Evangelischen Mission 2008, 308 p., ISBN 13-978-3-921900-31-4

Björn Krondorfer, **Men and Masculinities in Christianity and Judaism. A Critical Reader**, London: SCM Press 2009, 400 p., ISBN 978-0-334-04191-7, £ 25,00

Kathleen McGarvey, **Christian and Muslim Women in Dialogue. The Case of Northern Nigeria**, Religions and Discourse 42, Frankfurt a. M. / New York / Oxford /

Wien: Peter Lang 2009, 450 p., ISBN 978-3-03911-417-7, € 65,60 (D) / € 67,40 (A) / SFR 96,00

Elisabeth Moltmann-Wendel, **Frauen um Jesus**, Gütersloh: Gütersloher Verlagshaus 2009, 188 p., ISBN 978-3-579-06488-8, ca. € 34,95 (D) / € 36,00 (A) / SFR 59,90

Elisabeth Moltmann-Wendel (Hg.), **Feministische Theologie – Wo steht sie? Wohin geht sie?** Theologie interdisziplinär 5, Neukirchen-Vluyn: Neukirchener 2008, 107 p., ISBN 978-3-7887-2296-8, € 19,90

Nefissa Naguib, **Women, Water and Memory. Recasting Lives in Palestine**, Women and Gender: The Middle East and the Islamic World 6, Leiden: Brill 2009, 176 p., ISBN 978 90 04 16778 0, € 59,00

Jamal J. Ahmad Nasir, **The Status of Women under Islamic Law and Modern Islamic Legislation**, Brill's Arab and Islamic Laws Series 3, Leiden: Brill 2009, 228 p., ISBN 978 90 04 17273 9, € 102,00

Birgit Peters, **LiebesArten. Im theologischen Gespräch mit Ingeborg Bachmann**, Theologie und Literatur 21, Mainz: Grünewald 2009, 208 p., ISBN 978-3-7867-2762-0, € 24,90

Ina Praetorius, **Gott dazwischen. Eine unfertige Theologie**, Mainz: Grünewald 2008, 144 p., ISBN 978-3-7867-2734-7, € 14,90

Nawab Faizunnesa's Rupjalal, Translated and commented by Fayeza S. Hasanat, Women and Gender: The Middle East and the Islamic World 7, Leiden: Brill 2008, 228 p., ISBN 978 90 04 16780 3, € 59,00

Martina Schmidhuber, **Warum ist Armut weiblich? Philosophische Reflexionen auf Basis des Fähigkeitenansatzes nach Amartya Sen und Martha Nussbaum**, Saarbrücken: VDM Verlag 2009, ISBN 978-3639116205, € 59,00

Ishaq Tijani, **Male Domination, Female Revolt. Race, Class, and Gender in Kuwaiti Women's Fiction**, Women and Gender: The Middle East and the Islamic World 8, Leiden: Brill 2009, 176 p., ISBN 978 90 04 16779 7, € 69,00

Alice Peace Tuyizere, **Gender and development. The role of religion and culture**, Kampala: Fountain Publishing 2007, 447 p., ISBN 978-9970-02-618-0, $ 6,70

Heike Walz / David Plüss (Hg.), **Theologie und Geschlecht. Dialoge querbeet**, Theologie und Geschlecht 1, Münster: LIT 2008, 296 p., ISBN 3-03735-222-9, € 25,90

Book market
Büchermarkt
Feria de Libros

Sue Yore, **The Mystic Way in Postmodernity. Transcending Theological Boundaries in the Writings of Iris Murdoch, Denise Levertov and Annie Dillard**, Religions and Discourse 43, Frankfurt a. M. / New York / Oxford / Wien: Peter Lang, 2009, 334 p., ISBN 978-3-03911-536-5, € 42,80 (D) / € 44,00 (A) / SFR 62,00.

III.4 Praktische Theologie, Spiritualität, Liturgiewissenschaft, Religionspädagogik, Homiletik, Ethik / Pastoral theology, teaching, homiletics, spirituality, liturgy, ethics / Teología pastoral, Espiritualidad, Liturgia, Pedagogía de la Religión, Homilética, Ética

Maria Elisabeth Aigner / Hans Pock (Hg.), **Geschlecht quer gedacht. Widerstandspotenziale und Gestaltungsmöglichkeiten in kirchlicher Praxis**, Werkstatt Theologie. Praxisorientierte Studien und Diskurse 13, Münster: LIT 2009, 304 p., ISBN 978-3-8258-1654-4, € 29,90 (D)

Ruth Albrecht / Annette Bühler-Dietrich / Florentine Strzelczyk (Hg.), **Glaube und Geschlecht. Fromme Frauen – Spirituelle Erfahrungen – Religiöse Traditionen**, Köln: Böhlau Verlag 2008, 384 p., ISBN 978-3-412-07906-2, € 29,90 (D) / € 30,80 (A)

Kristin Aune / Sonya Sharma / Giselle Vincett (eds), **Women and Religion in the West. Challenging Secularization,** Theology and Religion in Interdisciplinary Perspective Series in Association with the BSA Sociology of Religion Study Group, London: Ashgate 2009, 242 p., ISBN 978-0-7546-5870-2 £55,00, eBook 978-0-7546-9023-8 www.ashgate.com/ebooks

Sigrid Eder / Irmtraud Fischer (Hg.), **"… männlich und weiblich schuf er sie…" (Gen 1,27). Zur Brisanz der Geschlechterfrage in Religion und Gesellschaft**, Theologie im kulturellen Dialog 16, Innsbruck/Wien: Tyrolia-Verlag 2009, 326 p., ISBN 978-3-7022-2931-3, € 29,90 (D) / SFR 49,90

Brigitte Enzner-Probst, **Frauenliturgien als Performance. Die Bedeutung von Corporealität in der liturgischen Praxis von Frauen**, Neukirchen-Vluyn: Neukirchener 2008, 499 p., ISBN 978-3-7887-2249-4, € 39,90 / CHF 69,00

*Annette Esser / Andrea Günter / Rajah Scheepers (Hg.), **Kinder haben – Kind sein – Geboren sein: Philosophische und theologische Beiträge zu Kindheit und Geburt**, Königstein/Taunus: Ulrike-Helmer-Verlag 2008, 307 p., ISBN 978-3-89741-273-6, € 24,90 / CHF 44,00

Bibliographie
Bibliography
Bibliografía

Anna Findl-Ludescher / Johannes Panhofer / Veronika Prüller-Jagenteufel (Hg.), **Weil nichts so bleibt, wie es ist. Theologische Beiträge zum ambivalenten Phänomen Wandel**, Kommunikative Theologie 11, Mainz: Grünewald 2009, 200 p., ISBN 978-3-7867-2761-3, € 24,90

Ingeborg Gabriel (Hg.), **Politik und Theologie in Europa. Perspektiven ökumenischer Sozialethik**, Ostfildern: Grünewald 2008, 425 p., ISBN 978-3-7867-2746-0, € 25,00

Mother Tongue Ink (Hg.), **We'Moon – mit Gaia den Rhythmus finden. 2010: Das Rad neu erfinden**, Rüsselsheim: Christel Göttert 2009, 272 p., ISBN 978 3 939623 16 8, € 18,50

Margaret Farley, **Just Love. A Framework for Christian Sexual Ethics**, London: T&T Clark 2008, 336 p., PB 978 0 8264 2924 7, $19,95

Lidia Guzy / Anja Mihr / Rajah Scheepers (Hg.), **Wohin mit uns? Wissenschaftlerinnen und Wissenschaftler der Zukunft**, Frankfurt am Main u. a.: Peter Lang 2009, 192 p., ISBN 978-3-631-58114-8, € 39,00, SFR 57,00

*Lamya Kaddor / Rabeya Müller / Harun Behr, **Saphir 5/6. Religionsbuch für junge Musliminnen und Muslime**, München: Kösel Verlag 2008, ISBN 978-3-466-50782-5, € 14,95

*Gisela Matthiae / Renate Jost / Claudia Janssen / Annette Mehlhorn / Antje Röckemann, **Feministische Theologie. Initiativen, Kirchen, Universitäten – eine Erfolgsgeschichte**, Gütersloh: Gütersloher Verlagshaus 2008, 405 p., ISBN 978-3-579-08032-1, € 39,95 (D) / € 41,10 (A) / SFR 68,90

Cristina Mazzoni, **The Women in God's Kitchen. Cooking, Eating, and Spiritual Writing**, London: T&T Clark 2006, 232 p., PB 978 0 8264 1912 5, $ 16,95

Margarete Ney, **Orte gesellschaftlichen Lernens. Frauenhäuser in Luxemburg als Aufgabenfeld der katholischen Kirche**, Übergänge. Studien zur katholischen und evangelischen Theologie / Religionspädagogik 8, Frankfurt a. M. / New York / Oxford / Wien: Peter Lang 2008, 211 p., ISBN 978-3-631-56341-0, € 39,00 (D) / € 40,00 (A) / SFR 57,00

Annebelle Pithan / Silvia Arzt / Monika Jakobs / Thorsten Knauth (Hg.), **Gender – Religion – Bildung. Beiträge zur Religionspädagogik der Vielfalt**, Gütersloh: Gütersloher Verlagshaus 2009, ca. 400 p., ISBN 978-3-579-08093-2, ca. € 39,95 (D) / € 41,10 (A) / SFR 68,90

Book market
Büchermarkt
Feria de Libros

Uta Pohl-Patalong, **Bibliolog. Impulse für Gottesdienst, Gemeinde und Schule, Band 1: Grundformen**, Stuttgart: Kohlhammer 2009, 176 p., ISBN 978-3-17-020920-6, € 22,00 (D) / SFR 37,90

Uta Pohl-Patalong / Maria Elisabeth Aigner, **Bibliolog. Impulse für Gottesdienst, Gemeinde und Schule, Band 2: Aufbauformen**, ca. 150 p., Stuttgart: Kohlhammer 2009, ISBN 978-3-17-020921-3, ca. € 20,00 / ca. SFR 34,50

Stefanie Rieger-Goertz, **Geschlechterbilder in katholischer Erwachsenenbildung**, Bielefeld: Bertelsmann 2008, 463 p., ISBN 9783763936533, € 35,90 (D)

Kerstin Rödiger, **Der Sprung in die Wirklichkeit... Impulse aus dem rhetorischen Ansatz Elisabeth Schüssler Fiorenzas für die Rezeption biblischer Texte in narrativer Sozialethik**, Ethik im theologischen Diskurs / Ethics in Theological Discourse 18, Münster: LIT 2009, 328 p., ISBN 978-3-8258-1744-2, € 31,90

Ulrike Wagner-Rau, **Auf der Schwelle. Das Pfarramt im Prozess kirchlichen Wandels**, Stuttgart: Kohlhammer 2009, 144 p., ISBN 978-3-17-019703-9, € 18,00 (D) / SFR 32,90.

IV. BOOK REVIEWS – REZENSIONEN – RECENSIONES

IV.1 Exegese (Erstes Testament, Neues Testament, Jüdische und frühchristliche Schriften) und Hermeneutik / Biblical Studies (Old Testament, New Testament, Literature of Early Judaism and Early Christianity) and Hermeneutics / Exégesis (Antiguo Testamento, Nuevo Testamento, escritos judíos y del cristianismo primitivo) y Hermenéutica

Sigrid Eder, *Wie Frauen und Männer Macht ausüben. Eine feministisch-narratologische Analyse von Ri 4*, Herders Biblische Studien 54, Freiburg u.a. 2008, 384 p., ISBN 978-3-451-29784-7, € 60,00 / SFR 99,90

Das Thema „Macht" stand am Anfang der feministischen Bewegung und feministischer Theorien in den 70er Jahren. Als Thema Feministischer Theologie und Exegese hat es erst in den letzten Jahren zunehmend an Bedeutung gewonnen (vgl. hierzu z. B. meine eigene Untersuchung „Gender, Sexualität und Macht in der Anthropologie des Richterbuches", Stuttgart 2006). Das vorliegende Buch von Sigrid Eder bietet einen weiteren Zugang zum Thema Macht und Geschlecht. Dabei steht wieder der schon häufig behandelte Text aus dem 4. Kapitel des alttestamentlichen Richterbuches im Mittelpunkt der Auslegung. Der ausgewählte Text erzählt von dem gewaltvollen und kriegerischen Konflikt zwischen Kanaan und dem Volk Israel. Bei der Rettung Israels und dem Untergang seiner Feinde sind zwei Frauen (Debora und Jaël) sowie zwei Männer (Barak und Sisera) ProtagonistInnen. In der Einleitung des vorliegenden Buches (Teil I) klärt Sigrid Eder zunächst ihre hermeneutischen Prämissen und Herangehensweisen und stellt anschließend ihre methodologischen Grundlagen (Teil II) vor. Zusammenfassend leitet sie zur Darstellung des narratologischen Analysemodells von Mike Bal über, das sie in ihrer Arbeit verwendet. In Teil III führt sie in das Buch der Richter ein und legt in Teil IV Ri 4 mit Hilfe syntaktischer und semantischer Beobachtungen aus. Teil V bietet unter dem Stichwort „Macht und Geschlecht in Richter 4" eine Zusammenschau der Forschungserträge aus der syntaktischen und semantischen Analyse sowie Ergebnisse aus der narratologischen Untersuchung.

Dabei stehen die Erkenntnisse im Hinblick auf die Machtkonstellationen des Textes im Mittelpunkt.

In der Analyse von Ri 4 kommt Eder zu dem Ergebnis, dass es hier nicht einfach um übermächtige Täter oder ohnmächtige Opfer geht, sondern viele unterschiedliche Weisen dargestellt werden, an Macht zu partizipieren und sie handelnd auszuüben. Eine geschlechtsspezifische Zuschreibung sei ebenfalls nicht auszumachen. Eder versucht aufzuzeigen, dass durch den Text der Blick der LeserInnen auf das Schicksal der jeweils Unterlegenen gelenkt werde. Dabei spiele die Partei und Zugehörigkeit der einzelnen Personen keine Rolle. Eder kommt dabei zu der überraschenden These, dass Ri 4 ein gewaltkritischer Text sei. Die Erzählung nehme in jeder Szene die Situation der Unterdrückung wahr und lenke den Blick auf die jeweils Unterlegenen, unabhängig vom Geschlecht und ihrer Zugehörigkeit zu Kanaan oder Israel. Auf diesem Hintergrund decke die Erzählung Gewalt auf, wende sich gegen die Leben zerstörende Gewalt und biete somit einen konstruktiven Umgang mit Macht und für eine gewaltfreie Konfliktlösung.

Für LiebhaberInnen narratologischer Exegese bietet die Analyse Sigrid Eders sicherlich interessante und neue Einblicke. Ihre Lesart einer gewaltkritischen Tendenz in Ri 4 bedarf jedoch noch einer weiteren Überprüfung. Ebenso lässt sich fragen, ob eine Parteilichkeit für die jeweils Unterlegenen im Text, die die Autorin postuliert, ohne die Rekonstruktion eines sozialgeschichtlichen Hintergrundes möglich und sinnvoll ist. Auf jeden Fall leistet die methodisch strukturierte Studie einen lesenswerten Beitrag zur Exegese von Ri 4 und zum Thema Macht in der Bibel.

Renate Jost (Neuendettelsau – Germany)

Anni Hentschel, *Diakonia im Neuen Testament. Studien zur Semantik unter besonderer Berücksichtigung der Rolle von Frauen*, Wissenschaftliche Untersuchungen zum Neuen Testament 2. Reihe, Bd. 226, Tübingen: Mohr Siebeck 2007, 498 p., ISBN 978-3-16-149086-6, € 79,00

Was *Diakonia* ist, scheint nicht besonders strittig. In den Kirchen – und besonders in den deutschen protestantischen Kirchen – wird mit dem Wort „Diakonie" das sozial-karitative Engagement bezeichnet, und das zugehörige Amt wird als ein Dienstamt der Nächstenliebe verstanden (1). Dies wird in der Regel auf das neutestamentliche Wortfeld *diakonia ktl* zurückgeführt, von dem alle „irgendwie" wissen, was es bedeutet.

Book Reviews
Rezensionen
Recensiones

Anni Hentschel zeigt in ihrer von Oda Wischmeyer (Erlangen) betreuten und im Kontext des Würzburger Graduiertenkollegs zur „Wahrnehmung der Geschlechterdifferenz in religiösen Symbolsystemen" (Bernhard Heininger) erstellten Dissertation, dass dieser scheinbare Konsens ein Trugschluss ist. Er beruht auf einem Bedeutungsspektrum des Wortfeldes, wie er sich grundlegend in dem Artikel von *Hermann Wolfgang Beyer* im *Theologischen Wörterbuch zum Neuen Testament* von 1934 findet. *Diakoneo ktl* bedeute demnach „den niedrigen, untergeordneten Dienst von Frauen und Sklaven, insbesondere als Tischdienst, und sei im Neuen Testament v. a. als Dienst der Barmherzigkeit und Nächstenliebe gemäß dem Vorbild Jesu Christi in seiner Bedeutung spezifiziert worden" (1-2). Unterschiede im Verständnis der *Diakonia* ergeben sich vor allem im Verständnis des daraus abgeleiteten Aufgabengebietes, und zwar sowohl im Blick auf heutige ekklesiologische Vorstellungen, als auch im Blick auf die neutestamentlichen Gemeinden. Während es bei Männern meist im Sinne eines Amtes verstanden wird, wird es, sobald man sich Frauen darunter vorstellt, viel eher mit unspezifischen karitativen Liebestätigkeiten verbunden.

Die vorliegende Untersuchung weist nach, dass das von *Beyer* und zahllosen Nachfolgestudien vorausgesetzte Bedeutungsspektrum des Wortfeldes weder dem außerbiblischen noch dem biblischen Sprachgebrauch gerecht wird und dass dies natürlich weitreichende Folgen für das Verständnis der entsprechenden neutestamentlichen Texte hat. Dazu skizziert sie in einem ersten Kapitel zunächst den neutestamentlichen Befund (6-11), portraitiert einige wegweisende Forschungspositionen, darunter auch feministische wie *Luise Schottroff* und *Elisabeth Schüssler Fiorenza* sowie die für ihre Arbeit grundlegenden von *Dieter Georgi* und *John N. Collins* (11-24), stellt einige methodologische Überlegungen zur semantischen Untersuchung an (24-34) und wendet sich sodann der Wortgruppe in profangriechischen (34-61) sowie jüdisch-hellenistischen Schriften zu (61-85). Dabei kommt sie – in weitgehender Übereinstimmung mit *Collins* – zum Ergebnis, dass die insgesamt eher selten begegnende Wortgruppe nicht zur Alltagssprache gehört und auch „nicht grundsätzlich die niedere Hausarbeit oder den Tischdienst von Frauen und Sklaven bezeichnet" (85). Sondern zentral ist der Aspekt der *Beauftragung*. Entsprechend meint das Verb *diakoneo* meist „eine Tätigkeit, die im Auftrag einer weiteren Person zu erledigen ist" (86), und ein *diakonos* ist derjenige, der als Beauftragter diesen Auftrag ordnungsgemäß, schnell und zuverlässig erledigt. Dies kann im Bereich der Übermittlung von Nachrichten, der Ausführung von Botengängen und verschiedensten Aufträgen – oder auch im Bereich der Hausarbeit und Aufwartung sein. Zwar steht der Beauftragte in einem hierarchischen Verhältnis zu seinem Auftraggeber, doch kann er gegenüber seinen Adressaten durchaus mit entsprechender Autorität auftreten, um seinen Auftrag auszuführen. Das Lexem gibt dabei per se keinerlei Auskunft über den Status oder das Geschlecht des Beauftragten; es können sowohl Könige als auch Sklaven, oder Frauen ebenso wie Männer als *diakonos* bezeichnet werden. Insgesamt ist stets der genaue Kontext zu analysieren, um die jeweilige Bedeutung des schillernden Begriffs herauszuarbeiten. Dies gilt auch und gerade für die neutestamentlichen Texte, für die sich zeigen lässt, dass sie gerade *nicht* einen Begriff der Alltagssprache aufnehmen und ihn in spezifischer Weise für religiöse Zusammenhänge umprägen, sondern dass sie den Begriff – wiewohl je unterschiedlich – analog zur außerbiblischen Verwendung gebrauchen. So muss ein *diakonos* keinesfalls von einer Grundbedeutung des Tischdienstes her erklärt werden, sondern ist im Horizont der griechischen Sprache als ein – wofür auch immer – *Beauftragter* zu verstehen.

Diese Erkenntnisse haben Konsequenzen für die Lektüre neutestamentlicher Texte. Diese werden in den Kapiteln 2-5, die zweifellos den Schwerpunkt der Untersuchung bilden, ausgelotet. Die Untersuchung lässt sich dabei – durchaus angemessen – von der Häufigkeit und Bedeutung des Vorkommens der Wortgruppe in den neutestamentlichen Texten leiten. Kapitel 2 widmet sich daher dem Wortgebrauch in den authentischen paulinischen Briefen (90-184). Kapitel 3 wendet sich dem Lukasevangelium (185-295) und Kapitel 4 der Apostelgeschichte (298-382) zu. Ein etwas kleineres 5. Kapitel beschäftigt sich mit der Verwendung der Wortgruppe in den deuteropaulinischen Briefen sowie der Didache, dem ersten Clemensbrief und den Ignatiusbriefen (383-432). Eine ausführliche Zusammenfassung, eine umfangreiche Bibliographie und ein dreiteiliges Register runden das Buch ab.

Die Arbeit spannt einen Bogen über sehr viele und sehr unterschiedliche Texte, verliert aber trotz ihrer Gründlichkeit und Detailgenauigkeit nie den roten Faden aus den Augen. Zusammenfassungen nach allen wichtigen Untersuchungsschritten sowie eine klare und verständliche Sprache machen die Dissertation zu einem sehr gut lesbaren Buch. Die Ergebnisse sind dazu angetan, manche neutestamentlichen Texte in ein neues Licht rücken zu lassen.

Paulus kann zunächst in einem sehr breiten Sinne „alle Aufgabenbereiche der Gemeinde, von der Leitung über die Verkündigung bis hin zu organisatorischen und karitativen Tätigkeiten als *diakoníai*, als offizielle Beauftragungen im Namen Christi, charakterisieren (1 Kor 12,5)" (434). Mit Hilfe des Verbalsubstantivs *diakonos* kann er „seine Rolle als von Gott beauftragter und autorisierter Botschafter des Evangeliums sowie den damit verbundenen Autoritäts- und Wahrheitsanspruch seiner Mission ausdrücken" (435) – und dies besonders, wenn seine eigene Arbeit in Zweifel gezogen wird (2 Kor 3-6; 11). Semantisch rückt der Begriff damit in die Nähe des Aposteltitels, wobei bei diesem nicht so sehr der Aspekt der Beauftragung, als vielmehr die Sendung im Zentrum steht. Paulus verwendet diesen Begriff aber nicht nur für sich selbst, sondern auch für andere Menschen, die mit ihm oder unabhängig von ihm in der Verkündigung arbeiteten. Das deutet darauf hin, dass der Begriff grundsätzlich dazu geeignet war, Personen zu bezeichnen, die im Auftrag Gottes bzw. Christi das Evangelium an Menschen übermittelten, und dass er als *eine* Funktionsbezeichnung neben anderen für GemeindeleiterInnen und MissionarInnen verwendet wurde. In diesem Horizont sind auch die Tätigkeit Phöbes als *diakonos* der Gemeinde von Kenchreä (Röm 16,1-2) sowie die *diakonoi* aus Phil 1,1 zu interpretieren, wobei letztere keineswegs nur als reine Männergruppe vorzustellen sind, wie nicht zuletzt die besondere Erwähnung von Evodia und Syntyche in Phil 4,2 deutlich macht.

Das lukanische Doppelwerk zeigt zwar in einigen Aspekten, besonders in der Apostelgeschichte, eine große Nähe zur Wortverwendung bei Paulus, weist aber auch deutliche Unterschiede zu dieser auf. So wird die *Diakonia* im Sinne der von Gott legitimierten Verkündigung auf Paulus und die Zwölf beschränkt, was einen eklatanten Unterschied zum Wortgebrauch in den Paulusbriefen darstellt. Außerdem wird das Verbalsubstantiv *diakonos* nicht verwendet, obwohl vorauszusetzen ist, dass der Verfasser entsprechende Bezeichnungen für GemeindeleiterInnen kannte. In einer Zeit der Gefährdung der Überlieferung durch abweichende Lehren, so Hentschels These, vermeide es Lukas auf diese Weise, den GemeindeleiterInnen der eigenen Zeit Identifikationsfiguren vor Augen zu stellen, auf die sie sich als „Vorgänger im Amt" berufen könnten (in der Miletrede Apg 20 werden – im Unterschied zu ihrer späteren Rezeption – gerade *keine* „Nachfolger" des Paulus eingesetzt). Denn die Zeit der von Gott autorisierten Verkündigung durch Paulus und die Zwölf sei nach Lukas definitiv abgeschlossen, und die gegenwärtigen Funktionsträger in den Gemeinden sollen ihre Aufgaben „nicht als Herrscher, sondern als Beauftragte pflichtgemäß und ohne falsches Statusstreben" ausüben (439).

Im Blick auf die Rolle der Frauen im lukanischen Doppelwerk und insbesondere im Lukasevangelium kommt Hentschel (im Unterschied zur 1998 erschienenen Untersuchung der Rezensentin) zum Schluss, dass Lukas durch seine Art und Weise des Erzählens die Rolle von Frauen auf praktisch-materielle Unterstützung reduziere und für sie keinerlei Leitungs- oder Verkündigungsaufgaben vorsehe (vgl. die Kritik an der *diakonia* der Marta in Lk 10,38-42). Damit stellt sie Lukas in eine Linie mit der in den Pastoralbriefen zu beobachtenden restriktiven Tendenz gegenüber Frauen. Doch während nach Hentschel Texte wie 1 Tim 2,11f Frauen für die Zukunft aus entsprechenden Gemeindefunktionen ausschließen wollten, lösche Lukas die Erinnerung an Frauen aus, die in der Nachfolge Jesu und in der frühchristlichen Mission als beauftragte Verkünderinnen und Zeuginnen aktiv waren.

Als eine weitere lukanische Besonderheit muss die metaphorische Verwendung des Lexems im Sinne des Tischdienstes angesehen werden. Damit hat Lukas „einen entscheidenden Beitrag dazu geleistet, dass neben der Betonung der Autorität eines Amtsträgers die verpflichtende und sich auf praktisch-materielle Verantwortung erstreckende Dimension eines christlichen Amtsverständnisses nicht übersehen werden darf" (441).

In der spätneutestamentlichen und nachneutestamentlichen Briefliteratur lässt sich schließlich beobachten, dass *diakonos* sich zu einem Amtsbegriff mit leitenden Funktionen und insbesondere mit Verkündigungsverantwortung entwickelt. Jedoch geschieht die Beauftragung nicht mehr direkt durch Gott bzw. Christus, sondern zunehmend ist die Vorstellung einer Einsetzung durch die Gemeinde oder deren Leiter zu beobachten. Und da letztere zunehmend an Tugend- und Rollenvorstellungen der Zeit gemessen werden, gehört dazu mehr und mehr die Erwartung, dass diese Gemeindeverantwortlichen *Männer* sind.

Ein sehr lesenswertes Buch!

Sabine Bieberstein (Bamberg / Eichstätt – Germany)

IV.2 Kirchen- und Religionsgeschichte / Church history and history of religions / Historia de la Iglesia y de las Religiones

Christiana de Groot / Marion Ann Taylor (eds), *Recovering Nineteenth-Century Women Interpreters of the Bible*, Society of Biblical Literature Symposium Series 38, Leiden: Brill u.a. 2007, 244 p., ISBN 978-90-04-15109-3, € 93,00 / US$ 139,00

Seit vielen Jahrhunderten lesen, reflektieren und schreiben Frauen über die Bibel. Oft sind ihre Einsichten verloren gegangen oder in Vergessenheit geraten. 1993 hat die Historikerin Gerda Lerner Frauen dargestellt, die sich im 19. Jahrhundert in der US-amerikanischen Frauenrechtsbewegung engagiert haben und sich dabei auf die Bibel beriefen. Das vorliegende Buch knüpft an Lerner an und beschränkt sich dabei ebenfalls auf Frauen des 19. Jahrhunderts aus dem englischen Sprachraum. Erklärtes Ziel beider in den USA lehrenden Biblikerinnen ist es dabei, nur solche Frauen zu behandeln, die bisher nicht als Auslegerinnen der Bibel in den Blick traten. Dreizehn Frauen aus verschiedenen kirchlichen Traditionen werden vorgestellt; zum Teil ist ihr Name und Lebenslauf weit über England oder die USA hinaus bekannt, allerdings wegen anderer Aktivitäten: so etwa Florence Nightingale (als Verwundetenpflegerin im Krimkrieg), Josephine Butler (als Sozialreformerin und Frauenrechtlerin), Harriet Beecher Stowe (als Autorin), Christina Rosetti (als Poetin) oder Annie Besant (als Freidenkerin und politische Aktivistin).

Alle beschriebenen Frauen haben Werke verfasst, in denen sie Schriftstellen kommentiert haben. Die Gattungen sind dabei – mit Blick auf den unterschiedlichen Adressatenkreis – sehr unterschiedlich und reichen von Kommentaren zu einzelnen Büchern der Bibel (Mary Ann Schimmelpenninck über die Psalmen, Christina Rosetti über die Offenbarung des Johannes), über katechetische Werke mit erzieherischem Anliegen (Sarah Trimmer, Mary Cornwallis, Sarah Ewing Hall) hin zur tagebuchartigen, nur für den persönlichen Gebrauch bestimmten Kommentierungen der eigenen Bibel (Florence Nightingale). Auch das Maß der Aneignung der historisch-kritischen Methode ist sehr unterschiedlich; so entschieden sich Mary Ann Schimmelpenninck für ihren Psalmenkommentar und Elizabeth Rundle Charles trotz Kenntnis der in ihrer Zeit aufkommenden kritischen Bibelwissenschaft für eine vorkritische, so genannte „figurative" Bibelauslegung, da sie ihnen offensichtlich eine spirituellere Auslegung und so eine Verbindung zwischen den Bibeltexten und ihrem eigenen Leben ermöglichte. Viele lesen das Erste im Lichte des Zweiten Testaments. Manche konzentrieren sich in ihren Auslegungen auf solche Bibelstellen, die sie vom liturgischen Gebrauch her kannten (Trimmer); eine Frau wie Catherine McAuley, die Begründerin der Sisters of Mercy in Irland, ließ sich für ihre Gemeinschaft von Leben und Lehre Jesu inspirieren und nahm dabei manche heutigen Ansätze und Fragen der Schriftinterpretation vorweg (77-79). Die meisten Frauen beherrschten neben ihrer hohen Bildung die klassischen Sprachen. Sie wurden von ihren Vätern oder Ehemännern in der Bibellektüre bestärkt und gefördert. Manche Frauen identifizierten sich mit biblischen Frauen (starke Mütter bei Beecher Stowe, Hagar bei Butler) oder erkannten in Christus mütterliche Züge Gottes; andere wählten Männer als ihre

Identifikationsfigur (Joseph, Sohn Rachels und Jakobs, bei Nightingale). Eine Frau wandte sich der Theosophie zu, da für sie die Bibel zu sehr ein Zeugnis des Patriarchats war (Besant).

Die Auswahl der Frauen richtete sich nicht nach dem Reifegrad ihres Feminismus; bei manchen – wie etwa bei Mary Cornwallis – ist lediglich die Rede von einem „embryonic feminism" (49). Andere wurden durch ihre Arbeit und ihren Einfluss – bisweilen ungewollt – Vorreiterinnen der Frauenemanzipation (so etwa die Tochter und Schwester eines Bischofs, Elizabeth Wordsworth, die 1878-1909 erste Rektorin des anglikanischen Studentinnenheims Lady Margaret Hall in Oxford wurde und eine wichtige Rolle für das Frauenstudium spielte). Auffällig ist jedoch, dass die allermeisten der hier behandelten Frauen – ganz gleich, ob sie an der im 19. Jahrhundert üblichen Frauenrolle festhalten, sie betonen (Beecher Stowe) oder sie durch ihr Handeln in Frage stellen (Nightingale) – die Bibel als Bestärkung ihres Anspruchs auf Auslegung der Schrift und ihres Handelns benutzen (so etwa McAuley).

Das Buch ist ausgesprochen gut lektoriert; meine Kritik beschränkt sich auf Kleinigkeiten, wie die überflüssigen Fußnoten 19 und 20 auf S. 143 (hier hätte je ein Verweis auf den Beitrag im gleichen Buch genügt) oder den fehlenden Hinweis, dass das Zisterzienserinnenkloster Port-Royal auf königlichen Befehl zerstört und nicht lediglich aufgelöst wurde (85).

Der Band enthält eine instruktive Einführung der Herausgeberinnen (1-17), einen „Index of Ancient Sources" (aus Bibel, Antike und vormoderner Zeit, 235-240) sowie ein Verzeichnis moderner Autorinnen und Autoren (241-244). De Groot und Taylor betreten Neuland und machen Lust auf die Wieder-Entdeckung weiterer Frauen und ihrer Bibelauslegungen in anderen Kulturen und Sprachen.

Angela Berlis (Haarlem – The Netherlands)

IV.3 Systematische Theologie, Ökumene und Interreligiöser Dialog / Systematic Theology and Interreligious Dialogue / Teología sistemática, Ecumenismo y Diálogo interreligioso

Christina von Braun / Bettina Mathes, *Verschleierte Wirklichkeit. Die Frau, der Islam und der Westen*, Berlin: Aufbau Verlag 2007, 476 p., ISBN 978-3-351-02643-1, € 24,95 / SFR 47,60

Nur selten wird ein Werk der Genderforschung in der öffentlichen Debatte dermaßen kontrovers zur Kenntnis genommen wie die „Verschleierte

Wirklichkeit". „Mondial" nennt es zum Beispiel Susanne Mayer in der Zeit (DIE ZEIT, 22.03.2007 Nr. 13). Sie liest es als „Partitur eines ungewöhnlichen wissenschaftlichen Konzerts, das Klängen aus Orient und Okzident aufs Erstaunlichste Raum gibt". Pauschal verdammt wird dagegen die vermeintliche „Apologie des Schamtuchs" von Regina Mönch in der FAZ. Ein „Manifest philologischer Verstiegenheit" sieht sie darin, mit dem die Autorinnen die „politische Debatte um den Islam hierzulande umdeuten in eine der Ignoranz vor großen Kulturleistungen des Orients" (FAZ, 30.04.2007).

Ähnlich wie im Fall der „Bibel in gerechter Sprache" scheint es den Autorinnen gelungen zu sein, durch eine umfassende Verknüpfung der Geschlechterfrage mit Geschichte und Gegenwart von Religion(en) die Gemüter in Wallung zu bringen. Allen Frauen, denen diese Verknüpfung am Herzen liegt, sei das Buch schon deshalb zur Lektüre empfohlen. Doch es gibt auch zwei Jahre nach seinem Erscheinen weitere Gründe, diese – wenn auch manchmal ausufernd materialreiche und komplexe – Studie zu studieren.

Religiöse Prägungen der Geschlechterordnungen im Gegenüber von Orient und Okzident werden hier einer umfassenden kulturwissenschaftlichen Betrachtung unterzogen. Insbesondere am Beispiel des Schleiers – aber auch an vielen anderen Weisen der Ent- oder Verhüllung zwischen Verbildlichung und Abstraktion – werden kulturelle Muster von Orient und Okzident ineinander gespiegelt. Dabei treten jene des Orients als geheimer Subtext der Selbstbilder des Westens zu Tage, als Inbegriff des eigenen verdrängten Anderen und Fremden.

Ein vermeintlich objektiver Blick des Westens auf die orientalische Kultur dient, so zeigen die Autorinnen, der Verhüllung von „unter dem Schleier" verborgenen Wahrheiten. Genau hieraus resultiert die Aufregung rund um das Kopftuch und ein neu erwachtes islamisches Selbstbewusstsein, das gerade auch unter jungen und gebildeten Frauen zu beobachten ist: Eine im Westen verschleierte Wirklichkeit, nämlich jene der ansonsten verdeckt verhandelten Geschlechterordnung der eigenen Kultur, wird im Symbol des Schleiers offenbar. Im Schleier blickt die westliche Gesellschaft sozusagen „nackt" auf ihre eigenen bisher verdrängten Prinzipien. Diese sind nicht ohne den Enthüllungsprozess des weiblichen Körpers im Verlauf des vergangenen Jahrhunderts und ebenso wenig ohne andere Schichten der Entblößung und Bemächtigung zu verstehen.

Christina von Braun und Bettina Mathes geht es nicht um die Rechtfertigung der Geschlechterordnung islamischer Kulturen. Vielmehr zeigen sie, wie das

Geschlechterverhältnis in Orient und Okzident auf grundlegend andere Weise geregelt wird, und wie Begegnungen und Überlagerung beider Kulturen – sowohl im Dienst an patriarchalen als auch an emanzipatorischen Interessen – zu interessanten neuen Kollisionen, aber auch Koalitionen führen können.

Dazu unternehmen die Autorinnen einen wahrhaft atemberaubenden Ritt durch Welten und Horizonte von Geschichte, Themen, Theorien. Bisweilen ist dieser Ritt durchaus „schwindelerregend" zu nennen. Gelegentliches Taumeln bleibt dabei ebenso wenig aus, wie Stolperpartien oder Verstiegenheiten. Und doch wird die Reise für die Leserin zwar lang, aber nicht langweilig – führt sie doch Stationen zusammen, die in den letzten Jahren auch in anderen Zusammenhängen gelegentlich auf der Tagesordnung aktueller Debatten standen. Die Bedeutung oraler und schriftlicher Kultur mit ihren jeweiligen Auswirkungen auf Leiblichkeit und die Geschlechterordnung gehört ebenso dazu wie die Rolle des Sehens und die Entwicklung optischer Instrumente im Gegenüber zu religiösen und kulturellen Traditionen und ihren jeweiligen Geschlechterordnungen. Auch die unterschiedlichen Weisen des Wissens in Orient und Okzident kommen zur Sprache und deren verschiedenen Auswirkungen auf den Umgang mit Geld und Geschlecht. So kommen religiöse und kulturelle Tiefenstrukturen in den Blick, die eigentlich erst im Gegenüber und in der Abstoßung des einander Fremden offensichtlich werden können.

Letzteres mag als Absolution dafür gelten, dass die Studie trotz gegenläufigen Beteuerungen in *eine* Falle am Ende doch tappt: Sie bleibt bei einer polaren Gegenüberstellung von Orient und Okzident weitgehend stehen. Dadurch treten die vielen Überschneidungs- und Vermischungsformen in den Hintergrund, die es zwischen diesen Kulturen gerade dort gegeben hat, wo die Begegnung weniger durch koloniales Herrschaftsgebaren als durch gegenseitige Bereicherung und Befruchtung geprägt waren (und sind!).

Eine interreligiös und politisch engagierte Feministin würde sich wohl Auskünfte darüber wünschen, wie sich emanzipatorische Bemühungen in der Begegnung unterschiedlich geprägter Kulturen ergänzen und anregen können. Darin liegt aber weniger die Zielrichtung dieses Buches. Vielmehr unternehmen die Autorinnen den Versuch, Paradoxien der westlichen Kultur in Worten und Bildern zu präsentieren, um sie auf ihre eigenen Subtexte zurückzuverweisen. Dabei kommen scharfe Anfragen auf den Tisch: Etwa nach dem sehr unterschiedlichen Aufmerksamkeitsniveau, das Ehren- und sogenannte „Liebes"morde, Zwangsheirat und Sextourismus oder geschlechtsspezifischer Menschenhandel im Westen erfahren. Auch der Missbrauch feministischer Anliegen im Dienst an patriarchalen Interessen und der Ruf nach notwendiger Selbstaufklärung feministischen Denkens wird zu Gehör gebracht.

Die Lektüre dieses fast 500 Seiten starken Werkes fordert der geneigten Leserin die Bereitschaft ab, sich auf ungewöhnliche Perspektiven einzulassen. Auch mag sie sich gelegentlich fragen, ob hier ein ultimativer und umfassender Welterklärungsversuch aus der Geschlechterperspektive unternommen werden soll. Doch alles in allem liegt in diesem Buch ein äußerst spannender Impuls für neue Perspektiven auf die Genderdebatte im Dialog zwischen unterschiedlichen Religionen und Kulturen vor. Besonders interessant könnte die Reaktion kritischer und feministisch engagierter Musliminnen auf dieses Buch sein. Auf eine erneute Rezension durch eine von ihnen in einer der nächsten Ausgaben des Jahrbuches der ESWTR wäre ich neugierig.

Annette Mehlhorn (Rüsselsheim – Germany)

Annette Esser / Andrea Günter / Rajah Scheppers (Hg.), *Kinder haben, Kind sein, Geboren sein. Philosophische und Theologische Beiträge zu Kindheit und Geburt*, Königstein/Taunus, Ulrike-Helmer-Verlag 2008, 307 p., ISBN 978-3-89741-273-6, € 24,90 / CHF 44,00.

Der vorliegende Aufsatzband hatte mehrere Anlässe seiner Geburt. Eine wichtige Triebfeder des Nachdenkens stellte die (Selbst-)beobachtung einzelner Wissenschaftlerinnen zur erneuten Privatisierung des „Kinderthemas" nach einzelnen Erfolgen seiner Vergesellschaftung in der Frauenbewegung dar. Dies bot Anlass, die Fragen nach Geburt und Gebären in den Mittelpunkt einer nationalen Tagung der ESWTR Deutschland 2006 zu stellen. In Reflexion und wissenschaftlicher Einholung galt es, das Thema neu zu besichtigen, und dabei auch vor der spirituellen Dimension der „Kinder Gottes" nicht Halt zu machen. Daneben und dazu trat die Auseinandersetzung mit Hannah Arendt und ihrem Konzept der Geburtlichkeit pünktlich zu ihrem 100. Geburtstag.

Einen weiten Bogen haben die Herausgeberinnen damit gespannt. Nach biographisch gefärbten Erforschungen (in Abschnitt I: Kinder haben oder keine) werden Aspekte des Kindseins seit der Antike bis in die Gegenwart der Religionspädagogik aufgegriffen (in Abschnitt II: Kind sein – Kindheit).

Dann wendet sich das Nachdenken ganz unterschiedlichen Elternschaften zu (in Abschnitt III: Kinderhaben: Elternschaft, Gebären, Mutter sein) und nimmt schließlich in einem letzten Schritt das Konzept Hannah Arendts genauer in den Blick (Abschnitt IV: Gebürtigkeit, nicht nur bei Hannah Arendt).

Dabei wurden ganz verschiedene Stile des Darstellens gewählt: Die durch die Aufführungspraxis des Kabaretts während der Tagung pointiert überspitzten O-Töne von Frauen mit und ohne Kinder kommen neben detailgenauen Beobachtungen zu historischen Einzelfragen (wie etwa Ute Eisen, Spielen und Arbeiten – Kinder in der römischen Antike), meditativeren Annäherungen (z. B. Hanna Strack, Die Metapher vom Gewebe – Schwesternschaften mit einem Gedicht Hannah Arendts) und grundsätzlichen Themeneinblicken (wie Andrea Günter, Philosophie der Gebürtigkeit in ethischer Perspektive) zum Stehen.

Wer zwischen den Kapiteln spaziert, dem und der bieten sich spannende Entdeckungen, wie z. B. mir ganz neu über Johann Friedrich Starcks Gebetbuch für Schwangere zusammen die Vorstellung der Verborgenheit einer Leibesfrucht vor der Erfindung der modernen Medizin (in Christine Globig, Angst vor den Schmerzen, Angst vor dem Sterben – was kann da trösten? Seelsorge an Schwangeren im 18. Jahrhundert). Die Einladung zur Tour d'horizont ist also wirklich gelungen. Vielen einzelnen Überlegungen ist zu wünschen, dass an sie angeknüpft, mit ihnen weiter gedacht wird. Leider ist dem Band nicht zu genau zu entnehmen, welche Referate schon im Tagungszusammenhang gehalten wurden. Wo das Gespräch zwischen den hier Versammelten schon begonnen hat, hätte ich gerne gewusst.

Nicht wenige Zugänge legitimieren sich über die biographische Erfahrung der Schwangerschaft. In der Pluralität dieser Texte zeigt sich damit eine Spur, bei der nicht sicher ist, ob die Autorinnen sie legen wollten. Insgesamt nämlich erscheint die reale Leiblichkeit des Vorgangs der Geburt damit mächtiger in diesem Themenfeld weiter zu wirken als alle Kontexte, Umformatierungen und Gegenlesarten. Auch diesseits der Privatheit bleibt die Frage, wie normativ die Möglichkeit des Gebärens mit der Vorstellung von Frausein insgesamt zu verschränken ist bzw. verschränkt wird. Schade, dass zu dieser sehr grundsätzlichen Frage (die gewiss keine einheitliche Antwort erwarten lässt) keine Statements der Herausgeberinnen zu finden sind. Sie hätten die Möglichkeiten, in dem Buch flanieren zu können, noch wohltuend abgerundet.

Brigitte Becker (Boldern – Switzerland)

Book Reviews
Rezensionen
Recensiones

IV.4 Praktische Theologie, Spiritualität, Liturgiewissenschaft, Religionspädagogik, Homiletik, Ethik / Pastoral theology, teaching, homiletics, spirituality, liturgy, ethics / Teología pastoral, Espiritualidad, Liturgia, Pedagogía de la Religión, Homilética, Ética

Lamya Kaddor / Rabeya Müller / Harun Behr, *Saphir 5/6. Religionsbuch für junge Musliminnen und Muslime*, München: Kösel Verlag 2008, ISBN 978-3-466-50782-5, € 14,95

Das vorliegende Schulbuch ist das erste Unterrichtswerk für den islamischen Religionsunterricht der 5 und 6. Klassen. Es wurde nicht nur von den zuvor genannten Autoren erarbeitet, sondern auch von drei Lehrergruppen in Bayern, Niedersachsen und Nordrhein-Westfalen. Die das Judentum betreffenden Abschnitte wurden von der Berlinerin Rachel Herweg gegengelesen.

Da die bisher angelaufenen Modellversuche zum islamischen Religionsunterricht ohne ein eigenes Schulbuch auskommen mussten, wenn die Lehrer nicht zu im Ausland erarbeiteten Schulbüchern greifen wollten, wurde das nun vorgelegte Unterrichtswerk mit besonderen Erwartungen belastet.

Es muss daher auf Autoren wie Lektoren geradezu entlastend gewirkt haben, als sie in fast allen Medien gelobt wurden. Selbst aus der ansonsten eher skeptischen Ecke der politischen Nörgler ließ sich kaum etwas Kritisches hören. Der herausgebende Kösel Verlag konnte in jeder Hinsicht zufrieden sein, denn wann ist schon einmal ein Schulbuch und dann noch für den Religionsunterricht in den Feuilletons der überregionalen Zeitungen besprochen worden? Der „Saphir", so lautet der Titel des Buches, erstrahlte, wie ihn sich PR-Abteilungen nur wünschen konnten.

Allein, die islamischen Verbände hielten und halten sich zurück. So erschien zu einer der Pressekonferenzen gerade einer von ihnen, ohne sich inhaltlich zu äußern.

In seiner Rezension hat der Nürnberger Hansjörg Biener den kritischen Punkt erfasst, als er schrieb, dass sich der Herausgeber und seine Autoren mit der Konzeption eine Gratwanderung leisteten. Da standen auf der einen Seite die ministeriellen und modernen didaktischen (Heraus-)Forderungen, die Kalam (christlich: Theologie) orientiert waren, und auf der anderen die Tradition der Orthopraxie der Muslime in den Moschee-Vereinen. Hinzu kamen die scheinbar unantastbaren Rollenverständnisse nicht nur der Geschlechter, sondern ebenso der Höflichkeitssysteme orientalischer Einwanderergeneration(en) und die Individuum betonte Normativität gesellschaftlicher Formlosigkeit in den Aufnahmegesellschaften; und schließlich galt es die durch die Katastrophen des vergangenen Jahrhundertes sensibilisierte Haltung zur Pluralität zu beachten und die Einmaligkeit des geoffenbarten Glaubens zu bezeugen. Schließlich ist Mohammed für jeden Muslim der letzte Prophet.

Die Gratwanderung gelang wohl durch die verlegerische Routine bei den Photos, Bildern und den guten deutschen Texten, die dem Spiel zwischen Schüler(in) und Lehrer(in) zahlreiche Anregungen zum Fragen bzw. Nachfragen geben. Dies ist eine für den klassischen Koranunterricht ungewohnte Didaktik. Man wird daher abwarten müssen, wie die Vereine damit zu Recht kommen werden, wenn Jungen und Mädchen nicht nur eine Tradition befragen, sondern auch den ehrwürdigen Text.

Aus den Familien ist bisher keinerlei Reaktion zu hören. Die Lehrer, die bereits nach dem Buch unterrichten, berichten nur, dass die Eltern sich über den Unterricht freuen.

Man wird daher abwarten müssen, ab wann die Älteren auf die Aussagen der Schulbuchtexte reagieren. Das Problem ist nicht das Fragen an sich, sondern der Stil.

In jedem Koran-Unterricht kann gefragt werden, aber die Fragende fragt so, dass die (Glaubens-)Wahrheit nicht in Frage gestellt wird. Im Fragen moderner Didaktik nagt der prüfende Zweifel. Irrt der Lehrer, wenn er sagt, dass Haribo Gummibärchen haram (nicht erlaubt) seien? Gibt es kommunikativ vermittelbar vernünftige Gründe dafür?

Die Autoren des „Saphir" haben den Edelstein am deutschen Alltag abgeschliffen. Die Folge ist, dass z. B. kaum „Orientalismen" zu finden sind. So tragen zwar betende Mädchen ein Kopftuch, aber auf anderen Bildern sitzen oder spielen Mädchen mit und ohne Kopftuch miteinander bzw. mit den Jungen zusammen. Gleichzeitig sucht man vergeblich nach populären deutschen Aktivitäten gleich dem Schwimmen. So wird die Frage nach der werdenden Identität der Heranwachsenden in aller Behutsamkeit gestellt, ohne in die „Freizügigkeit" hinüber zu gleiten. Es ist daher zu fragen, ob wesentliche Teile der Genderentwicklung allein dem Biologie-Unterricht überlassen bleiben sollen, der doch von den muslimischen Eltern seit langer Zeit problematisiert wird?

Diese nicht-konfrontative Grundhaltung der Autoren, um ein Wort des Nürnbergers Johannes Lähnemanns aufzugreifen, trägt vor allem dort, wo es um die Vielfalt der Religionen geht. So wird auf den Seiten 112 und 113 die kalamische, theologische Aufforderung zum Lesen, iqra, in einer Weise umgesetzt, die alle Grundsätze heutiger Didaktik und gesellschaftlicher Normativität gleichwertig zur Geltung bringt: Jüdische Jungen lesen aus der Thora, Jungen und Mädchen stehen am Altar, die Hände eines Blinden lesen, Mädchen mit und ohne Kopfbedeckung lesen; und optisch mittig gesetzt wird das Wort „al-Quŕan" erläutert. In anderen islamischen Religionsbüchern taucht mindestens in diesem Kontext das Bild einer islamischen Autorität auf, die meist einem Jungen beim Lesen hilft. Die Saphir Autorinnen und Autoren verweisen auf die Eltern der Jungen und Mädchen, aber andere religiöse Bezugspersonen sind nicht einmal bei der Frage nach den Vorbildern zu sehen. Die Jungen und Mädchen, an die sich dieses Religionsbuch wendet, sind und bleiben auf sich gestellt, wobei der Lehrer bzw. die Lehrerin als Moderator(in) im Hintergrund steht. Es ist eben ein deutsches Schulbuch, dessen Lektüre eine Reihe von Fragen provoziert.

So findet man keinen Hinweis auf den Umgang mit Rückfragen aus der Familie bzw. der Moschee z. B. hinsichtlich der Sunna. Dabei muss man nicht gleich an die großen Rollenkonflikte denken, sondern vielfach geht es um so schlichte Dinge wie den Verzehr von Süßigkeiten, die die einen für haram erklärt bekommen und die anderen nicht. Die non-konfrontative Grundhaltung der Autoren verlagert insbesondere bei jungen Frauen die Konfliktlösung in die Identitätssuche der reifenden Persönlichkeit. Ein Blick in die Blogs junger Muslima macht die Schwierigkeiten deutlich. Daher kann man den Lehrerinnen und Lehrern nur empfehlen, an Elterabenden den „Saphir" in die Hand zu nehmen, um von seinen Texten aus das Gespräch zu suchen. Anregungen gibt es genug.

Dieser Gedanke führt zum zweiten Fragenkomplex: dem Lehrerhandbuch bzw. der Lehrerfortbildung. Letztere fand bisher an den Lehrstühlen für islamische Pädagogik statt, an denen kaum Frauen tätig waren. Und wer den schulischen Alltag kennt, der weiß, wie abhängig jeglicher Unterricht von der Persönlichkeit des/der Unterrichtenden ist. So kann der Unterricht non-verbal die Absichten einer Rahmenrichtlinie und eines Schulbuches konterkarieren. Auch im Religionsunterricht lässt sich diskriminieren, da hilft selbst das beste Schulbuch nicht. Ein gutes Lehrerhandbuch vermag hier zu helfen.

Mit dem „Saphir" ist „der" Islam in der Wirklichkeit der Schule angekommen, was nicht nur für das Klassenzimmer gilt, vielmehr ebenso für die Gespräche im Kollegium. Dort begegnet die Religionslehrerin bzw. der Religionslehrer nicht nur dem deutschstämmigen Kollegen, sondern auch dem türkischstämmigen des muttersprachlichen Unterrichtes, der sich an ein anderes Curriculum gebunden fühlt, in dem die Religion (vielleicht) keine Bedeutung hat. Und er steht vor der Herausforderung für die Schulbibliothek den „Saphir" ergänzende Literatur zu bestellen, die die Aussagen bisheriger Schulbücher korrigiert bzw. ergänzt.

Wenn die religiöse Distanz betonende Attitude das eine Ende einer Dimension der Einstellung zum Islam ist, dann stehen die Vertreter eines Ilmihal (orthopraktischer Katechismus) für das andere. Die Autorinnen und der Autor des „Saphir" haben keinen Ort in dieser alten Dimension. Sie versuchen eine eigenständige Sichtweise auf den ihnen teuren Glauben, die dem Islam und den Muslimen in diesem Lande eine Zukunft öffnet, anzubieten. Dazu zählt die Diskursfähigkeit der heranwachsenden Muslime. Und sie steht im Zentrum der Bemühungen der Herausgeberinnen und Herausgeber.

Wolf D. Ahmed Aries (Hannover – Germany)

Gisela Matthiae / Renate Jost / Claudia Janssen / Antje Röckemann / Annette Mehlhorn in Verbindung mit Kristin Bergmann, Angelika Fromm, Mieke Korenhof, Anna-Karena Müller, *Feministische Theologie. Initiativen, Kirchen, Universitäten – eine Erfolgsgeschichte,* Gütersloh: Gütersloher Verlagshaus 2008, 405 p.; ISBN 97808032, € 39,95

This collaborative book project documents the thirty year history of feminist theology in Germany and assesses its successes (and failures) at institutionalization. Feminist theology, the editors assert in the introduction, has taken root in three different institutional contexts: the churches, the universities and at the grassroots in the form of feminist networks and autonomous organizations. Feminist theology developed within this "velvet triangle" of the patriarchal structures of church(es) and academia and/or in newly forged organizations, such as women's bookstores, publications and publishing houses, feminist retreat centers and support networks. The theoretical framework of "velvet triangle" (p. 378-383) is exceptionally helpful to assess the institutional niches in which feminist religious thought and practice has flourished.

The idea for this project was hatched by the Aktionsbündnis *Tempo,* an alliance of activists committed to speed up the pace of institutionalization in German theology departments and concerned over budget cuts in the churches that disproportionately affect women's projects. Feeling alarmed by the backlash, the "action alliance" decided to conduct a broad analysis of past successes and failures at institutionalization. To do this, they set out to retrace projects, collect names, dates, and initiatives in order to gain a comprehensive lay of the land. As a historical documentation project, this book could not have come at a better time. Much of the movement's history is oral and subject to the vagaries of memory. Few feminist activists had bothered to archive relevant materials, to record the administrative decisions or document changing leadership. Now that memory begins to fade and there is no longer any one person who could possibly overlook the various initiatives and programs, this history was (once again) threatened by erasure: it took 60 authors to (re)assemble the histories of various projects and the ensuing synopsis provides compelling proof of the enormous productivity and enterprising creativity of feminist theologians over the last decades.

What lessons emerge from this comprehensive data gathering? Most striking from the perspective of this American reviewer is the extent to which politics and institutional structures shape the possibilities of individual feminist generativity. For Protestant women, faced with stiff resistance from academic theology department, the ordained path into church ministry proved to be most hospitable. Feminist Protestant clergy initiated multiple support networks and developed feminist resources for congregations that have transformed the nature of the church. The few Protestant theology department (only 7%-12% of university faculty are female) that are offering courses in feminist theology, do so because the Protestant churches has provided financial resources and mandated the establishment of endowed chairs. In the absence of external funding, university departments have successfully rebuffed feminist theology, maintaining masculinist environments and androcentric theological orientations. For Roman Catholic women, given the lack of progress on women's ordination, academic theology remain attractive despite enormous (and increasing) hurdles put up by the Vatican and Roman Catholic hierarchy. Some university departments provide feminist theology through adjuncts or on rotating lecturer appointments, arrangements that actively discourage younger women from pursuing feminist theological scholarship.

This dismal academic situation, however, also explain the vibrancy and dynamism of "grassroots" feminist initiatives, such as retreat centers, workshops, networks and publishing houses. In contrast to the United States where feminist theology has comfortably (?) been absorbed by academia, European feminists continue to depend on and to support a variety of autonomous organizations. In the US, feminist theologians gather within the framework of mainstream professional associations such as the AAR (American Academy of Religion). This professionalization has turned time into a most precious commodity and the demands of scholarly productivity undermine the community-oriented and political aspects of feminist theology.

The notion of the "velvet triangle" helps to explain the state of feminist theology in different cultural, political and economic contexts. In countries,

Book market
Büchermarkt
Feria de Libros

where the university remains inhospitable, the churches provide the niches for feminist theology (and vice versa); where access to church employment remains blocked, grassroots initiatives prevail; when the economy threatens the survival of autonomous institutions, another vectors of the triangle will be emphasized. Success will be measured by feminist theology's continued flexibility in responding to shifting conditions and changed circumstances. Knowing how successfully feminist theology organized along the three vectors of the "velvet triangle" is very encouraging and gives rise to the hope that the movement will be able to navigate the looming challenges on both the national (German) and global levels in the future.

Katharina von Kellenbach (Maryland – USA)

EUROPEAN SOCIETY OF WOMEN IN THEOLOGICAL RESEARCH

EUROPÄISCHE GESELLSCHAFT FÜR THEOLOGISCHE FORSCHUNG VON FRAUEN

SOCIEDAD EUROPEA DE MUJERES EN LA INVESTIGACIÓN TEOLÓGICA

President – Präsidentin – Président:
Prof. Dr. Angela Berlis, Haarlem, The Netherlands

Vice-President – Vize-Präsidentin – Vice-Président:
Prof. Dr. Lisa Isherwood, Neath, West Glamorgan, U.K.

Secretary – Sekretärin – Secrétaire:
Lucia Ramòn Carbonell, Valencia, Spain

Vice-Secretary – Vize-Sekretärin – Vice-Serétaire:
Dr. Rajah Scheepers, Berlin, Germany

Treasurer – Schatzmeisterin – Trésorière:
Annukka Kalske M.Th., Helsinki, Finland

Vice-Treasurer – Vize-Schatzmeisterin – Vice-Trésorière
Sylvia Grevel, Arnhem, The Netherlands

Networking
Martá Bódo, Cluj, Rumania

Journal – Jahrbuch – Annuaire
Prof. Dr. Sabine Bieberstein, Bamberg and Eichstätt, Germany
Christine Gasser, Wien, Austria

Contact for the ESWTR Bulletin:
Dr. Rajah Scheepers,
Muthesiusstraße 14, D- 12163 Berlin

Journal of the European Society of Women in Theological Research

1 **Luise Schottroff, Annette Esser**, *Feministische Theologie im europäischen Kontext – Feminist Theology in a European Context – Théologie féministe dans un contexte européen*, 1993, 255 p., ISBN: 90-390-0047-6
[out of print]

2 **Mary Grey, Elisabeth Green**, *Ecofeminism and Theology – Ökofeminismus und Theologie – Ecoféminisme et Théologie*, 1994, 145 p., ISBN: 90-390-0204-5
23 EURO

3 **Angela Berlis, Julie Hopkins, Hedwig Meyer-Wilmes, Caroline Vander Stichele**, *Women Churches: Networking and Reflection in the European Context – Frauenkirchen: Vernetzung und Reflexion im europäischen Kontext – Eglises de femmes: réseaux et réflections dans le contexte européen*, 1995, 215 p., ISBN: 90-390-0213-4
23 EURO

4 **Ulrike Wagener, Andrea Günter**, *What Does it Mean Today to Be a Feminist Theologian? – Was bedeutet es heute, feministische Theologin zu sein? – Etre théologienne féministe aujourd'hui: Qu'est-ce que cela veut dire?*, 1996, 192 p., ISBN: 90-390-0262-2
23 EURO

5 **Elisabeth Hartlieb, Charlotte Methuen**, *Sources and Resources of Feminist Theologies – Quellen feministischer Theologien – Sources et resources des théologies féministes*, 1997, 286 p., ISBN: 90-390-0215-0
23 EURO

6 **Hedwig Meyer-Wilmes, Lieve Troch, Riet Bons-Storm**, *Feminist Pespectives in Pastoral Theology – Feministische Perspektiven in Pastoraltheologie – Des perspectives féministes en théologie pastorale*, 1998, 161 p., ISBN: 90-429-0675-8
23 EURO

7 **Charlotte Methuen**, *Time – Utopia – Eschatology. Zeit – Utopie – Eschatologie. Temps – Utopie – Eschatologie*, 1999, 177 p., ISBN: 90-429-0775-4
23 EURO

8   Angela Berlis, Charlotte Methuen, *Feminist Perspectives on History and Religion – Feministische Zugänge zu Geschichte und Religion – Approches féministes de l'histoire et de la religion*, 2000, 318 p., ISBN: 90-429-0903-X
    [out of print]

9   Susan K. Roll, Annette Esser, Brigitte Enzner-Probst, Charlotte Methuen, Angela Berlis, *Women, Ritual and Liturgy – Ritual und Liturgie von Frauen – Femmes, la liturgie et le rituel*, 2001, 312 p., ISBN: 90-429-1028-9
    23 EURO

10 Charlotte Methuen, Angela Berlis, *The End of Liberation? Liberation in the End! – Befreiung am Ende? Am Ende Befreiung! – La libération, est-elle à sa fin? Enfin la libération*, 2002, 304 p., ISBN: 90-429-1028-9
    23 EURO

11 Elżbieta Adamiak, Rebeka J. Anić, Kornélia Buday with Charlottte Methuen and Angela Berlis, *Theologische Frauenforschung in Mittel-Ost-Europa – Theological Women's Studies in Central/Eastern Europe – Recherche théologique des femmes en Europe orientale et centrale*, 2003, 270 p., ISBN: 90-429-1378-9
    23 EURO

12 Charlotte Methuen, Angela Berlis, Sabine Bieberstein, Anne-Claire Mulder and Magda Misset-van de Weg, *Holy Texts: Authority and Language – Heilige Texte: Autorität und Sprache – Textes Sacrés: Autorité et Langue*, 2004, 313 p., ISBN: 90-429-1528-X
    23 EURO

13 Valeria Ferrari Schiefer, Adriana Valerio, Angela Berlis, Sabine Bieberstein, *Theological Women's Studies in Southern Europe – Theologische Frauenforschung in Südeuropa – Recherche théologique des femmes en Europe Méridionale*, 2005, 255 p., ISBN: 90-429-1696-6
    23 EURO

14 Sabine Bieberstein, Kornélia Buday, Ursula Rapp, *Building Bridges in a Multifaceted Europe. Religious Origins, Traditions, Contexts, and Identities – Brücken bauen in einem vielgestaltigen Europa. Religiöse Ursprünge, Traditionen, Kontexte und Identitäten – Construire des ponts dans une Europe multiforme. Origines, traditions, contextes et identités religieux*, 2006, 257 p. ISBN 978-90-429-1895-5
    23 EURO

15 **Hanna Stenström, Elina Vuola, Sabine Bieberstein, Ursula Rapp**,
   Scandinavian Critique of Anglo-American Feminist Theology – Skandinavische Kritik angloamerikanischer feministischer Theologie – Critique scandinave de la théologie féministe anglo-américaine, 2007, 292 p. ISBN 978-90-429-1974-7
   23 EURO

16 **Sabine Bieberstein, Christine Gasser, Marinella Perroni, Ursula Rapp**,
   Becoming Living Communities – Construyendo comunidades vivas – Lebendige Gemeinschaften werden, 2008, 241 p. ISBN 978-90-429-2208-2
   35 EURO

All volumes of the Journal of the ESWTR can be ordered from Peeters Publishers,
Bondgenotenlaan 153, B-3000 Leuven
Fax: +32 16 22 85 00; e-mail: order@peeters-leuven.be

The volumes of the Journal of the ESWTR are also available online at
http://poj.peeters-leuven.be